Toward a Future Theatre

RELATED TITLES

Toward a Future Theatre

Conversations during a Pandemic

Caridad Svich

methuen | drama

LONDON · NEW YORK · OXFORD · NEW DELHI · SYDNEY

METHUEN DRAMA
Bloomsbury Publishing Plc
50 Bedford Square, London, WC1B 3DP, UK
1385 Broadway, New York, NY 10018, USA
29 Earlsfort Terrace, Dublin 2, Ireland

BLOOMSBURY, METHUEN DRAMA and the Methuen Drama logo are
trademarks of Bloomsbury Publishing Plc

First published in Great Britain 2022

Cover design: Ben Anslow
Cover image: Sydney Opera House Keeps Ghost Lights On Across Theatres
During Coronavirus Closure (© James D. Morgan / Getty Images

A catalogue record for this book is available from the British Library.

Library of Congress Cataloging-in-Publication Data
Names: Svich, Caridad, author.
Title: Toward a future theatre : conversations during a pandemic / Caridad Svich.
Description: London ; New York : Methuen Drama, 2021. | Series: Theatre makers |
Includes bibliographical references and index.
Identifiers: LCCN 2021020336 (print) | LCCN 2021020337 (ebook) |
ISBN 9781350241060 (hardback) | ISBN 9781350241053 (paperback) |
ISBN 9781350241077 (ebook) | ISBN 9781350241084 (epub)
Subjects: LCSH: Theater–Philosophy. | Theatrical producers and
directors–Interviews. | Theater and society–United States. |
Theater and society–Great Britain.
Classification: LCC PN2039 .S94 2021 (print) |
LCC PN2039 (ebook) | DDC 792.01–dc23
LC record available at https://lccn.loc.gov/2021020336
LC ebook record available at https://lccn.loc.gov/2021020337

ISBN: HB: 978-1-3502-4106-0
PB: 978-1-3502-4105-3
ePDF: 978-1-3502-4107-7
eBook: 978-1-3502-4108-4

Series: Theatre Makers

Typeset by Newgen KnowledgeWorks Pvt. Ltd., Chennai, India

To find out more about our authors and books visit www.bloomsbury.com
and sign up for our newsletters.

CONTENTS

Introduction

Caridad Svich

What do you get when you ask sixty UK and US theatre makers to speak about how the Covid-19 pandemic, the Black Liberation Movement and the reawakened spirit of the Occupy movement have deepened and/or radically shifted how they think about and make public-facing theatre? What happens when digital, horizontally thought work becomes one of the necessary ways forward for many who have not been working in digital or remote social theatre before Covid-19 shuttered the possibility of in-person, indoor site-based theatres in March 2020? How can DIY non-hierarchical forms of online and installation theatre replace and/or reform existing broken, ableist, industrial systems? What does the space/time axis around which centuries of live theatre been made mean from a practical, ontological and philosophical perspective during the time of socially distant theatre, be it live and/or streamed live to a virtual audience? In the age of Brexit, Donald Trump and Boris Johnson, escalating climate change due to environmental racism, severe economic injustice and a collapsing theatre industry that has laid bare the fault lines of racial and class hierarchies that exist inside the precariat class, what kind of theatre is to be fought for and how does one re-dream a new theatre? These questions are at the heart of this collection, which features conversations sustained with playwrights, artistic directors, movement directors, dramaturges and critics between July 2020 and December 2020.

While the conversations in this book are records of a 'moment in historical time', and a death-haunted, radically unique 'moment' at that, global and simultaneous in its traumatic scale, the observations, struggles, practical advice, lessons and hopes articulated herein point towards ways forward for the field as it reckons with structural and systemic racism, misogyny, questions about accessibility (on all fronts) and who theatre is for on local and large stages. The conversations herein serve, thus, as a prism from which present and future practitioners can learn about what it is like to make theatre in the time of massive reckoning. Theatre makers and thinkers in this collection consider the necessity of theatre in the first place, and how in times of crisis (expected and not) artist-citizens are tested and challenged to recalibrate the art form in powerful and sometimes innovative ways. The intergenerational dialogue in this book charts too the special political and theatrical relationship between US and UK artists living under fascist-leaning leaderships while the reality of death from Covid-19 and the simultaneous death of theatre threw the entire field into an urgent moral quandary.

The catalytic event of the murder of George Floyd on 25 May 2020 in Minneapolis at the hands of the police ignited global Black Lives Matter protests, which sparked, in turn, field-wide calls to action for white-dominant theatres to dismantle white supremacist structures and adopt anti-racist language and practices. The social tumult and political fire of the Covid-19 era, especially its first few months of detection and lockdown in the United States and the UK, evoked the spirit of both the 1968 revolutions centred on civil rights, racial justice and healing, gender equality and LGBTQIA rights and the volatile, fractious 2008 Occupy movement. Yet, it also felt like the tectonic plates of the entire world were shifting, reeling from hundreds of years of the effects of colonialism and late capitalism's Chicago School of Economics' neoliberal economic paradigm, as artists and citizens articulated a renewed sense of purpose and solidarity with long-standing global anti-colonial, anti-racist and anti-fascist movements that had long been fighting for the indigenization of teaching, learning and cultural spaces.

The conversations in this book reflect varied perspectives on the many fault lines exposed in the weighted apparatus of much of the corporate-modelled, capitalist white-dominant theatre industry. A few of the conversations address the problematic nature of those struggling in-and-against the system, expressing a discrete alignment with views articulated by both, to single out two thinkers in this area, sociologist John Holloway in his book *Crack Capitalism* (2010) and Stuart Hall in his essays collected and edited by Kobena Mercer in *The Fateful Triangle: Race, Ethnicity, Nation* (2017) – in effect, (a) that the struggle to stay within the system perpetuates capitalism itself and its commitment to labour subordinate to the demands of the market, and (b) that there are deadly consequences to the contemporary politics of identification that reinscribe systems of power rather than wrestle the discursive terms reflective of such power. Hovering above and through most of the conversations is also the inescapable subject of climate change and theatre's complex relationship towards the continued erosion of the environment and the hastening of climate disruption.

All artists in this collection were asked four core questions:

How has lockdown been for you?
What advice do you have for people entering the field
 right now?
What hopes and dreams do you have for theatre's future?
In times of crisis and profound multivalent traumas, how can
 theatre be a vector for healing and heal itself from damages
 that mostly white cishet male-led dominant theatres have
 incurred against Black, Indigenous, ethnically diverse people,
 people of colour, LGBTQIA+ folx, working-class and
 differently abled practitioners?

The answers that the thinkers in this book offer in response to these four core questions (and more) are wide-ranging and vulnerable, and by no means definitive, but in their totality, they are honest, lucid, engaging and provide fiery food for thought. The reformative and regenerative impulses, especially around the question of hopes and dreams, speak to the creative optimism exhibited by all the practitioners, administrators, critics and academics in this collection, even when blunt and dire realities are faced by them. The absolute necessity for racial healing and parsing through intersectional racism and classism towards the rebuilding of a new theatre ecosystem, one that is also ecologically conscious, is expressed with vitality and purpose.

Questions of and around the centrality and/or ubiquity of digital theatre, the Zoom platform stage, transmedia work and also gender parity (a subject that weaves its way through the pieces in subtle and less subtle ways) are positioned throughout the collection, specific to the working processes of each contributor. What the book points towards in these conversations that spanned six months in the United States and the UK – six months that saw a huge, revolutionary pivot in the field around online, streaming theatre and its access to audiences (with Wi-Fi, of course, which opens up the debate around audiences without) globally – is a recalibrated field, one where parallel programming – live and digital – 'suddenly' became the new usual not only for unusual times but likely for always.

The only non-transatlantic voices in this collection hail from Aotearoa-New Zealand, and specifically, a director/playwright team that works at the Auckland Theatre Company. Their inclusion in this collection may at the outset seem as if they are an outlier. Yet, given that New Zealand was the first country to truly rein in the effects of Covid-19 through a severe and early lockdown imposed by Prime Minister Jacinda Ardern, their perspective is invaluable. Also, they were one of the first companies to effectively innovate with the properties available through Zoom to reimagine their staging of Anton Chekhov's *The Seagull* for the Covid-19 era. Playfully called 'the Zoom Seagull', the work of Eleanor Bishop and Eli Kent, adapting the piece for a cast of Indigenous and Anglophone actors in a contemporary setting, set a new standard for what was possible for text-based work created for the online medium.

The time capsule aspect of this book also exposes the fragility and mortality of theatre itself – the seemingly indestructible beast that has been part of cultures for centuries. Is theatre dying? Or better yet, is theatre always dying to be reborn? How to keep theatre alive and present and open for everyone when structures and systems quickly seem to calcify access entry points and its operating procedures, especially within a caste- and race-based neoliberal economic context? Is being on the weary hamster wheel of late capitalism the default for many theatre organizations and National Portfolio Organizations (NPOs), or could they find, or even lead, the way towards modelling a post-capitalist state?

The other elements that are part of the time capsule nature of this book, even as it imagines ways forward (sometimes by looking backwards towards older, ancient ways of doing and making art), are less easy to pinpoint and have much to do with the nature of the Covid-19 era itself – its unpredictability, volatility, loneliness and anxiety. Practitioners in this book range from artistic directors of small, mid-size and larger companies and NPOs to critics to freelance artists working in the gig worker economy, where gigs suddenly disappeared as soon as theatres shuttered in March 2020 (some never to return). A great percentage of the artists in this collection had shows cancelled or postponed, others saw projects in development stop in their tracks, while others were forced into a position of questioning why there were making theatre and live art in the first place. Other artists are immunocompromised and were wrestling with the reality and/or potentiality of the disease affecting them or their loved ones and neighbours. There is a lot of hurt expressed in this book. And panic. And, also, joy. The work in this volume, as it speaks to and points towards a future theatre, thus, is also the physical, emotional and spiritual labour that was being undergone (and that continues) for the artists in this collection. Illuminating the difficult areas of this kind of emotional and spiritual labour has been crucial. Often this work is invisible to audiences viewing and experiencing public-facing art. Rendering it visible, while also being respectful of the artists' privacy, has been one of the goals in the making of this book. Why? Because there is the work that is seen and the work unseen, and both are part of the work. And so is the dreaming.

The five chapters in this book are structured around issues related to locality; virtuality; political, aesthetic, artistic and linguistic resistances; interstitial spaces of communion; and necessary r/evolutions. The book begins with layers of historical sediment metaphorically laid out by British playwright, director and theatre maker Tim Crouch, as he dissects political forces that led to the initial writing of his play *I, Cinna (The Poet)* from its initial staging with the Royal Shakespeare Company to a reimagined staging at the Unicorn Theatre in London, pre-lockdown, and then a live, Zoom interpretation during lockdown. Crouch calibrates a litany of rage and revolution in the story of the poet that bears witness to the ravages and damages of a rapidly accelerating age of catastrophe and inequity, and tasks themselves with writing down what they see and how it is that they see what they see. As theatre is both a seeing and listening place, Crouch throws down the gauntlet right at the start of the book for the reader to contend with the images of a desolate, despairing Republic, and how artist-poets need to remain vigilant and alert to the shifting, and often erratic, tides of their times. Crouch's fiery provocation sets the stage for the chapters that follow.

In this first chapter, the central theme that courses through the conversations is the fire of r/evolution itself. In the sudden fallout from Covid-19, the field was thrust into a 'temporary autonomous zone' (to quote anarchist writer and poet Hakim Bey). What could this mean for a process of liberation and reformation? Could the revolutionary wheel be broken to enable true evolution in the field? Could theatre disentangle itself from the clutches of the 'culture industry', and its dominant economies, embedded, as they mostly are, within an economic, neoliberal framework that capitalizes (pun intended) and, therefore, politically neuters its evolutionary potential?

The second chapter centres on local and hyperlocal theatre, focusing on artists and companies embedded within specific communities, often, but not always, at the ground level – physical, live, socially distanced – and work that is theatre but may not always be a play in the conventional sense. This is work that takes the form of drawing classes, open space forums, jamborees in parking lots, remote online socials, escape rooms or virtual online one-on-one conversations, co-created live art experiences and yes, sometimes, plays, too.

The third chapter focuses on virtuality, and it explores the digital highways of theatre – where it has been, where it is or may be going and how Zoom and other platforms allow for an illusion of intimacy even within its box-like frames, and how sound and light installations, immersive video podcasts, online game experiences, travelogues and the cultures that thrive on TikTok, YouTube and Twitch are pushing the field to places it maybe never thought it could go at such an accelerated pace, out of urgency, necessity and fearlessness. In the fourth chapter, resistance as an artistic and political tool is examined. This chapter centres on artists and thinkers who work to hold spaces of radical difference, racial healing from structural, cis-het, patriarchal, ableist and racist practices in theatres, and who are actively engaged in individual and/or circle-based collective projects that seek to resist commodification and the lure of celebrity. The last chapter focuses on communion – how artists, critics and audiences share and hold space together, and indeed, how they may do so during a pandemic, with all its mitigating factors, and after too, when theatre returns, hopefully, without the health and safety measures of social distancing. In this chapter practitioners speak about building or rebuilding process-based private-facing and public-facing artistic thought experiments through the reimagining of what the essential communion between an artwork and an audience is and can be. Could theatre debuild to rebuild? Could theatre do its level best to leave the edifices behind and go out into the world, and what kind of world would that be? The unbearable racial and class injustices that have governed much of the colonial arms of theatre present in the United States and the UK find themselves at a breaking point or tipping point in the Covid-19 era. At the same time, the twinned spectres of climate grief and climate change haunt our stages – political, social and theatrical. It is one thing to debuild or dismantle the corporate, capitalist, Oxbridge/Ivy League-driven, caste-based industry and another to also reckon with the fact that the dismantling need to be led with and by an ecologically conscious vision. In other words, if there is not a planet, then there is no future for a dismantled theatre.

Social justice writer adrienne maree brown in her book *Emergent Strategy: Shaping Change, Changing Worlds* (2017) offers a biometric, permaculture approach to social design projects centred on the liberation of Black, Indigenous and ethnically diverse people of colour. McKenzie Wark in *Capital Is Dead: Is This Something Worse?* (2019) argues that the post-broadcast era has made the consumer the product, and that it is the consumer that must refind their way to becoming a citizen again rather than a product/client and liberate themselves from the production line, which includes their own bodies and data mined for rentier capitalist and post-capitalist profit. Braiding these two divergent strands for a moment, is it possible to conceive of an evolutionary theatre that leads with an ecologically conscious, ethically responsible, pleasurable, biometric and non-consumer-based way of moving through an ever-changing world?

If so, what might that theatre look like? Might it look a bit like the Purple Door Theatre in Liverpool set to open in the spring of 2021, which is billed as the UK's first 'truly free theatre' and is subsidized by bar sales and social impact funding? Will it take a tip from the legendary days of the Shunt collective when they were at The Vaults, where a £5 note was your cover for entry to the bar and along the way one was enticed to check out the work happening 'next door'? Might it be a podcast series that one listens to, an audio piece in your ear as you ride the underground line, a play garden where a theatre piece occurs with tools from a nearby shed or a colouring book that asks its audience to fill in the colours of the story being told? How many ways could we dream theatres' future?

The conversations documented in these pages do not offer all the answers. How could they? But I do think that in their totality, speaking from the broken spaces and places of the 'death' of theatre, surrounded by the concrete reality of shuttered, darkened buildings, and individual artists struggling with the fiscal and emotional after-effects of a severely unbalanced playing field, they may offer ways forward for the theatre to attend to the multiple emergencies of not only the field of theatre but also its position in and relationship to the planet and its many people and inhabitants. When I use the word 'attend', I mean 'to listen, to give attention to' but I also mean to show up, 'to attend and regard', just as an audience attends the theatre.

I started this book way before these conversations came to light. It was late one night before the 'end times' of the Covid-19 era. I was on Twitter. Yes, a rentier capitalist platform. But I was thinking about how I could treat the platform as a utility for something else: a writing project. One that would play with the language of address and attention. I wrote the words 'Dear theatre'. After those words began a series of tweets that evolved into thousands of tweets – virtual letters sent to the intangible body of theatre writ large. Sometimes those short missives were taunts. Sometimes they were provocations. At other times they were caresses, and at others, they were dreams. Each missive unfolded onto the next in a nonlinear cyber scroll built on the praxis of hope.

As you travel metaphorically through these pages, dipping into an artist's house in Brighton, and another's in Brooklyn, and so on, I invite you to think about how each conversation is part of a larger network of dreams, and how these momentary glimpses of trouble, struggle, despair, passion, irreverence and humility are also built on this praxis, addressing theatre as one would a confidante, and not an industrial machine. The collective, dissensual 'we' in these pages are all sending signs in the dark, illuminated by a hope in the future. They are staring at theatre's mortality in the face and talking through and from a state of emergence. All we ask is that you show up.

A poet dreams: Three earth samples

Tim Crouch

Tim Crouch is a British playwright and theatre-maker. These opening remarks, written in November 2020, reflect upon his piece *I, Cinna (the Poet)* from its first staging in 2012 through its restaging at the Unicorn Theatre pre-lockdown to its live online presentation during lockdown in the summer of 2020.

Analyse a sample of the earth we stood on at the start of 2012. Before Trump; before Boris Johnson, Brexit, Antifa, QAnon, Black Lives Matter, Covid-19. Before Zoom had even launched its software.

2012. Before modern era.

Our sample would tell us, in the UK at least, that we liberal-leaning theatre-makers thought we had it pretty bad back then. What did we know? Labour had lost the general election in 2010 and the Tories's commitment to austerity ensured that wealth was being kept firmly in the hands of the few. In 2011, the UK had seen three days of rioting in response to a police killing in Tottenham – riots fuelled by racial tensions, spending cuts, youth unemployment, social divisions. They inspired the then mayor of London, one Boris Johnson, to buy some water cannons. It was around the time of the riots that the RSC commissioned *I, Cinna (the Poet)*, a play for audiences aged 11+, scheduled for production in 2012. The play I wrote felt deeply rooted in the core sample of that moment.

My Cinna the poet is also Shakespeare's Cinna the poet – based on what information we get from his seventeen lines in *Julius Caesar*. Both dreamers. Both watching big political events unfold from the safety of their homes. Both ill-fated. Both killed arbitrarily and violently. Both Cinnas have 'no will wander forth of doors' and who can blame them? The world outside is in revolt. Democracy is threatened. Society is polarized. Civil war feels imminent. My Cinna has writer's block – a premonitionary sense of a poem he's failing to write. He invites his audience to write with him. To write reactively at first and then slowly to engage with their own position. He invites the audience to write the name of the country where they live, the name of the leader of that country and then one word that describes that leader. Cinna then asks his audience to share some of those words out loud. Back in 2012, the UK prime minister was David Cameron, and the words were relatively restrained: *privileged, rich, powerful, important, greedy*. Towards the end of the play, each audience member is invited to write a poem about the defining action of Cinna's short life: his death. The defining texts in *I, Cinna (the Poet)* are not written by the playwright.

Fast forward eight years and analyse a sample of the earth we stood on at the start of February 2020. This was the month a new production of *I, Cinna (the Poet)* opened at the Unicorn Theatre in London. The core sample has a completely different chemical constitution. It's like it's from another planet. How could a play from 2012 sustain life in that? At the start of 2020, the liberal-leaning theatre-makers could hardly lift their jaws from the floor.

What happened in those eight years?

In 2012, the London Olympics felt like the final death rattle of the UK's cultural connectedness to the world. In 2016, the UK electorate voted to leave the European Union and, with that, they almost single-handedly gifted global populism its future on a plate. On the eve of the EU referendum, Labour politician Jo Cox was shot and stabbed to death by a neo-Nazi shouting 'Britain First' as he attacked. ('Speak, hands, for me,' says Casca, as he plunges his dagger into Caesar.) Later in 2016 a self-confessed sexual predator was elected president of the United States. In his one term of office, he attempted to destroy democracy and undermine the free press. Back in the UK, Boris 'Water-Cannon' Johnson became prime minister – a man who was once secretly recorded conspiring to have a journalist beaten up; who compared women wearing burqas to 'letter boxes'; who burnt to cinders the 'oven-ready' EU deal he'd promised us.

Our earth sample in February 2020 shows us that we were blissfully unaware of an approaching pandemic but depressingly aware of the direction of political travel in the world. For the RSC in 2012, I'd been writer and director but not the performer. For the Unicorn in 2020, I was the writer and performer but not the director. The director's role was taken by Naomi Wirthner and the conversations we had in the run up to rehearsals were as much about the state of the world as they were about the play. We agreed that the change to this new *Cinna* would be less to the text and more to the *con*text – an understanding that if the audience writes the defining texts in the play then it would be the audience (and the world they lived in) that would supply its contemporary meaning. In 2012, the original production of the play was interspliced with film footage of the UK riots of the previous year. In 2020, we widened our video palette to accommodate the widening global crisis – violent protest in Ukraine, Hong Kong, Palestine, Syria, Charlottesville, Catalonia, Lebanon and Chile. And, in turn, the words elicited from the audience to describe their country's leader also widened: *buffoon, inept, opportunist, fool, arrogant.*

And then Covid-19 arrived. The first UK lockdown came on 23 March – two weeks after the end of the London *Cinna* run. The enforced confinement felt energized by its newness. But the newness didn't last long, and people started dying. Some people who got ill stayed ill. The virus became a magnifier of all the shit that had been building up over the years, the toxins in the earth: the lie of austerity, the failure of populism, the reality of racial discrimination, of class inequality, the underfunding of the health service. Political incompetence could now be measured in surplus deaths.

Our third and final core sample comes from July 2020 – four months on from that first lockdown – and the mass spectrometer can't believe its isotopes. Over those five months, the world had become almost unrecognizable. In April, Boris Johnson spent a week in intensive care with Covid-19 and his senior advisor broke and thereby completely undermined the rules of the lockdown by driving 250 miles to his second home. In May, the slow-motion police execution of George Floyd ignited a global movement that was to be described by Donald Trump as 'toxic propaganda'. In June, Trump ordered the teargassing of peaceful protestors to facilitate a photo op in front of a church. In London in June, neo-Nazis gave Hitler salutes as they claimed to protect a statue of Winston Churchill from 'terrorists'.

There were no liberal-leaning theatre-makers as there was no liberal-leaning theatre to make. No theatre period. The UK became a country without live public culture. But also, a country where the bird song was louder, where the skies were empty, the roads were quiet. Midway through the first lockdown I wrote a provocation for a UK arts organization where I attempted to identify new possibilities afforded to us by the pandemic: a desperate act of optimism. I suggested that we were living in one 'big Brechtian gesture' – a potentially productive process of verfremdungseffekt, of 'making strange'; that the restrictions we found ourselves in could be the 'prompt for new thinking' and that distance had its benefits. The provocation ended:

> Stay strange, everyone. Keep the strangeness. Even as we eventually get to hold each other tightly, stay strange. And as the strange becomes familiar, find the new strange.

In July 2020, at the time of our final sample – a time when our real-life communities were shattered and exhausted – a live rendition of the Unicorn production of *I, Cinna (the Poet)* was staged on Zoom. The form of this digital iteration was rooted firmly in the strange and socially distanced soil of its time. I performed alone in a Unicorn rehearsal room with a Zoom host sitting in the corridor outside and an operator/stage manager sitting four miles away in their home. Two monitors, two webcams, a phone and an invisible audience behind their screens, scattered around the world. In the play, Cinna unpacks the idea of a 'republic'. 'Is this a republic?' he asks. 'Are we equal here? I want us to be equal.' This question felt big in a theatre with an audience present – a consideration of democracy and autocracy in the live performance space. On Zoom, it took on a whole new dimension. The play reached into the digital terrain in which we'd been living for the last five months and the question felt genuine and profound: who's in charge here?

Zoom's Webinar function enabled the audience's presence to be acknowledged. They could raise their digital hands. They could speak – we opened microphone to hear voices from the ether explain what they would die for, what they would kill for. Zoom also enabled the audience to see itself in a way it couldn't in the theatre. At the end of the performance, the Zoom host promoted the audience to participants and invited them to open their cameras. Slowly, one by one, they appeared – in their homes, on their sofas, with their families, their partners, engaged, witnessing, writing. The words they wrote spoke of the time they lived in. The words for their countries' leaders came fast and furious on the Zoom Q&A function: *fascist, amoral, scared, buffoon, dictator, dumbass, opportunist, racist, stupid, liar, wanker, overrated, right-wing clown, puppet master, twat, cruel, pig.* The defining texts not written by the playwright. The defining texts giving voice to a hitherto voiceless audience. In a world seemingly headed towards totalitarianism the audience each night were fighting for the republic.

And then there were the poems that they wrote. Hundreds of them, collated by the Unicorn Theatre into a digital book. A public specimen. A cross section of a moment in time – culturally, politically, poetically. It's not in the spirit of a republic to single out any one in particular but this, written by someone called Ella, age unstated, punched like a fist.

Cut the binds
Sharpen the knife
Spill the blood
Whatever it takes
To release some of this tension.

1

R/evolution

Jessica Blank and Erik Jensen

Jessica Blank and Erik Jensen are American theatre-makers specializing in documentary theatre. They are writers, actors and directors and together, they are the authors of *The Exonerated* (2002), *How to Be a Rock Critic* and *Aftermath* (2009). Their piece *Coal Country*, with music by Steve Earle, premiered at The Public Theater in New York City, when Covid-19 lockdown began in New York in mid-March 2020. Their piece *The Line* premiered on 8 July 2020 online at The Public Theater, with music composition by Aimee Mann and Jonathan Coulton, and music produced by Michael Penn. This interview was conducted over Zoom on 18 August 2020. Audio transcription by Maya Quetzali Gonzalez.

CS *How has lockdown been for you?*

JB *Coal Country*, which we'd been working on for four years, had just opened at The Public Theater on 3 March 2020. We'd been in previews for a few weeks before that, but we'd just opened. We were right at the beginning of that crest and then everything suddenly changed in one day.

The story of the Upper Big Branch Mine disaster that *Coal Country* tells was sort of a microcosm of the story of what was happening in the first days of the lockdown because it really tells the story of how, when corporate interests and monied interests and the interests of power systematically over time undercut institutions and systems that are put in place to protect ordinary people that one crisis can come along and completely decimate a community.

When our show was suddenly closed, we were stunned and trying to get our bearings. And then the producers of the 24-Hour Plays called us and asked us to do a monologue for their Viral Monologues series. We interviewed a New York City hospital nurse about what she was experiencing. This was during the first days of the peak, when they were changing the rules about PPE every day. It was a moving and intense interview. At the same time, we were still in almost daily contact with The Public Theater and we pitched them this idea of a rapid-response documentary play called *The Line* based on interviews with frontline New York City medical workers. A few weeks later, The Public said 'yes'.

EJ The urgency of the moment kept pushing us forward. My anger too, at the total lack of an executive branch, federal response, bothered me down to the soles of my shoes. My great-grandfather was a judge, and my grandfather was a cop, and I was raised in a household in the Midwest that taught me that the government was there to help, that there was equality under the law and that we're all in this together. To wake up and realize that we're not in this together and we can't get it together without leadership was shocking and disturbing to me.

JB George Floyd was murdered just as we had completed the interviews. While we couldn't start all the interviews over from scratch at that point, it was really imperative that we include the reckoning that happened in the wake of his murder as part of the moment we were talking about in the play. We reinterviewed a few people, so those resonances are also in there.

EJ I consider the people I interview as teachers. Making *The Exonerated*, twenty years ago, was my entry into the justice system and how it really works and how inherently racist it is. It was my entry into learning that there is no equanimity in the judicial system, and it doesn't work, and it is broken. Seeing the public execution of George Floyd take place in my hometown of Minneapolis rocked me to the core. I realized the system was not merely broken but it was doing the things that it was designed to do. Making *The Line*, I realized that that system just did not exist in policing, it also existed in our hospitals. *The Line* for me became a bit of a rallying cry because I was waking up and I wanted other people to wake up with me. That is what all writers want.

CS *What are your hopes and dreams for theatre's future?*

EJ Let me answer your question in a weird way. When I was in college, I attended my first Grateful Dead concert. Structurally, *The Exonerated* (for me internally, anyway) was based on that Grateful Dead concert. One song leading into the next, actors playing off each other, a direct audience address, that sort of breathing that the band and us experience together. My hope for the theatre is that it becomes more communal and captures more of our real experience and casts a wider net. Digital opportunities have created a situation where audiences are potentially more multi-ethnic now. We can get younger audiences in now. It's like listening to a Beatles record instead of going to see the band. One thing feeds the other. One doesn't take away from the other. My hope is that that communal experience is spread out like a net and captures as many imaginations as possible.

JB As a director, I think about my rehearsal rooms or sets like a 'temporary autonomous zone' – that's not my term, it's from the author Hakim Bey (original name Peter Lamborn Wilson) and his 1991 book of the same name. The idea is: institutions take on their own sort of life over time and become confining, oppressive, etc.; but in a temporary space we can reinvent the rules. When I run a room, I'm trying to do that every day. In the most idealistic of worlds, if we use it right, the theatre itself could become a Temporary Autonomous Zone, because of its transitory, impermanent nature. We have opportunities all the time to create microcosms of what an equitable and just organization of human beings could look like, to experiment with interacting creatively and productively in ways that are non-oppressive. As Erik was saying, our system is inherently oppressive and must be completely reinvented, right? All of us must unpack and deprogramme the ways we've been conditioned by the system we've been raised in, which is an ongoing process. But art is an iterative process of doing that. We've got a little petri dish we can all work in together. In the best of all possible worlds, that is what we do.

EJ The virus exposed systems. It focused us all to take a pause while dealing with grief and fear and forced us to re-evaluate what our place in that system is. As a cis white male who is in the most privileged position, that means I need to evolve, and adjust my ideas about how I'm listening and who I'm listening to. The virus is forcing our whole country to do that work, and to see it for what it really is and not to live in the fantasy of it. Theatre is fantasy and imagination, but we do not want to perpetuate the fantasy of our society with it. We want to address it, change it and evolve it. The only way to beat a virus is to evolve faster and change quicker than it.

CS *What advice do you have for people that are entering the field now?*

JB Keep making work. I came to New York and started out as an actor just before 9/11, which was like another moment that was seismic. When 9/11 happened, we'd just had the first readings of *Exonerated* and that project was just starting, and there was this moment where people were like, 'Are we ever going to make theatre again?' We didn't know. We just kept putting one foot in front of the other and kept making things. We didn't have resources. Except for people. We called everybody we knew, and asked them for help, and if they wanted to collaborate. The advice is to make stuff, build community and take care of your community. Mutual aid.

EJ I had a teacher in high school named Dennis Swanson who saved me from a difficult family situation (in conjunction with the second teacher that I had in college, named Victoria Santa Cruz).
      Dennis taught me what I needed to know innately, that I had a voice and that I had something to say and that there was a conduit for that. Victoria taught me that I didn't know how to listen yet. The advice that a lot of young writers get is the write what you know thing and I never found that to be helpful. I spend far too much time with myself for that to be interesting. It is what I don't know that feeds me. Living and not knowing is okay. You must stay curious in that not knowing.

JB And learn to love it. Erik said to me incredibly early on in our relationship/collaboration the three most beautiful words in the English language next to 'I love you' are 'I don't know'. That is a guiding principle for us creatively. It is something I teach. We must make friends with it.

EJ Traumas teach us things. It's like a tree. A tree bends in the wind and it cracks, and you can hear it crack, and hear it get hurt as it moves in a big storm. But what is happening is all those little cracks in the tree are healing. It is coming out stronger. The not knowing and the pause that we are in right now is a real opportunity for us to examine what is important. People have started to suss out what is important are other people. Because other people have been taken away from us. Some people are realizing their values and some people are just starting to realize that they have been had and that they bought into an illusion. In the not knowing and in the fear, we are like those trees. We are cracking and bending, and it hurts, but ultimately, next year we are going to grow that extra layer and get a little taller and a little stronger.

JB Theatre is ritual. There is a ritual structure to making a new play and rehearsing it and putting it up and riding the run and then closing it. That ritual was interrupted. There's something that feels wrong about that. I know that we will find – I don't know what form it is going to come in – but we'll find ways to complete that circle. When it's safe to breathe the same air again.

Michael Garcés

Michael Garcés is a Cuban-American playwright and director and artistic director of Cornerstone Theatre Company in Los Angeles. This interview was conducted on Zoom on 6 November 2020.

CS *How has lockdown been for you?*

MG This pandemic is one that everyone in the world has experienced collectively, yet each of us is having such a highly individual experience. There's a dissonance between the self and the existential threat we share in common. As an artist, I've found it to be a time for me for reflection and response. For the company it's been a galvanizing time. Cornerstone had a crisis of contraction which was mostly financial two years before the pandemic hit. We lost two of our major funders here in California; both stopped funding the arts altogether. It was a huge blow for us because we lost a big chunk of our income. Property values also rose astronomically in our neighbourhood. So, we lost our space. This all happened pre pandemic.

There's still a tremendous amount of uncertainty and fragility in any not-for-profit, but our mission is more vital than ever. We've had very robust conversations among our ensemble and company members and board, looking at the roots of our company, and at overcoming what in our company – intentionally or not – mirrors white supremacist structure. The truth of the company's DNA is that we were started by a group of young idealistic white people from Harvard as a response against more conventional LORT theatre structures while at the same time not entirely disengaging from those structures. We've been really trying to see what about our structure and practice we can and should change.

CS *What are your hopes and dreams for the field?*

MG I'm trying to think about this time as not about before and after, but rather as simply part of a continuum in which we're living. We're coming through things and we'll enter new phases, but we're in a years-long continuum of grappling with what we've done to the climate, and our necessary and inevitable reckoning with history continues unabated.

There have been plagues before in human history and this one won't be the last. My hope is that we will take advantage of the forced awakening from the sort of somnolence that many of us were in as a society. This can only be a boon for theatre artists in terms of their own awareness and awakening as they hopefully grapple with an audience that is eager to explore similar questions about existence.

Theatre works best when the critique of whatever is happening on stage is one that the audience is hungry for and for which they might not agree with the answers. Right now, we're all very open for the critique, and we're also open to celebrate together and mourn together. This is potentially a moment in which great art can flourish.

I think about some of the theatre and live experiences I was privileged to see in Chile after Augusto Pinochet left power. There was this eruption of performance art and theatre because our audience was hungry for new work. I'm not saying audiences in Chile then liked everything they saw, but the curiosity and hunger was strong because the entire society was coming out of a very turbulent and yet deeply repressed time, and as sentient beings they were seeking to gather in theatres to grapple with questions around what the country had endured.

I'm hopeful that we as a field lean into that kind of hunger instead of settling for specious ideas around the bourgeois contempt for political theatre, which has been a real inhibitor for many years for artists in this country. There were formulas we lazily repeated, ideas about how things 'had' to work; we accepted as fact that the systems in which we worked were inevitable.

We understand how these systems are not a given. We understand that these systems and structures are weak and brittle. In that breakability there's limitless possibility. I'm optimistic that as artists we can be part of a social movement towards shattering those brittle, inflexible systems and creating new, supple, fluid, inclusive, open structures.

Maybe we can finally make work where there is deep engagement with other human beings on their own terms and have conversations we enter innocent of and genuinely curious about the outcome as opposed to engaging in conversations which are really just a devious form of marketing in which we – the instigators – knew exactly what we want and are just trying to trick people into thinking there was a genuine give and take. That's a lie and the kind of lie that's deadly in the theatre – as opposed to the lie we all accept together in mutual consent because we want to make something beautiful that's alive and created with reciprocity of feeling. When the lie of theatre is not one of mutuality but of deceit, then it is corrosive. It prevents authentic vulnerability, kills the possibility of breakthrough.

CS   *What about Cornerstone? Future goals?*

MG   The only constant at Cornerstone is change. I think our response to the uprising following the murder of George Floyd surfaced some concerns for us about things we had not been talking about as a company quite as deeply as we should. It's made a lot of our conversations as a company take on a greater sense of importance as opposed to urgency, because urgency is only about getting things done quickly, whereas importance means that we must have this conversation and a greater commitment to be reflective.

We've always been grappling with issues of agency in the work. Who's telling the story and who is centred, and when we sit in circles, how do we truly have a circle that is all Circumference and no Centre? How do we have leadership that is horizontal and not vertical? How do I as artistic director do no harm, lead well, and make choices and decisions that are equitable?

CS   *Any advice for those entering the field right now?*

MG   This is a field where every artist is always entering. Even without a pandemic going on. The fact of being always in enter mode can lead to burnout and frustration but can also lead to inspiration and rebirth and rejuvenation. We're in a capitalist system. We reward each other by giving each other capital. The field is and has always been about the haves and have nots. Now the gaps are greater between them. But everyone still has their own path, their own *camino* through this business. To be rigorous with your practice is important and centring yourself in love and trust in your work. Now more than ever it's going to be required for people to own that themselves because they're going to be fewer structural handholds. The field is going to be more horizontal, which will mean that the economic models will change. People will still be hungry for work that engages them and their communities. There will be a need for processing what has happened and a need for celebration and critique. We'll come out of this collective pandemic that we've all experienced highly individually and very differently in different parts of the world in different parts of the country and in different racial classes (I hate to use the word race because it's such a lie, the lie that we have used to punish ourselves and each other for centuries, but it is a lie we'll make real in our interactions and willed perceptions until we don't) ready to engage in good, deep, rigorous work that doesn't necessarily find its centre through commodification. I hope for a less vertical field. The so-called narrative of the American Dream assumes that a person's singularity and specialness will single them out to climb the ladder of success. Everybody wants to be a star. Everybody wants to be *sobre-saliente*.

You walk into most theatres and the structure is hierarchical and it's a pyramid. The artistic director (or whatever the title) is on top. And while the optics may change in terms of who has power, the pyramid stays the same, which means nothing has changed. It's a class hierarchy.

Capitalist theatres will not change capitalism.

CS *How do you build nurturing work environment while also negotiating trauma and the dramaturgy of trauma?*

MG Western theatre always involves the lever of trauma in that it requires that the human move through crisis to enlightenment or at least resolution. The centrality of this kind of dramaturgy, a cis-male paradigm, has in and of itself caused a great deal of damage because it is a narrative that has dominated the field and has disallowed other ways of thinking about dramaturgy. Not all plays have to be about the pornography of trauma. Even plays that are set in the aftermath of trauma centre trauma! A dramaturgy of empathy and compassion can push back against a dramaturgy of trauma. If we're all listening to each other and truly hearing and seeing each other everybody feels listened to and heard in the process. Then you're naturally going to be taking care of each other. This kind of approach can lead to bigger, more interesting, more challenging and ambiguous – and ambitious – possibilities. We need to seek other ways of seeing that create paths towards empathy or opportunities for empathy and lead us on a path towards compassion.

James Graham

James Graham is an Oliver Award-winning British playwright, screenwriter and librettist. This interview was conducted over email during November 2020.

CS *How has lockdown been for you?*

JG Like a lot of creative people, I've finally gotten over the guilt and the shame I felt about, at best, inconsistent and, at worst, non-existent productivity. I have been baffled by why this specific condition – which is in theory ideally suited to writing (private, quiet, no distractions, focused) – is the least productive I've been since I first became a professional writer over fifteen years ago. My only explanation is that enforced solitude makes you naturally inclined to crave connections – on social media, news updates, messages. And that, unlike novelists, dramatists thrive on the juxtaposition of private and public experiences.

One of the strangest aspects of my own experience, during this very isolated time, was having to be often extremely 'public', as part of the campaign to win emergency relief funding from the government. The fight to get the disproportionately devastating impact of the virus on live arts into the public conversation, into the media and onto the desk of politicians, lasted for a couple of gruelling months and there was no guarantee the funding was coming, up until the last minute. As a lover of our industry, I often found it emotionally exhausting. As a political playwright however, I often found the insights into lobbying and power completely fascinating! And as a human being, I was strangely grateful to be involved in the conversation with my peers and industry leaders as, quite frankly, it made me feel part of something during a detached time.

A consensus has never been reached about *what* the best arguments to make for public funding are. If you're trying to win over – in this instance – Conservative ministers, do you go hard on the economic value (we return more to the exchequer than they invest, etc.), or is the social good a local theatre can do, or the importance of mass entertainment on our mental health, or is it the enhancing of our international reputation?

All these ranging thoughts were raging around my brain when I found myself sat on the set of the TV show *Question Time* in May. It felt like things were coming to a head, and the government were yet to even acknowledge the scale of the crisis. It was a week where, through some casual coordinating by various artistic directors, certain members of our community were writing newspaper features, appearing on the radio ... and I was booked onto the BBC's centrepiece political debate show. Facing a Conservative minister, I decided to begin on the economy, attempting to put to bed the false notion that arts funding will cost hospital beds, when it in fact pays for them. It's a profit-making, growth sector (ugh, this all sounds so cold, I know, but we were trying to win!). And then I tried to infuse my passion for what I thought art and storytelling could do on an emotional level.

Honestly, I was bracing myself for a negative reaction on social media – the new public square. But I think something about the way in which drama and entertainment had really helped people through lockdown meant many were incredibly receptive to financial aid. When Southampton and Plymouth began announcing news of theatre closures and redundancies, I felt like that was a real turning point. It wasn't celebrities or 'luvvies' calling on the government to help by then, it was local people. Constituents tweeting and writing to their MPs. I was incredibly moved. We think of our work as a constant battle to justify its place, but it turns out (for now at least), a lot of people really don't like the idea of seeing their local theatre boarded up and closed, whether they attend regularly or not.

CS *What advice do you have for young people entering the field right now?*

JG Young people are going to be told that the world of performance arts and theatre is no longer a viable path for them, that post-pandemic the private consumption of entertainment on personal devices proves that live art isn't as desirable or necessary ... and nothing could be further from the truth. What lockdown has reminded most people is the value of physical community, collective action and communal sharing.

The economic environment they will step into will be hugely challenging – but nothing has proven better the mental, social and emotional benefits of storytelling and art than this pandemic. It is what got millions of people, across class, ethnic and cultural divides, through the trauma.

My advice is to have confidence in your viability, and your importance. The creative sector is not some niche, unsubstantial thing, it is one of the most important, worthwhile and vital, on a personal, a local and a national level.

Oh, and that it has got to be fun as well. We have to remember to have fun, against the bleak backdrop unfolding. That's why they call it a 'play'.

CS *What are your hopes and dreams for theatre's future?*

JG I dream sentimentally and ridiculously that theatres can become these vital spaces for people to return to, from isolation, and become physical communities again. That they're open and inclusive and mean something to everyone. In urban centre, and particularly the capital, it's hard to explain to people that many smaller cities, towns and suburbs just don't have enough of these public spaces to meet and 'be' with others anymore. The libraries, the community centres, the youth clubs, the leisure centres, even the pubs are vanishing. Our public sphere is diminished. My stupid dream is theatres and arts centres could be those places. Yes, putting on work at '7.30', but it's what surrounds the work as well, all day long.

Like everyone else, I dream of a substantial reset in the structures and the processes that meant, in the old world, certain groups or communities felt less able to make and share work, sustain careers, and certain audiences didn't conceive of theatre as something for them. Now is the time.

CS *During a time of global collective trauma, what are theatre's healing properties, if any?*

JG Theatre is strong but also weak in this area. At times of trauma – whether that be plague or war or austerity or civil unrest – British theatre tends to revive the classics. Old narratives that can act as allegories, as metaphors. There is power in this of course. Setting *Henry V* in the sands of Iraq or *King Lear* against the backdrop of a kingdom infighting reminds us of society's constancy, that things go around in circles, and there's comfort and perspective in that.

Theatre to me isn't heritage. It isn't something that needs conserving. We also need an urgent theatre, a responsive theatre, a radical theatre that is new and alive not roped off and preserved.

Imagine a world where on a stressful day for your community or the nation, your first instinct is to go to your theatre. I know – dream on. But imagine that was where most average people were pulled. To be around others, to drink and talk and debate. To hear talks and lectures and provocations in the foyer, a kind of Speaker's Corner, and then to watch a show, and debate that afterwards, against the backdrop of live music.

CS   *What are your thoughts on digital theatre?*

JG   For me, the revelation this summer, as theatres and grassroot artists began sharing masses of old and new work online, is that theatre's greatest asset can still be retained in this new digital world – its *liveness*. Theatre has two main superpowers that other artforms don't. Liveness and physical proximity. You are 'there', while they are 'doing it'. Digital theatre cannot replicate one of those – the physical aspect – but it can totally retain the liveness; the joy you get from knowing what you are watching is happening *right now*; that those performers are going through those emotions in *real time* and that you are watching this collectively along with many others across the country and the world *at the same time*.

When I experimented briefly with the digital capture of live work – *Bubble*, for the Nottingham Playhouse, a same-sex pandemic rom-com (there's a new genre for you) – this was what excited me, and the socially distanced audience in the auditorium. Seeing the cameras and knowing that we were sharing this with e-ticket holders across the world.

CS   *In what ways are you energized, galvanized or demoralized at the moment?*

JG   I feel demoralized and broken at the thought that we are losing so many skilled people who can't survive without income and will go to work somewhere else. I feel exhausted by the notion that so many of our dynamic companies and buildings are now so weighed down with debt and paralyzed by uncertainty. I feel so frustrated that so many of us spent so long trying to make even gradual reforms for good in terms of access to the arts, and now we're fighting for just any part of the sector to survive in whatever form.

If you believe that art and plays can help us make sense of the world, and ourselves, that it can both provoke and unite, and that the simple of act of getting people together to tell a story, watched by other people, is a deeply moving thing to happen ... then I suppose you could argue there'll never be a more important time for drama. People need to heal, society needs to be rebuilt, a new purpose and sense of the collective need be attained. Let's get to work and start telling stories about ourselves.

Miranda Haymon

Miranda Haymon is a Black American director and playwright, and resident director at the Roundabout Theatre Company in New York City. This interview was conducted on Zoom on 16 October 2020.

CS *How has lockdown been for you?*

MH Being on lockdown feels like an intervention for me. I don't think that I'd be seeing my potential for risk or new ideas or any new ways or modes of working without quarantine. A lot of my growth as an artist has been vertical and being in quarantine is making me think more horizontally. At the beginning of lockdown, I was, like, freaking out because I thought to myself 'who am I without like going to rehearsal every day and being in a dark room all the time?' But then I started to see that cool stuff was happening outside theatre. I'm living in an artistic and existential question. Do I go back to making art the way I did before or differently? As a Black artist working right now, what does sustainability look like? I am twenty-seven years old, and I'm already exhausted. I've also been breaking down a lot of myths about my understanding of my relationship to New York as a theatre artist. I'm seeing an opportunity for a polyamorous relationship between New York and several other cities in relationship to my artistic work and craft. I really moved into identifying more as an artist during this time than as a theatre maker. I don't think that the life that I was living before this was sustainable in any way and that's because of the industry and that's because of how I was living and that's how I viewed success and forward movement and growth. Although I hate to say it, quarantine was the intervention that I never knew I needed. It took a pandemic to slow me down and I want to make sure that I am giving myself the opportunity to slow down at other times.

CS *Are things happening now in the field that you think are vector points for what theatre may look like in the future, especially because we are also in the middle of massive climate change?*

MH People are in the stage of quarantine where they are ready for new things. At the start of lockdown, I saw a lot of adaptation of live performance happening on Zoom as opposed to intentional work being created on Zoom. I'm not interested in just seeing adaptations of live performance and I mean adaptation because if we thought about it like an adaptation then a lot of the Zoom theatre that we're seeing would be 100 times better. People are afraid of Zoom theatre because there might be some things about it that shows us what we could have been doing all along, especially in terms of access.

As a director, I want to keep asking myself how to move the form forward and interrogate why we are doing things the way we do them, but I'm also beginning to move away from thinking myself as a director because directors aren't really nurtured or respected or mentored in the way that directors need. I don't want to identify only as a director because I want to begin to break away from it. We can't go back to business as usual. It's unacceptable. It never was acceptable. But now it's not even benefiting anybody to do business as usual. From a marketing and budgeting perspective, it's a bad business choice. I'm curious about how theatre will change the 'business as usual' model. Some of our greatest culturally specific organizations and the ones that were doing the work and have been doing the work and have been committed to BIPOC and trans and disabled artists still rehearse six days a week and still don't pay anyone. Artists don't want to go back to that. This summer the rage and sadness and disappointment that I feel is infinite. Especially as a Black artist. I value myself differently now and my worst fear is being inauthentic.

CS *We are also dealing or going to be with audiences that are carrying fear in their bodies.*

MH What's going to make me feel comfortable going to the theatre again? The metrics of it are still hazy. I'm going to go steal a phrase from my dear friend Seonjae Kim: the only thing that seems the most 'business as usual' to me is toxic productivity. I don't understand why theatre artists are so obsessed with toxic productivity and this was before Covid-19. The constant need to be working on something is vicious. It is obviously rooted in white supremacy and capitalism and our scarcity mentality.

The low wages in our industry force people into a mode of constant hustle for work. Mid-career directors are only making on average $70,000 and 16 per cent of that income is from theatre directing. I do miss the theatre. Yet I can't stomach the obsession and the money and capitalist intentions that are behind it. In response to the We See You White American Theater demands and pleas for social and systemic change, I don't think anybody's talking about how much work and labour this has been for people that have had their hours cut or have been furloughed. We are both in the exact position to be able to have these conversations because nothing's going on, and yet the additional labour that comes into people's work while also trying to brainstorm Zoom programming and also how to make the programming that you had before happen. I do not feel like we are talking about that especially how it relates to BIPOC staff in terms of their labour. I wish there were a budget line for emotional labour. Hopefully, significant change will occur simply on that level.

CS *You are working on a piece about Brecht called* bb brecht *at the 2020 Prelude Festival at the Martin E. Segal Theatre Center at CUNY Graduate Center, where you are co-curator. Can you talk about it?*

MH I am obsessed with Brecht. He is my problematic fave. I had a shrine of him in undergrad. I think a lot about what Brecht would have to say about Instagram and influencer culture and performances on Tik Tok. I am eager to take like a Brechtian lens on the state of Art. *bb brecht*, then, is more of an alter ego. It also is an opportunity for me to merge my love of him and his theory and my own obsessions as a millennial. I am also trying to figure out how to find Joy again. I also think a lot about like how much I miss something that I never had: Dada Cabaret. We need a twenty-first-century Dadaist Cabaret and I am positive that it takes place on Instagram. I want to carve out a space for my Black body in Dadaist Cabaret.

CS *What are your hopes and dreams for the field?*

MH I want artists and administrators in the field to be able to have a life. I keep telling my therapist that I have no hobbies and it makes me want to cast off the Trigorin-like mask that being an artist is about having a sickness – the inability to have a life, because you are always looking at life as a source for your artmaking. I wish that every single undertaking that I had as a human person did not have to turn into a product. I hope that we continue to support artists and generate artists and curate artists and make space for ourselves. The word that comes to mind is ephemerality. We are in the business of making something that we know will die.

Simeilia Hodge-Dallaway

Simeilia Hodge-Dallaway is a Black British arts leader, director, activist, founder and artistic director at Beyond the Canon and Artistic Directors of the Future, and co-founder at Black Lives, Black Words International Project. This interview was conducted on Zoom on 26 August 2020, and it was audio-transcribed by Emily Ezzo.

CS   *How has lockdown been for you?*

SHD   Similar to many people in the arts, a few of my projects were cancelled due to the pandemic. When some of your liberties are taken away, it makes you hone even more deeply into your core values, acknowledge where your privilege lies in terms of material and non-material things and identify how you can use your privilege to support other people in the industry. The reality was my workload increased and not lessened during the pandemic. Therefore, what was most important to me was to establish how to take better care of myself, support my staff and assess how much to pivot and respond to the impact of the pandemic and BLM uprising.

Although my work and founded organizations are designed to redress the balance of Black, Asian and POC leaders and artists in the arts industry, the lockdown allowed time to implement necessary changes in my leadership practice and organizational structure. For instance, at the end of 2019, I had the intention of focusing the work carried out at ADF with less attention on partnerships with mainstream institutions, instead recognizing our own agency by creating a more flat-lined leadership practice with shared leadership opportunities for ADF members, online leadership resources and in-house training for my staff and board – I am happy to say, all of these things were achieved. There has always been a high duty of care for my employees, ADF members and wider POC artistic communities; however, I was able to share my knowledge, networks and resources in a different way, for instance, I was able to secure a partnership with Bloomsbury, Oberon and Playwrights Canada Press to offer free published plays written by POC writers to students and artists at a time when their education and training was disrupted. So, I guess you can say, the lockdown and heightened attention to the Black Lives Matter movement helped to validate my work even more.

CS *Can you talk about your companies?*

SHD I run Artistic Directors of the Future (ADF), which is a registered charity dedicated to increase the number of ethnically diverse cultural leaders in the arts industry. I also run Beyond the Canon, a limited company that aims to increase the knowledge of published and produced plays by Black, Asian and POC writers to enable that work to be valued, accessible and revived. Beyond The Canon was inspired by my work as project manager on the Black Play Archive, initiated by Kwame Kwei-Armah, at the National Theatre, independent research of plays by international contemporary POC playwrights and my monologue anthologies for POC actors.

I am also co-founder of Black Lives, Black Words International Project, which I run with my husband Reginald Edmund, which speaks to Black Lives Matter issues using art as a form of activism to create social change and healing.

CS *The Black Play Archive: was it meant to just be an archive? Or was there some idea that the National would do these plays at some point?*

SHD Funded by the National Theatre and Arts Council England the Black Play Archive was designed to be a digital archive, featuring audio-recorded extracts from each of the plays as well as video recordings of ten full-length plays. Unfortunately, we were never able to complete the project as it was cut prematurely by the National Theatre due to financial cuts and a lack of prioritization. That really relates to where we are today: the hope is that when we rebuild the arts industry post-pandemic, we do so with a commitment to equitable practices, a fair allocation of adequate resources and a genuine investment to transformative projects. There was no commitment from the National Theatre to produce any of the plays. However, I brought the 1957 play *Moon on a*

Rainbow Shawl by Errol John to their attention and pleased to say, it received a revival in 2012; in addition, I was responsible for the revival of *Strange Fruit* (1981) by Caryl Phillips, *Leave Taking* (1987) by Winsome Pinnock and *Chiaroscuro* (1986) by Jackie Kay at the Bush Theatre.

CS   *What are your hopes and dreams for theatre's future?*

SHD   Firstly, there is no better time than now for us to articulate what we want when we demand equitable practices and a change in organizational culture, attitudes, structures and systems.

There are a lot of people within our communities that are more than qualified for leadership positions at theatre organizations. I have seen some steps in the right direction, and I have also seen some choices that are detrimental to progressive, actionable steps. There are a lot of white men and white women who hold so much influence and power. Their voices silence others. My hope goes beyond performance activism – half-baked statements on websites to show solidarity to BLM movement – instead, what is needed is an honest 360 look at arts organizations: the leadership; who's in charge of day-to-day decision-making, recruitment and programming and the organizational structures and systems that are broken and for those in power to truly invest in change – short, med and long (ongoing) change. Change with teeth and multi-year financial support.

I also would love for us to give less power to large institutions. That comes down to funding. Mainstream organizations still have the power in their hands resulting in smaller organizations constantly at risk of being exploited. There is no pathway for small-scale organization to evolve, so they remain small with limited funds and resources dependent on large-scale organizations, white-led funding bodies and project-focused funding.

Also, let us use language with efficacy. An 'Associate Director', for instance, means so many things, depending on what organization you are in. An 'Assistant Director' – what does that mean now? Let us stop pretending that these roles are pathways to leadership if they are not pathways to leadership. If an 'Assistant Director' is really meant to be a pathway to become a director then more attention is needed to establish what that role should really entail. It shouldn't be okay for that person just to be the person who makes tea or coffee, or to be the person who just offers that cultural perspective to make whoever's directing the show feel more at ease when directing our stories.

We need to unpack terms such as 'partnership'. It should be an exchange. Small organizations need set their own terms and leave with more resources, increased profile and investment opportunities. There is a toxic nature in the DNA of larger establishment who are rewarded for giving crumbs to POC artistic communities off the back of receiving large investments from funding bodies.

We need to ensure that Black leaders and artists are getting the same wage as their white counterparts with the same level of agency and influence. Too often, succession roles given to POC artists and leaders are diluted, powerless and underpaid. On the same note, we need to be financially compensated for any consultation for our time, our energy, our expertise and our lived experiences. Any, and all, advice is consultation. Our knowledge is not free. Pay us the equivalent that you would pay any other consultant that comes in to strengthen your organization.

Employ the right person from our communities and pay us fairly. If you are going to employ us, don't do it out of pity. Don't do it just because it looks good for your organization. Widen your talent pools and employ the right person. Don't discredit us. Do not undermine us.

CS *What advice do you have for people entering the field right now?*

SHD We're living at a time of crisis and uprising, which will be subsequently followed by restructuring and rebuilding. It is an unprecedented time for the industry to reflect, learn and change and to be held to account. There is no better time than now, to be a part of the solution.

New people entering the industry are fundamental to support the process of reimagination to ensure the industry becomes more inclusive, equitable, relevant and representative of the society we are living in.

A high level of consciousness is needed now more than ever to help the industry think outside the box, find ways to sustain itself, engage with technology, diversify their practices, and workforce.

I would encourage anyone entering the industry to use this small window of time to connect to your community, read to familiarize yourself with our history, plays and theatre organizations and to connect with people in the industry. We cannot afford for the next generation to be ignorant to the many shoulders of POC artists and leaders that we all stand on, social and political injustices and barriers and successes within our own communities. In order to mitigate the risk of repeating history and build a new progressive industry, you must know what has gone before you and use that knowledge to leverage and create with audacity.

Tarek Iskander

Tarek Iskander is a London-based artistic director of Battersea Arts Centre in London. This interview was conducted via email on 27 September 2020.

CS *How has lockdown been for you?*

TI On the one hand, home life has been easy, thankfully, but work has been both relentless and brutal. The challenges BAC has been grappling with have been extreme. Staff, freelancers, artists, our local communities, all have been experiencing extreme pain and we have been on the receiving end of a lot of desperation with limited means to respond in the way we would want to. We have had to make endless choices on impossible trade-offs. I was in the job less than a year when Covid-19 struck and have been working almost continuously since then with our wonderful team to try to steady the ship.

A lot of the dialogue currently in our sector is about dismantling hierarchies, breaking boundaries and reimaging leadership. On a personal level I have felt that a lot of people have been yearning for a rather old-fashioned kind of 'leadership' from my AD role at a time of crisis like this. I have also had to question what 'kindness' means for someone in my role because it is clearly what the times demand. For now, kindness has sometimes meant making an 'unkind' decision alone and owning it, so other people do not need to carry that responsibility. At a time when my position is (rightly) constantly in question I have felt a responsibility to inhabit it and try to 'lead' in a way that does not come naturally. I have tried to be as constructive and as positive and as visible as possible, while remaining authentic to what I believe.

CS *What advice do you have for people entering the field right now?*

TI   There was never a playbook – never a right way of doing things, never a model path to follow, never a race to keep up with. This was always a fallacy and trap, but the sense of missing out, of not being where I need to be on this imaginary career path is real and corrosive. Everyone has their own journey. It's not a competition. Often, just finding a way to stay in the game is enough.

The pandemic, however, has made things much harder for people in the early parts of their careers, but it has also made things easier in some ways. The things we normally lean on for opportunities, like theatre venues, are extremely shaky right now. If you want an opportunity and are not finding it, or getting constant knock-backs my advice is go out, work with others and create the opportunity for yourself and those around you.

CS   *What are your hopes and dreams for theatre's future?*

TI   Dreaming is the work for all of us right now. We can and will build something better, I am confident of that, but we need to aim for the stars, so we can hit the ground.

There was so much that was beautiful about theatre and performance that we may never get back – and we are rightly mourning – but there was so much broken that we can fix. For starters, it was never 'for everyone'. Theatre had so many unnecessary rituals (pay a lot of money, buy a ticket, queue up here, sit in silence) that it was alienating the many and serving only the few. With BAC becoming a 'relaxed venue' we were learning that we can be more open just by doing less. Being inclusive does not have to be hard work, it can be as liberating as tidying up a room that has become so cluttered that you're tripping up everywhere. And you quickly find up that by making the door just that little bit wider, just that little bit more welcoming for some people, you are really making that door a little bit wider for everyone.

We need to create more agency for artists, communities and young people – they are the creative foundations of all our work, the doctors and nurses of our sector. They need to be valued, nurtured and renumerated properly because of the social value they bring. We do not need so many stuffy buildings everywhere; we need a thriving 'grassroots' ecology of all shapes and sizes that brings creativity to everyone's doorstep. Our sector has to be more responsive to communities and their cultural needs. We cannot play it safe. We need to be a hub for innovative practice and thinking the unthinkable and speaking to power and to ourselves. Silos must be broken down and collective collaboration properly supported and incentivized by funders.

What we have too much of in our sector is negativity and anger and projecting frustrations onto others. Irreverence and mischievous thinking will help us all right now. The needs are urgent, but if you are looking at the whole cultural sector, you need take the long view. Baby steps matter and should be cheered as much as any toddler careering across the floor for the first time.

CS *Theatre is often seen as a healing place (in certain branches of theatre history), but when theatre is also in trauma (fiscal, emotional, etc.), in what ways do you think it can locate its healing powers again?*

TI My sense of care and dealing with trauma is of course heavily influenced by many of years of working in the National Health Service (NHS). What the health service does much better than theatre is it sees people as unique, as individuals that you need to understand with and engage with as a whole. You cannot be helpful to someone unless you are responsive to them and their specific needs, unless you see them holistically, the interconnectedness within and without.

The theatre and live performance sector are particularly bad at this. We don't really see people: audiences, artists, participants. We establish rituals, hurdles and restrictive parameters at every opportunity and expect everyone to fit into these (then get angry when they don't turn up). It's not inclusive, it's not creatively productive, it's not the best version of ourselves. The word theatre comes from the ancient Greek word 'to behold' but we don't do much 'seeing' of others these days.

You don't treat a patient by wilful optimism, though. We won't improve things with a false diagnosis or peddling false hope. Courage is the only helpful response to trauma, and the foundation of every kind of care.

CS *What futures do you envision for digital and/or transmedia theatre?*

TI   The future is always more surprising than any one of us can think of, because it is curated collectively. A lot of pioneering practice in the last few decades has been about disrupting power structures by giving different people in the process more agency. We've seen it evolve in immersive theatre and experiences, VR, performance-as-games, audience role-play and so on. These have really activated audiences in new ways and the results have been thrilling. I'm calling to mind Punchdrunk's famous *Masque of the Red Death* (2007) at BAC or a play like Nassim Soulaimanpour's *White Rabbit Red Rabbit* (2010).

The parameters for these works are set by the creative artists involved – like a video game gives you a bounded reality to work within. What is interesting about this pandemic is it hasn't really impacted the content of what can be explored by art, as much as it's changed the context of what is possible. It's now such a struggle to put anything on, that the sheer ability to create any kind of circumstances for creativity to happen is a massive achievement. We're in the business of sharing space and making connections at a time doing those things feels impossibly difficult.

I'm wondering if in future decades we will take things further and the focus will be on creating the 'conditions' from which creative people (artists and audiences and participants combined on an equal footing) can engage creatively. I'm thinking about the work BAC has been doing nationally and internationally with the Co-Creating Change Network here. It's less about creating a frame for others to play in, as much as creating the conditions for creative connections to happen of their own accord and letting that run free in radically unanticipated ways. For me, this seems the natural evolution of where we were getting to coupled with a pandemic accelerating that kind of practice. I also think AI can radically transform our creative practice in the performing arts.

CS   *Poetry is the language of resistance. It can serve many functions (praise, elegy, celebration, articulation of different kinds of love, etc.), and during the pandemic, even more so.*

TI   There is a short essay by Ben Okri titled 'Of Poets and Their Antagonists' that is not widely known, but which I return to often. In it Okri celebrates the unique ability of poets and the poetic to redefine and reimagine the world – to create connections where none existed, to manifest things that were previously impossible.

In it he writes:

The antagonists of poetry cannot win. The world seems resistant, but it carries within it forever to be transformed into something higher. The world may seem unyielding but, like certain forces in the air, it merely awaits imagination and will to unloosen the magic within itself. The poet is not a creator, but an alchemist. Poets are helplessly on the side of greater forces, the greatest causes, the highest and most just future.[1]

That is the work for us now – all of us. And we need poetry in all its forms to help us imagine and dream that world. And theatre and live performance, to me, is poetry in living form, inhabited by us, in shared communion, experienced collective. Poetry, like art will be our way to a more just future. It matters now as much as it ever has; it matters more than breath itself.

---

[1]Ben Okri, 'Of Poets and Their Antagonists', in Malcolm Bradbury and Judy Cooke (eds), *New Writing: v. 1*, 153–4 (London: Minerva, 1992).

David Jubb

David Jubb is the former artistic director of Battersea Arts Centre and is now parenting in Devon, England. This interview was conducted over Zoom on 2 October 2020.

CS *How has lockdown been for you?*

DJ My wife is a civil servant and works in London. Since the beginning of the pandemic, she has been working from home and that has been an upside for both of us. For me, as a parent of a two- and a four-year-old, it means I get to have the occasional conversation with a grown-up! In addition to dad duties, I have written a few blogs about arts funding, researched and presented a podcast series called #*CulturePlanB* and recently I've been doing a bit of work for Theatres Trust as part of their free advice service during the pandemic.

Since leaving Battersea Arts Centre in April 2019 I have also been pursuing interests which started at BAC but which I did not find a way to fully explore. This summer I became a co-director of an organization called the Sortition Foundation. It publicly advocates for real democracy and seeks to institutionalize Citizens' Assemblies inside democratic institutions. For example, instead of a House of Lords imagine a permanent Citizens' Assembly as part of the UK parliament.

CS *What will the field look like in the near future?*

DJ At the outset of the pandemic there were lots of conversations about how to change the sector into something more radically inclusive and relevant to more people's lives. Great networks emerged; from Freelancers Make Theatre Work to an alliance called We Shall Not Be Removed which created Seven Inclusive Principles for organizations to The Privilege Café set up by Mymuna Soleman.

For a moment, a less hierarchical cultural sector was visible. Instead of everyone working to deliver the priorities of funders and artistic directors, the sector's narrative was being led by freelancers or furloughed employees: individuals who were available and hungry to talk with each other, to explore ideas for change and to have ideas about the future. Allies found a space to unite and the opportunity to take centre stage. Because there was literally nothing else on stage.

In addition to all the talking, there were all the artists, makers and producers who continued to work in their local communities during the pandemic. The lack of day-to-day shows, exhibitions and festivals, by all the big players, ensured that the work of these community-based practitioners was given space and recognition. It felt like the sector experienced a collective wave of optimism and courage about a possible future.

But as time went on, the negative impacts of lockdown on the sector were increasingly exposed. Over the summer an air of anxiety and fear seemed to infect the spirit of optimism. Cultural press coverage turned to stories of closure, redundancies and an existential threat to the sector. At the other end of the spectrum, some London venues seemed to embark on a competitive race to reopen. The focus appeared to shift from making change happen to getting back to normality. The good news of the government's arts rescue package followed; but it became clear that the 'Cultural Recovery Fund' would only add to a cumulative deadening effect on the sector's willingness to change.

The Cultural Recovery Fund was conservative with a small 'c'; all about sustaining existing cultural infrastructure. It was also Conservative with a big 'C'; shaped by a government keen to support the sector's 'crown jewels'. The fund was conceived using a classic top-down approach: a panel was appointed, largely made up of a group of leaders from established institutions and given the title of the 'Cultural Renewal Task Force'. Like many top-down decisions, the structure of the rescue package turned out to be an act of self-harm for the cultural sector. Important organizations were rescued. But the fund failed to recognize that the best creative ideas have always emerged from independent artists and members of communities (e.g. local communities, identity-based communities or interest-based communities) and certainly not from the business plans of funded institutions. By opting to only fund cultural organizations, and by giving them the opportunity to do nothing (except live to see another day) the Cultural Recovery Fund missed the opportunity to activate a renaissance. Instead, it bought the sector a £1.57 billion deep freeze.

Despite the valiant efforts of some visionary, brilliant and dedicated organizations, who are using their funds to work with artists and community groups, the Cultural Recovery Fund has further severed the connections between cultural organizations, individual artists and community groups, which were already hanging by a thread. The distribution of this top-down fund has been unsurprisingly uneven. For example, over 32 per cent of funding distributed by Arts Council England was awarded to organizations in London. That is the equivalent of around £16 per head of population in London versus around £4.50 in the East Midlands. The idea that there are fewer cultural 'crown jewels' in the East Midlands is offensive.

How many great creative ideas will never be developed or shared because the Cultural Recovery Fund failed to support artists and community groups? How many ways of making the sector more inclusive will not be developed because the sector's focus has switched to getting back to normal? How many artists and community groups will be forced to disengage from the cultural sector because of a lack of support during the pandemic?

It is easy to point a finger at government and express frustration. It is less easy to look at ourselves and the way that the pandemic has highlighted a long-standing imbalance between cultural organizations and funders on the one hand and freelancers and community groups on the other. The story of the last nine months has illustrated that the people with power in the cultural sector do not have a strong enough desire to reform it. Many have carried out redundancy programs to survive. But their Boards, their Executives and their Senior Management teams remain; to preserve their modus operandi for future generations.

During the early days of the pandemic many of the voices calling for change were coming from the periphery of the sector, while those at the centre sat tight.

CS *How is Brexit affecting and going to affect all of this?*

DJ In 2016 I wrote [in a blog piece] that the discontent which led to the Leave vote didn't simply highlight a failure of our political system, but it also highlighted how other parts of the UK establishment, such as the funded cultural sector, have failed to listen to and work with communities.

In this model, the majority of regular funding has gone to support ever larger organizations which seem to spend more time trying to outdo each other's art, competing for the attention of national broadcasters and journalists, instead of serving the needs and passions of communities. To understand just how far the arts establishment has removed itself from the lives of everyday people, you need only listen to a mainstream arts journalist describe a community arts project. This is because our values, as an entire sector, have become more concerned with what does and does not make 'great art' instead of cultivating a genuine interest in people and communities, and how we can creatively support them.

As many have argued, some of the discontent which led to Brexit derived from the 1980s when industries were dismantled, and jobs and livelihoods were destroyed. There was no investment or creative idea about what happened next for thousands of communities; villages, towns and cities were left behind. This catastrophe of governance, not just in the 1980s but in the decades that followed, caused generations of children to grow up hungry. It also tore a cultural way of life to shreds because when large employers shut up shop much of the resource, support and capacity for social and cultural activities evaporated. It is little wonder that people were seeking change and latched on to the Brexit campaign.

I was not part of a working-class community in the 1980s. I risk misrepresenting this story; and neither was I part of the cultural sector at the time. Yet, I have been part of the publicly funded culture sector since the 1990s and since then we have done more to align ourselves with government and government policy than to connect with communities to serve their needs; especially the working-class communities which experienced such radical change in the 1980s.

Another version of this story of exclusion now plays out in many urban centres in which major arts organizations fail to represent working-class Black, South Asian, East Asian, African, Latin and other ethnic minorities. It is the same old story for a sector which has failed to serve and to be inclusive. The outcome, as illustrated by the Warwick Commission's research in 2015, is that the cultural sector is most used and accessed by the most socio-economically advantaged and educated people in society.

While the pandemic is not the same as the 1980s, it is presenting similar challenges: decimating some sectors and leaving many communities poorer and in a perilous state. Do we make the same mistakes as in recent decades and spend our time delivering government agendas and creating cultural programs for the most advantaged in society? Or do we direct our capacity, energy and resource on serving and supporting communities, in a more equitable way, across the country?

Currently, in England, a fifth of annual arts funding goes to just five organizations, while half goes to just over fifty organisations. Based on that kind of distribution model, it is hardly surprising that we are failing to connect with thousands of communities around the country. During lockdown, I described an alternative model in which we could use the same amount of funding to support 3,000 artists and community groups along with 500 community serving venues across England. The idea was to create a model which works on a more human scale, where independent artist and community relationships are at the heart of every funding agreement.

Instead of a top-down plan by government or the leaders or major arts organizations, what if we asked a representative group of citizens what they think public funding for culture could achieve? We know a vaccine is on its way for Covid-19 and is likely to have a positive impact during 2021. What if we take this time of disruption to hold a Citizens' Assembly for culture? We could invite a representative group of 100 people by gender, age, socio-economic background, disability, ethnicity and geography to assemble; to be paid for their time; to hear about the history of cultural funding; to hear about different ideas for the future of arts funding; and to ask those informed citizens to deliberate and to create recommendations for the future of cultural funding in England. That would be a creative and constructive way for the sector to emerge from this pandemic; with a citizen-led plan for culture.

Madeline Sayet

Madeline Sayet is a Native American theatre director, writer and performer. She is also executive director of the Yale Indigenous Performing Arts Program (YIPAP) at Yale University. This interview was conducted over email on 21 November 2020.

CS *How has lockdown been for you?*

MS I am part of one of the many generations of Mohegans who have lived here, on this river, and survived plague. This is the thought that comes to me most often over the last eight months of the pandemic. I spend a lot of time on the river, travelling up and down in the way my ancestors did and thinking about the place that I call home, what it means to be made of this earth and survive here. The world has stopped, and yet nothing stands still. On the river, life goes on. Yet there is constant fear now, knowing our loved ones could be lost at any moment. Each moment is dearer. A call from my mom or a note from my father can bring me to tears.

Time is different now. Place is different. People are different: they feel fragile, impermanent, in a way they have always been, but has never felt so present.

It is not worth hurting anyone to make theatre. Stories will still be told, one way or another.

In the early spring, I was devastated when I realized that theatre could suddenly cease to exist, then overjoyed as we found ways to collaborate online. In some ways online collaboration was even more liberating because for the first time, I had the luxury of sleeping in my own bed for six months in a row, of having routines, of spending time with my partner, being able to run errands for family. For the first time, my family could even see all the art I was making. I even made art with family. My mother and I co-wrote a series of radio plays reimagining moments in Mohegan history, asking questions about what our ancestors may have thought in times like these.

My biggest learning phase was coming to terms with what it would mean to be directing in person this fall. Knowing that, suddenly, I would be leaving home again, but this time I would be leaving home during the pandemic. The production itself was a new adaptation of *Antigone* that I wrote for Butler University, in which the plague had not yet left Thebes, inspired by the time we currently find ourselves in, and really interrogating the notion of martyrdom. What kind of a world would rather let young women die than listen to them? I felt this story was no longer about what we're willing to die for, but about getting to a place where justice doesn't require us to die. All my work considers how the stories we pass down shape our collective possible futures, and if I couldn't save Antigone, we needed to get closer than we were. We needed to come together, and at the very least remove Creon from power by the end of the play. We had to interrogate how we plant seeds for the liberation of future generations in this telling. I wrote masks and distance into the script. As an ensemble, we reminded each other how we were all responsible for each other and switched rehearsal rooms every thirty minutes for air circulation.

We decentralized the usual protagonists and shed light on how every individual citizen's role is equally important. What would it take for us to live in a just world?

CS   *Your solo piece* Where We Belong *is currently scheduled at the time of this writing at Woolly Mammoth Theatre Company's next season. You performed this piece at Shakespeare's Globe – the first Native American playwright to have your work performed in that space. Can you speak to the piece's gestation, development and if it will make it to Woolly post-pandemic?*

MS   *Where We Belong* was born out of flight and, very specifically, chronicles my journey of becoming a bird. Now that we are physically grounded the way I engage with some of its core questions is shifting. The sky is off limits now. But in some ways, life as a bird is simpler. I am everywhere and nowhere at the same time. My feet and spirit rest in Mohegan and my mind is everywhere else.

The piece began when I first moved back from the UK, where I was pursuing my PhD in Shakespeare. I felt unrooted, and was trying to figure out if, as a Mohegan, missing England made me a traitor. The question expanded to ask: as an Indigenous person in an age of globalization – is there a place that I get to belong?

The journey of the play is at once a struggle between Shakespeare and colonialism, being a wolf and a bird, and how my journey to England to pursue my PhD mirrors the journeys of my ancestors who travelled to England in the 1700s on diplomatic missions, in service to my people.

The story explores notions of flight, borders and globalization. I have been reinvestigating what those ideas mean, now, for the upcoming version. Whereas other elements – place, colonialism, language, ancestors, home – already feel more present in our current landscape.

The productions in Woolly's season all have digital options so that if we cannot meet in person we will not have to cancel the show. But we do not know what the state of the virus will be yet. If this pandemic has shifted one thing in my mind, it is that accessibility is more important than artistry. If we cannot gather safely, how do we tell the story in a way that can really reach the people who it may help? This piece has always been deeply personal, but now that we have workshop time dedicated to it, I am shifting the process to include my peers. Woolly has allowed me to bring other Native artists into the digital room to embody and explore the work, even though it's a solo show. To consider the story in community is important to me, particularly knowing there may not be a live audience this time. In London, it was for my ancestors, but here I find myself imagining it for the next generation of Native theatre artists who may go through similar struggles.

CS *Would you speak to specific challenges that you see Native American artists and organizations facing now given how the theatre industry is rebuilding?*

MS There has never been significant funding for Native Theatre. Yet, Native Theatre is thriving right now. Play readings that before reached an audience of twenty reach an audience of two thousand. Our people can gather in ways no longer constrained by our geography. It's a game changer. I never saw Native Theatre growing up, and I did not find out about it until I was in my final year of college because there was nowhere I could access it, at home. Now, people can access it from all over. We can collaborate with other Native artists far away from us. I can host a playwriting workshop for Native writers at Yale but invite Native writers from across the nation.

Native Theatre has never relied on big budgets, but on people coming together to tell stories in community with one another, and in some ways, community has never felt stronger. We have lost significant leaders in Native Theatre to Covid-19. But we have not lost Native Theatre to it. It is nimble and expansive, and I believe a lot can be learned from the expansion of accessibility during this time. I hope that the attention that has shifted to it, in this moment of anti-racist action, stays, because there is much to be learned from these stories. Native Theatre has been here since before the foundation of America and will be here long after. The pandemic, like all great struggles, triggered our people to come together in new and powerful ways. My hope looking forward is that we tell more stories beyond the white and Native dichotomy that exists in much of the narrative around colonialism and really lift up Black Indigenous artists and also the intersections between Black and Native stories and lives, because there is much more work needed to move toward our collective liberation.

CS   *What are your hopes and dreams for theatre's future?*

MS   Every time we tell a story, something shifts, and something deepens. I believe deeply in Story Medicine. That stories have the power to heal or harm and must be wielded with that in mind. We need great healing, so my dream for the field is that we think about the stories we are telling in a way that builds the bridge to not only still exist seven generations from now but also to thrive. What worlds are we conjuring for the next generation to dream themselves into?

CS   *What advice do you have for people entering the field now?*

MS   In this field, this moment is a great equalizer. The theatre spaces that were once treasured are no longer useful. No one knows what they are doing. And in many cases students have a better understanding of digital platforms and media than the professional theatre companies do. Decide what kind of story you want to tell and tell it. We have a lot to learn from the worlds you will dream into being.

Chris Thorpe

Chris Thorpe is a British playwright, performer and theatre-maker, whose works include *Status* (2018) and *Victory Condition* (2017). This interview was conducted over email on 20 October 2020.

CS *How has lockdown been for you?*

CT As a writer maybe the biggest challenge is that the world comes second-hand right now a lot more than it did, whether mediated by devices or in memory. Even conversations I'm having as research for future projects happen while my body is in my house. A lot of my stuff is based, implicitly or explicitly, on things I *do*. On *being there* – even if 'there' is being physically present while listening to someone else's experience, it's still an active form of witnessing that involves exchange, mutual presence, observation. Obviously, there are people I speak to in the 'normal' course of making who I can't be present with, for reasons of logistics or distance, and so it's not as if remote conversations weren't a feature, but not *everyone*. There's definitely a challenge in finding ways round that flatness, that constancy of context.

There's also a challenge to *not* make work too particular to the present moment. I've made work I wouldn't have made for sure, when I've been invited to as a direct response to the circumstances, but even then I've tried to avoid the temptation to address the specific moment *too* specifically because then it'll be useless next week or next month or even tomorrow. It's not that I think we shouldn't be making work about the pandemic during the pandemic – there are effective ways of doing that, and if you find one, knock yourself out – but human nature hasn't changed. The structures that were fucking us up or getting in the way of justice before the pandemic are still present. The pandemic moment is a lens to look at our flaws through, and a lot of the behaviours we're seeing are symptoms of those flaws expressing themselves in this particular set of circumstances. But if we describe the symptom like it's the disease then the work won't be useful beyond a certain point.

As a citizen, there's a similar challenge that relates to the idea of the world being 'second-hand' above. Not being able to interact with as many other citizens as I'd normally be able to, in our natural habitat, has made me more reliant on mediations of their behaviour and opinion given to me by remote sources. It can really screw with your perception of the possibilities of change. Even more so than in 'normal' times, repetition becomes fact, or bias becomes truth. It's a real challenge to keep a live engagement with what's going on when so much of 'what's going on' is received opinion rather than live conversation. And if everything becomes too one-sided – if you become too much of a receiver, who then forms opinions or acts according to an internal, one-sided conversation you're having with the ideas that you allow to be fed into you, from sources you can't be in dialogue with, then your decision-making world and your basis for drawing conclusions becomes incredibly limited.

CS *What advice do you have for people entering the field right now?*

CT If there's one useful difference between me and specifically 'young' people in the field right now it's maybe around the subjective experience of time. That's a particular danger now, when a lot of people seem to feel there's this mythical 'time' suddenly everywhere that can be magically filled with usefulness and creativity as if the only thing stopping our creative flow previously was having other shit to do. When really, the biggest waste of time is the time you spent punching yourself for not being as productive as you'd been taught to expect.

Other than that – don't worry about the shape of a career – we all internalize the idea of a hierarchy in this field, and if you don't resist that, you'll make choices in service of moving 'up' that hierarchy rather than choosing the projects and expressions that have a point, irrespective of whether they fit your idea of other people's idea of what you 'should' be doing. Oh, and try to tell the truth.

CS *What are your hopes and dreams for theatre's future?*

CT I dream/hope that we come out of whatever the fuck this is with a wider appetite for stuff theatres might have previously worried was too formally 'weird' – and that the whole concept of 'weirdness' becomes just a part of a much wider offer to a much wider audience. I dream/hope that all this watching stuff on screens has allowed us to put some clear space between the possibilities of the screen and the very different possibilities of liveness, rather than allowing them to overlap to the absolute detriment of liveness. And I hope/dream we come out of it determined to make the most of that difference. Because if this whole shitshow just drives theatre back into the perceived safety of the traditional then it probably shouldn't bother returning.

CS *During a time of collective trauma, what are theatre's healing properties, if any?*

CT I'm not sure 'healing' is what theatre should be doing – that reminds me a bit too much of religion, of patients miraculously 'healed' by the power of suggestion and intervention who then collapse in the street outside the church. Expecting artists to be constantly staring into their wounds for dramatic purposes seems like a limited use of the resource – the people in the room. Theatre can locate its healing power by looking underneath the sickness at what might have made us sick. And doing it in as linguistically and formally creative a way as possible, maybe even including some songs.

CS *How to centre the works of both immigrant and migrant and artists with visible and invisible disabilities during these precarious times, especially?*

CT This a perennial question that the pandemic's brought into sharper focus – but it existed before the pandemic, and it will still exist in whatever form the world, and theatre, are in when we're in a position to talk about the pandemic in the past tense. The answer to the question will remain substantially the same in a post-pandemic world (whatever that is) as it did before any of this happened. I'm not an immigrant/migrant in my particular place and time, and I'm not (yet) disabled – and obviously along with *not* experiencing those things, the world I *do* experience is substantially easier to navigate than it is for many people who are in those communities. Until the structural change happens to level that playing field in terms of convenience, access, opportunity, there should obviously be the option for artists from marginalised communities to foreground their identities, to speak particularly to those communities if that's what they want their art to encompass, but the toxic expectation that they *should* is one of the worst things about our art form. I can't relate to that pressure through personal experience because that pressure *doesn't exist* for me. It's a choice I *can* make, to foreground my identity in my work, but it's never expected of me. I'm given far more latitude to be weird. It might be a bit of a niche imbalance I guess, but the structural inequality it indicates is fucking huge.

As an artist whose identity isn't marginalized, and who doesn't have the implicit and explicit pressure to foreground that identity, I guess there are two possibilities I think about. One is – put that same pressure on yourself – maybe make some work that explicitly recognizes or leans into your *own* identity even though there's no external pressure to do so. That's something I've done in some of my work – usually the stuff that I'm going to be performing, because I'm a fact on that stage, so what I am might as well be a recognized fact. Then at least you can recognize the structural advantages of that identity from within it, so people who don't share it might have to spend less of their creative time pointing it out.

And then the other, and in some ways opposite approach is, if it's not me that's going to be performing a piece, I try not to write identity at all unless it's absolutely necessary. Partly because that's where I feel more comfortable, with character as an occasionally effective option rather than as a default, and partly because at least there's at least an inbuilt breadth there, in the number, identity, background of the people who might eventually execute the work.

CS   *What is poetry's relationship to resistance?*

CT   Poetry, like performance, is time outside. Whatever the function of a particular use of poetry, one of the necessities is that it puts language, and the experience of receiving that language, in a space beyond the 'normal' rules. There's an agreement, like there is in theatre, that we collude in stopping time, sealing off a bubble of reality from the mainstream – and then we step into that bubble, and we repurpose the codes and signals of the mainstream for an agreed amount of time, or participate in someone else's repurposing of them. There's a more urgent need for that now than there ever has been, in language and in form, because we need to work out how we're going to usefully cope with these times, and find a space outside coping to slow time, break apart our own thought processes, really dig into *how* we think rather than the constant barrage of *what* we think, and work out what we might want to change about the frameworks of thought and interaction and power rather than simply highlight or try to change their content. There isn't a better way of doing that than poetry – it's a way of highlighting the structures language is normally held in by bending and breaking those structures into different configurations. It's so much more useful now because it's easy to believe that there's a 'new normal' or the times are 'unprecedented' when actually it's just a new skin laid over the same old bones. Poetry can show that skin for what it is and get under it to the bones that were always there, and remain there, and maybe dislocate a few.

Stephanie Ybarra

Stephanie Ybarra is artistic director of Center Stage Theatre in Baltimore, Maryland. This interview was conducted over email on 10 September 2020.

CS *How has lockdown been for you?*

SY As quarantines go, mine has been on the easier side. My needs are met, and I have been fortunate to spend much of my time outdoors raising both a puppy and a garden. This is not to say I have not struggled. My anxiety and depression have escalated and the pressure to perform – to show up as a 'leader' – is almost too much to carry sometimes. All of this is compounded by the grief of losing my father last October – that heartache has dulled a bit but is still with me constantly. The more I read about how we humans respond to crisis, the more I understand just how normal all my struggles are. The more surprising challenge is that my creative energy is completely depleted. My imagination has always played a massive role in my life. I cannot remember a time when I did not have ideas and visions and musings multiplying in my head. Early in the lockdown I had all kinds of artistic impulses – I could see multiple pathways forward in programming and in our business practices. I took my creativity for granted, and now in October of 2020, I am challenged to activate my imagination in any meaningful way. I am trying to make peace with that discomfort and have patience with myself, but it is hard.

CS *What advice do you have for people entering the field right now?*

SY I started my career just a couple of years before 9/11. I was re-entering the field after graduate school in 2008 just as the financial crisis was starting to unfold. My tenure as an artistic director began eighteen months before a global pandemic. Each one of these events resulted in an 'unprecedented' disruption in our field. On a personal level, I felt that I was veering off course or away from my goals. In hindsight I can see now that my professional trajectory was not interrupted. Rather, it was emergent. I have not 'arrived' anywhere yet, and I am not expecting to. The heart of my advice is this: trust that the journey itself is abundant with opportunities for growth and learning. You must know what you are looking at when you see it. The knowledge that you are exactly where you need does wonders for one's resilience. The ground has shifted beneath us all, and that creates opportunities for each of us to survey the new landscape and adjust course, but we never stop journeying.

CS *What are your hope and dreams for the future of theatre?*

SY I do have hope that we are already creating the conditions for constant change and evolution in pursuit of eradicating all forms of oppression. With each new generation of theatre-makers comes a chance to build an arts sector that is so intentional in its dynamism that 'status quo' and 'best practice' are understood to be anathemas to our culture. When I dare to run headlong toward a dream for our field, I inevitably find myself staring into a future in which our arts institutions are deeply entangled civic participants. This is not to say everyone gets 'political', but it is to say that actively contributing to the civic life of a city, town and/or neighbourhood is well within our grasp; we are only limited by our own imagining of how non-profit theatres can fulfil their legal and ethical obligation to do public good.

CS *In a time of global collective trauma, what is theatre's role, if any, toward healing?*

SY While it is true that theatre is often seen as a healing space, we cannot authentically fill that aspiration until we better understand the ways theatre has been a deeply harmful space. It has been a space of exclusion, erasure, exploitation, appropriation, economic oppression, abuse, racial injustice, cultural extraction, power hoarding, and environmental destruction. The list goes on. For better and for worse, our theatres are a microcosm of our society, perpetuating so much of the harm we claim to reject. Before we can truly heal ourselves we have to first reckon with these hard truths; we must talk about them openly, to name them, to wrestle with them in order to ultimately move on from them. Our field is amid that reckoning right now – it is decades in the making and shamefully overdue.

Our artform is one that relies on relationships and community. Without our rehearsal rooms, green rooms, shops, performances and offices, it has become even more difficult to move through the world in an authentic relationship with one another. So, we adapt. We are already finding new ways to create community and with the proliferation of streaming options, we have even more pathways to reach across geographic locales to be in relationship with one another. As isolating as this pandemic has been, there are myriad ways we are more connected and aware of the national theatre ecology. It has forced an understanding of our interdependence and interconnectivity. If we do this moment right, then we just might come through it having begun to heal ourselves and our communities.

CS *In what ways do you instigate joy in your work process?*

SY Joy is central to my own process as a theatre-maker, and I'm fortunate to be surrounded by people who prioritize joy in their art. Understanding the role of joy as a core value in our work helps inform the stories we tell on stage, which means reaching for the full complement of human experiences and privileging stories that normalize BIPOC joy rather than solely centring pain. To do this, it is imperative to stay connected to levity, play and laughter off stage. Before the pandemic, you could walk into our artistic offices at any time and find any number of shenanigans taking place with a room full of people bringing their joy to bear on our work environment. That kind of culture leaves a mark – it helps create the conditions for centring work that centres joy.

It is worth noting this is a deeply personal quest for me as a Latinx woman. My father was a dark-skinned Mexican bookworm whose love for science fiction was rivalled only by his obsession with classical music and his family. As a second-generation American whose first language was Spanish, he knew plenty of pain. I witnessed the racism he experienced when I was finally old enough to understand what it was (he hid it from me well). But, if I were telling a story about him, it wouldn't centre that pain – it would iris in on his loving marriage to my (white) mother, the laughter he shared with his four younger siblings (none of whom speak Spanish), his trials and tribulations of raising three daughters. I have never seen his story on stage or screen. He is not represented anywhere in our cultural narrative about Latinx people. For that matter, neither am I.

CS *How did you pivot your programming during lockdown?*

SY Back in March 2020, when theatres around the country cancelled productions and closed doors, we were all scrambling to adapt our shows and other programming to a digital platform. We were no exception. We were about to go into tech for a co-production of Donetta Lavinia Grays's one-person play *Where We Stand*. We immediately contacted a Baltimore-based film crew and within seventy-two hours we had captured the show on film and sent everyone home. Simultaneously, we postponed our final show of the season – Anne Carson's *Bakkhai* (2017) – to the fall of 2021. And just like that, we had no more programming and no clear path forward in terms of connecting to our artform or our audiences. Instead, our costume shop workers immediately started making masks for a hospital down the street from our theatre, and our energy went from making theatre to supporting frontline health workers.

A couple of weeks later I had a fledgling idea about how we might activate live theatre at home – I reached out to my most trusted colleagues and together we fleshed out the idea for Play at Home. What began as a collaboration between Baltimore Center Stage, Long Wharf Theatre, Woolly Mammoth Theatre, St. Louis Rep and The Public became a national invitation for theatres of any size and scale to commission playwrights (at $500 each) to write a five- to ten-minute play designed to be read/performed at home. Within a matter of weeks, we had over 100 plays and $50,000 in artist commissions available to download for free. By all measurements, the project was a success and provided a real shot in the arm creatively. We were in the process of building a second wave of Play at Home activities when George Floyd was murdered in June.

The pain of that moment along with the national wakeup call of the century catapulted Baltimore Center Stage into another adaptive moment. We scrambled to safely open our lobby to protesters, trying to contribute to our community's call for racial justice in any way we could. Ultimately, that meant turning our gaze inward and continuing to deeply interrogate our ways of working. We have spent the last several months digging deeper into our equity practices, transforming them into antiracist practices. Using the seminal document, BIPOC Demands for the American Theatre from the We See You WAT collective, Baltimore Center Stage has been focused less on the products we can deliver to our audiences and more on the underlying processes we use to make our art. From curatorial choices and hiring practices to budget transparency to pay equity, our focus has shifted to evolving our organizational culture in service of creating the world we all want to see: a world free of racism, oppression and exclusion.

2

Local and hyperlocal

Naomi Alexander

Naomi Alexander is the artistic director of Brighton People's Theatre. This interview was conducted initially over Zoom on 4 November 2020 and additionally over email through mid-December 2020.

CS *How has lockdown been for you?*

NA I'm a single parent. My partner and I share our parenting of our son. This meant that save for Zoom I was alone for half the week. I felt a real sense of disconnect communicating over the computer all the time. I also found and still find, as we enter our second lockdown now in November 2020, the absence of cultural experiences really discombobulating. I had taken it for granted that I could be with people and be present at events with others and share in the power of coming together for a cultural experience. I hadn't fully appreciated that until it was taken away, just the energy of being at a live gig, or at the theatre, being *with* people, viscerally. It's like I can feel those experiences still reverberating in the cells of my body and I revisit them in my mind from time to time just to soak up the richness of those opportunities that I have had.

CS *What are your hopes and dreams for the field?*

NA I used to work for this organization called The Scarman Trust, which was an organization set up to promote active citizenship and we shared an office in London with Operation Black Vote and there was a poster up in the office that said, 'Power is never given.' You have to take power and to take power you have to be organized and you have to have resources. That's the challenge for changing the theatre sector – how do we get the resources, the power and the organization to come together and change things?

I want to see People's Theatres across the country, being part of the fabric of normal life. For theatre to be a natural part of how people come together to make sense of their experience of being human in this crazy world. I see communities being built through theatre. I see people from different backgrounds, with different perspectives, coming together through theatre and connecting in deep and powerful ways. I want to see this valued properly. Invested in properly. For it to be seen as part of the 'crown jewels' of the country's creative sector, not a tokenistic add-on to a theatre's participation department.

I feel hopeful that co-created work is being taken more seriously right now. There is a sense that ordinary people's creativity is being taken more seriously and people are being given platforms and opportunities slowly. One of the things that the pandemic has done is opened people's eyes to the glaring inequalities both in the sector in terms of the precarity with which freelance workers live and glaring inequalities in our society in terms of food insecurity, and the terrible pay and conditions that some key workers experience.

There have been people that have been working on food insecurity for decades. Working to improve workers' rights for decades. But it feels like the pandemic has done something to people's awareness. People are connecting more as human beings with kindness and generosity and an awareness of each other's fragility and vulnerability in a way that has the potential to open up spaces which are far more supportive and nurturing of other human beings and giving people a genuine chance rather than using people in a tokenistic way.

What I've seen a lot over the last couple of decades in participatory theatre work is that quite often people in communities will be used in a way to further an artist's vision. Over the last few years this is changing. People are finding the right mix of leadership skills to hold the space in a meaningful way to enable co-creation. Being honest about the expectations and motivations of everyone involved. Creating multiple ways for people to contribute. Being transparent about decision-making processes. Being open to learning and feedback. Being sensitive to the emotional journey of everyone involved. Equipping people with a greater sense of agency.

I strongly believe that being creative is a human right. Everyone has creativity and unbound creative potential inside them, but not many people have the conditions within which they can flourish and within which they can realize that potential because our society doesn't value that. Instead, it values profit. Ordinary people's creativity is not valued in that way, but I would love to believe that this will change in the future. My mission is to create the conditions to enable people to realize their creative potential.

CS *How is Brighton's arts scene doing during the pandemic?*

NA It's been devastating. In 2019 a University of Sussex study found that the creative industries in Greater Brighton generated more than £1.5 billion in annual turnover. So, the impact of Covid-19 has been profound. People estimate that over 50 per cent of jobs in the creative sector in the Greater Brighton region are expected to be lost. However, there's been a fantastic initiative with local arts networks establishing a participatory process involving arts professionals in the city to come together to draw up an action plan for recovery.

Yet, our capacity at BPT has been completely stripped back. At our company, we have gone from a small team of freelancers to the equivalent of one full-time member of staff during the pandemic. So, we have had our heads down just trying to figure things out. Where's our future? Where's the money coming from? How are we going to sustain ourselves so that we can realize our vision?

Brighton has a reputation for being a very sort of liberal open-minded creative city. But there is also a division in the city. There are plenty of people who feel completely excluded from that offer and that reality. We prioritize engaging with people who have had the fewest opportunities. So, our goal is to enable people to start a relationship with theatre through play reading or theatre clubs while also offering opportunities to make their own theatre through weekly theatre workshops. By the end of 2021 we plan to have six workshops running every week across the city. We want the majority of these to be in areas with high levels of social housing. The hope is that new cultural forms might be created or certainly new cultural products that might be experienced as being more accessible and more relevant. That's the *aim*.

CS *During the pandemic one of the things I think about the most is how much trauma we are carrying in our bodies. Art is a vehicle to not exploit but maybe to understand and recognize trauma(s).*

NA We did a show early on called *Tighten Our Belts* and it was about the cost of austerity to people in the city. I co-created the show with people over eighteen months with regular attendees at the Brighton Unemployed Center Families Project, which is an NGO in the city that works with people who are out of work long-term. And yes. People do carry trauma in their bodies and the experience of austerity was vicious.

It was vicious on the most vulnerable people in our society and I co-created a show with them about that. I tried really hard to put in place everything that I could to protect people and to support people. But inevitably the resonance is going to be there.

There were many things that were fantastic about the work and making it. People who were regular visitors at the centre saw the show and walked out of that theatre saying they felt ten feet tall because they felt like they'd been seen. Sociologist Nancy Fraser writes about social justice and she says that for social justice to happen you must have both recognition and redistribution. If you apply that to theatre, then you need to ensure that the stories that you tell generate recognition by people who don't normally recognize themselves on stage and you need to ensure that the resources to tell those stories are redistributed to those people that don't normally see themselves on stage. A part of the trauma was witnessed and there was a sense from a lot of people who witnessed that performance that they felt stronger as a result. We will never shy away from talking about the things that people want to talk about. But we will do our absolute utmost to find a way to do it in a way that is joyful and playful and that doesn't create too much traumatic resonance.

What we are going through right now is global collective trauma coupled with the existential threat of climate change, and alongside that, the experiences of the true costs of racism, capitalism and patriarchy. How do we sit together in the darkness of the theatre and acknowledge our shared vulnerabilities and frailties? Absolutely this is a question and there's a place for that. But if you are preoccupied about whether or not you have food in the house and if your children are going hungry, maybe sitting in the darkness with and about darkness as subject matter may not be what you are looking for. It's Maslow's hierarchy of needs. Certain things need to be in place in order for you to feel safe enough to sit and contemplate the existential threat. If you're in survival mode, you're not necessarily going to want to go and see a show that's asking you to sit and reflect on just how tough things are. The point of theatre is that it helps us figure out what it really means to be a human being in the most profound way because it enables us to unlock feelings and sensations and thoughts that are not capable of being expressed just through a conversation.

There's this photograph by a US-based artist that does public balloon-word-based art, and one of his pieces states that art is a radical act and so is joy. This summarizes a lot of my deeply held values and principles of working. It takes a lot of courage to be happy. You find joy and light in the middle of darkness and it opens you up and it strengthens you and it connects you to others. People need to be connected. Perhaps now more than ever.

Ned Glasier

Ned Glasier is a British theatre director and writer, working primarily with young people and non-professional makers and performers. He is founder and artistic director of Company Three in north London. This interview was conducted via email on 17 October 2020.

CS   *How has lockdown been for you?*

NG   It has been hard, of course, but so much better for me than a lot of people.

I still have my job and I am still able to do the things I am meant to do in my job. I am also just turned forty and I have a three-year-old, so in some ways I have been in a slow process of lockdown over the last few years, going out less! So, it has not hit me that hard. It is of course frustrating and annoying and boring, but I have been lucky not to have been affected in the way that so many have – I have been able in some senses to do the things I normally do, and I have been much more worried for other people than myself and my family.

CS   *What advice do you have for people entering the field now?*

NG   The main one is to be realistic. Set yourself small expectations, things you can really achieve. Try and tune out the noise that comes from those that seek to make this into a competition. I honestly think that a realistic expectation for everyone right now (I wrote a thread on twitter about this) is to still be in the same place in a few months' time. Moving forward when you're stuck in a huge impossible storm is a very tough thing to do.

Also, and connected with that – it's useful to understand that the process of becoming a theatre-maker involves doing things other than making theatre. I am supporting a brilliant young director right now and the thing we are working on is a kind of bucket list of things she really wants to do. Very few of them involve theatre and I think she will be a much richer artist for doing them.

CS   *What are your hopes and dreams for theatre's future?*

NG   I've written a bit about the potential I see in youth theatre to become a sprawling, national civic space in which young people can learn about the world, consider their place in it and communicate how they feel about both of those things to audiences of other young people and adults. In some ways that's a dream that you could expand to cover all the arts – imagine if the arts really did what some people in the arts claim it does in order to make themselves feel better about themselves. What if it was really a space of democracy, discovery, challenge and change? Of course, there are loads of examples of this happening right now, but not enough – it's not the dominant way that we think about arts and I think that is why there has been so little public outcry about the treatment of the arts during lockdown.

I was talking to Tarek Iskander at BAC and we were talking about what it would mean if all the arts events that ever took place were treated like parties – things which people curated and invited others too. What I am grasping at there is the idea of removing capital from the arts, returning them to a place of exchange and invitation.

CS   *During a time of global collective trauma, in what way can theatre locate its healing properties, if at all?*

NG   By listening. Too often people think theatre is a speaking artform, but I think it is a listening one. We need to spend more time in spaces without a specific agenda or outcome in mind. There is a lovely quote by Francois Matarasso at arestlessart.com which underpins a huge amount of our work – to really listen you must not know what the outcome is.

When you remove the outcome, the imperative is to listen much more keenly and carefully and to respond much more cautiously and sympathetically to everyone in the room, to follow the genuine need of the room rather than the ideas imposed by the lead artist.

I worry a little about talking about theatre as healing, because sometimes it is also usefully a place of rupture, though I guess in the

end we are constantly in a process of rupture and repair, so perhaps
I do think it is a healing place.

CS *Can you talk about your work currently as a theatre-maker
and community leader?*

NG   A positive element of the pandemic has been how robustly
Company Three's vision and mission has stood up and been relevant
during this hugely difficult time.

   We have not shifted what we want to achieve in any way, we
have just shifted how we have been trying to achieve it. So, we still
want to make a safe space for young people (needed more than ever,
of course), and we still want to make work that platforms their
voices and we still want to share our process with other people who
might make use of it.

   I feel galvanized by that. If our work stands up during a pandemic, it
will probably stand up after it. The projects we've run have accelerated
our connection with other companies of young people on a national
(and international) basis, which makes us feel like the possibility of
wider change is closer than perhaps it might have done otherwise.

   I am energized by the young people we work with, who remain
funny, passionate, resilient. We are back working with them in the
room, which is an absolute joy after all that time on Zoom – which
in some ways was great but exhausting in others. Over the last
couple of months, I feel like we have topped ourselves up again,
by working together in person – they are full of enthusiasm and
I have a much better sense of how they all are. Interestingly they are
largely doing fine – I wonder if the mental health crisis that I and
many others predicted is one that will burn slowly, especially when
we get deep into exam time next year.

   I was in the room with our members this week and we do a thing
where I read back to them my notes I wrote about the last session,
so they can see themselves as I've seen them and remember all the
things we talked about. And at the end one of the young people in
the room said something like if you read that to an adult they would
say that is not what a teenager would say, they wouldn't believe it.
And they are right – I do not think many adults would believe that
this group of teenagers could be so articulate and informed and
curious about the world. That they are gives me huge hope.

   Yet, I am demoralized about money and power. Not because C3
doesn't have any; we have enough, just about. But because of how

much more I could do with more of it – I watch the consultants failing to make Test and Trace work and I think, for your day's salary I could take fifty kids to the countryside for four days and it would be life-changing for some of them.

CS *In what ways do you instigate joy in your work processes?*

NG Joy feels to me to be a central currency in our work. It is both an essential ingredient in the creation of a space in which young people might feel comfortable to be themselves, and a mode through which young people might communicate their feelings about the world when they are onstage.

How do we instigate joy?

By meeting everyone for who they are, rather than who they will become.

By playing a lot of games.

By eating together, walking together, going away together.

By having three positive rules and no others.

By secretly always saying yes to any request made by a young person in my head before they finish their question, whatever it is.

By dancing.

By giving them space as often as possible just to spill out and connect with each other.

By having a lot of food around.

By presenting ourselves in a way that feels distinct from school. We have a joke that you get in loads of trouble in our work if you ever call an adult in our room 'miss' or 'sir' by mistake.

Love is a hugely important thing. I was talking to someone the other day who makes work with professional actors and she said the thing ultimately that binds them all together in a rehearsal room is money. Even if it is boring or going badly, everyone stays because they have a contract. But I do not have that, so I must work with something else, something much more tenuous and undefinable. I am wondering if that thing is love.

Love and joy are related, deeply. People often find it hard to love teenagers. Secondary schools are not places of love, like primary schools are. Even parents often act like they do not love their teenage children, so when you enter a space as a teenager which is full of love, then hopefully you will keep coming back.

In the context of the creation of work, your work will begin from a place in which you are able to be yourself, because out of joy and love comes honesty. That honesty is absolutely critical for our work – the more honest we can all be in the room, the more the work is likely to really reflect the opinions, ideas and tastes of the young people who make it. That work should contain joy – because they are *joyful*, but also because audiences are more moved, shifted, affected by joy than any other emotion on stage.

Conrad Murray

Conrad Murray is an Anglo Indian, London-based actor, writer, director, rapper, beatboxer, singer and theatre-maker. He is the artistic director and led the BAC Beatbox Academy since 2008. With Paul Cree he runs the company Beats & Elements. This interview was conducted over email on 28 November 2020.

CS   *How has lockdown been for you?*

CM   Lockdown has been a paradigm shift. I was supposed to be on a world tour with *Frankenstein: How to Make a Monster* (2019), the show I directed with the BAC Beatbox Academy. We were supposed to be in Brazil for six weeks and then off to the Sydney Opera house for a month. It's been difficult. Watching the cast see their tour, which is the result of hard work be cancelled is really sad.

I have also had to reassess my career. My work has mainly been working with real people and performing to audiences. Collaborating is truly my craft. But I have also started to see other ways and opportunities for performance. As well as Zoom, I have been able to start a performance platform using Camden People's Theatre's Instagram. We can utilize their audience and create opportunities for artists.

CS   *What advice do you have for young people entering the field right now?*

CM   Young people are more able to adapt. Theatre and performance are going to live on TikTok and other platforms unheard of.

There is no rule book for this period. But that is where the opportunity lies. They have the privilege of the old school not being able to tell them how to do it, because the older generations haven't got a clue.

Online platforms have opened so many possibilities, and lockdown have thrown us into the future. We will go back in time when lockdown ends, but we will have all this knowledge, and we won't be able to go back.

CS *During a time of global collective trauma, what are theatre's healing properties, if any?*

CM Theatre buildings should be seen as part of the community for *real*. I stay connected to my local theatre because I am part of that community. I walk down the street and see old students, friends, old teachers. Theatres should be a place to talk *and* listen. They should be functional and places of entertainment and dreams.

In this time, the dead wood, old and redundant ideas can be swept away.

A lot of theatres are not diverse places. For example, there is a lot of discrimination against religious people and religious communities. I have seen staff and performance pieces say off-hand anti-religious comments, which are tantamount to racism and prejudice. A lot of immigrant communities are religious, and they don't access many theatre and art buildings. How can middle-class venues proclaim to be open spaces, when they hold some of the most disgusting and reductive views?

This could be a time for revisioning and affirmation for the Theatre. In this time, it can remind itself of its healing properties – its place as part of society and put itself dead centre as the ritual and campfire.

CS *Can you talk about your work with BAC Beatbox Academy and with Beats & Elements?*

CM I have led the BAC Beatbox Academy since 2008. Initially I was part of a team, and then eventually I was the last man standing. The main reason for this was that I believed that the Academy was more than beatboxing, and that it had an important role in being a space for young people to come and develop, and that we could create some new and important performance/theatre.

Before getting seriously into theatre, I was getting into trouble and had been arrested. I carried a knife for years and had bought guns and thought I was probably going to end up in prison. My dad went to prison and so did other family members. I thought that this was going to be my path.

After being given opportunities by Battersea Arts Centre, I started to change my mind. Being allowed to be creative, and have some autonomy over my thoughts, made me see the power of creativity and having high aspirations for people – including myself.

The academy is about young people being able to come and be creative. The beatboxing is a conduit to get them in. Once they are there, they can share their stories, make friends and eat sweets. The minimum requirement is to create positive memories.

Since the lockdown, we have run weekly Zoom sessions. I expected the participants to come for around the first three weeks or so and then for the numbers drop off. Online, the sound lags, you can't beatbox together, and the picture is bad. Not only did the kids keep coming, but the numbers were probably a bit higher in some of the sessions. This could have been confusing, as WE COULD NOT BEATBOX.

What this showed is that our ritual, looking at each other in the eyes and sharing moments, is important. Each session has a purpose in and of itself. It is not the time to worry about grand outcomes, shows and reviews.

There is a problem with producers and other people asking 'What are the outcomes? Where is this going?' LOOK AROUND YOU. The outcomes are there! The process is everything, and as long as the weekly sessions are fun, then we are doing the right things.

Sometimes I feel like they are asking me to create *artists*. Wacky hairstyles shaved in a particular way. An affected way of speaking and gesticulating. (A lot of this is bound up in classism and racism.)

The world cannot all be beatboxers, rappers and spoken word artists. In the real world, we are teachers with the spirit of rappers, plumbers with the flow of a beatboxer and bus drivers with the veracity of a spoken word poet. And that is a beautiful thing that should be celebrated.

Me and Paul Cree started Beats & Elements as our own company, as a way to creative freedom. We would self-fund, fund raise and work for free. This would allow us to have no restraints on our work and vision. Hip-hop would be the aesthetic form which we would be working with. No one was asking for us to make this work, and it didn't seem like they cared about these stories either. Poor people in the UK aren't sexy enough.

CS *In what ways do you instigate joy in your work processes, especially when building work that centres Black, Indigenous and/ or POC performers?*

CM It is crucial that, whether I'm leading a participatory workshop, or whether it is an R&D, people are having fun and engaged in play. Creating memories and having a positive creative experience is part of my process, so joy is very much part of it.

We play drama games, where people can laugh at themselves. I give prompts such as *favourite TV shows, funny memories, dreams*. I have found that these often conjure up lighter material, that is still serious. We can see the performer, their bodies, and their voices. Often their race and class are inherent in the embodied performance. If a performer references their identity within the performance, it often takes them out of the experience. For them and for us the audience. Unfortunately, being totally on the nose in quite a gross way seems to be something the middle-class gaze salivates for.

I encourage personal stories that are honest and interesting. This could be that *so and so* went to the beach and something gentle and moving happened. It doesn't have to be that something traumatic or sensational transpired. This is often coerced by an industry that sometimes seems to only reward particular identity narratives. Middle-class people with privilege can tell any story, but young people and minorities seems to only be rewarded or commissioned when they tell victimized stories. This is part of a middle-class privilege. In many ways we must challenge the narrow view of POC writing and performing, and not play into the thirsty alleged allies who want us to talk about abuse and the make-believe abuse of the audience. We can never take away their privilege, so we must question why they pretend to beg for forgiveness for their 'whiteness' or 'privilege'. If we play this game, we are victims in perpetuity and they can wank off saying 'I'm bad, I'm so bad, tell me how bad I am', whilst poor white working-class people shoulder the blame, and the system stays EXACTLY THE SAME. This is complex, but twisting the narrative is very important.

CS *What are your hopes and dreams for theatre's future?*

CM I want it to become more accessible. More old people. More young people. Poor people. Theatre should be a place for people's stories. I feel like it has become about the institutions themselves. It is a ritual. The stigma of theatre should be taken away.

Let's have more different styles of theatre taught at GCSE. Why is it always the same old shit? We don't want it to be the same stuff in 100 years. What about the stories of now? And the new stories?

There is a place for classical texts, but it shouldn't be *all* that. Start them off with stuff they can relate to – work that has a purpose. The theatre that has a function for their souls.

The digital possibilities will allow theatre to be more accessible in a way that it hasn't before. The way that technology democratized the music industry it can do it for theatre. There can be live performances online, broadcast from anywhere to everywhere. And everyone with a computer or a phone can broadcast performance online. And make them more accessible to all.

Elizabeth Newman

Elizabeth Newman is a British theatre director and artistic director of Pitlochry Theatre in Scotland. This interview was conducted over Zoom on 28 September 2020.

CS *How has the first lockdown been for you?*

EN It has been hard. I live in the heart of the Highlands in Pitlochry and I am far away from my family. My close family have all been shielding. On a personal level, it has been really challenging. On a professional level, it has also been hard. This is the fourth company that I have run, and my third building, and I have been through restructures and capital campaigns but never a global pandemic and certainly not one that is resulted in so many redundancies. We have also had to make work in ways that we have never made work before and totally reimagine what we were doing. I'm one of the executives so my job with Chris, he's the executive director, was to lead the redundancy process. And we had to make forty people redundant and lay thirty-eight people off in an organization of a staff of a hundred, and those layoffs and redundancies don't include all of the artists and freelancers that we typically employ and work with as well. Our organization is on eleven acres of land and we've four buildings and every year we have 100,000 visitors. It is a turnover usually of £4.4 million, and box office is 85 per cent of our income. As soon as lockdown hit, it felt like we had fifteen minutes to reinvent everything just to stay afloat. It has just been unrelenting. On the one hand, I think that's really good, because it means you just have to keep going, and on the other hand, it means that I feel like at some point, it will stop, and that's when it will hit us. The way the UK approached the lockdown was not ideal. Neither was the way the UK approached furlough. I was in the car with a dear colleague when furlough was announced, and I remember crying so hard the car just shook for twenty minutes because of the relief that at least we'd be able to give people some money for a period of time.

CS *You were also in the middle of directing David Greig's* Adventures with the Painted People *at the time, yes?*

EN: Yes. We had to reconfigure it for audio. I used to run a theatre in Bolton, and Jon Claypole is chair of HOME theatre in Manchester. And the Director of Arts of the BBC called up and asked if we wanted to do something for their culture in quarantine series, and suggested we do the *Painted People* piece for BBC Sounds. I knew we had no way of doing it in person. It felt important both organizations to carry on making work anyway, and then I spoke to Matthew Sweet at Radio 3, and he said, 'let's put the piece on Radio 3', and that was it. We recorded it in fourteen days. They had never recorded Radio 3 drama remotely, but we all figured what is the worst that can happen? He paired us with a production company called Naked Productions, and we went for it! I think it worked because there was a real desire from everybody to make it work. David and I have known each other for a long time. And everyone else involved too. it was a positive experience.

CS *How did the digital theatre project* Shades of Tay *come to be?*

EN In December 2019, we launched Shades of Tay and a host of other projects. We had already been commissioning people but all the stuff that we commissioned was for work to be performed outdoors. When lockdown hit, we decided we are just going to mass commission now. To get money into artists' hands and to keep the work happening and the project itself going. Within two weeks we commissioned fifty artists. The goal was to put everything up online. We were only seven full-time staff and two part-time. But we felt we had to make it happen. As we headed into lockdown I asked myself 'what do people need right now?' People are lonely. They are going to be lonely. Hence, the Telephone project. All my friends with kids were asking what their kids could do during this time. We created an arts and crafts series where kids could Zoom in. The next thing was 'how do we look after artists'. If you could describe what people need during a global pandemic, what would be the three words that you use?

Light. Hope. Joy. That is where the Light Hope Joy project came from. Three times a day every day, you would have an artistic offering from the theatre that would in some way engage you or entertain you! Shades of Tay offers both of those things, but also it is an opportunity for artists to respond to nature. For me what became important was responding with urgency because it was an urgent situation.

CS *What advice or words do you have for people entering the field right now?*

EN It has always been hard and challenging like irrespective of a global pandemic. I think everyone at the start of their career feels entirely shut out and locked out unless they have some predestined kind of nepotism going on. We do not immediately assume this is all to do with the pandemic because it is not. But there are lots of things you can still be doing. Right now, what the industry is going to respond to is artistry and creativity. You have that in abundance. Now it is time for you to use it. If you are interested in getting an agent, they are still looking for clients. If you are interested in writing, people still want to read your work. The key thing for me remains the same, which is the advice that I was given by my mentor Annie Castledine. She said, 'You need to read all the plays. You need to see all the things. You need to be politicised.' The pandemic does not change that. Where the struggle comes in is that the form is changing. We do not have fully live theatre right now. You must adapt. There is no way around it. We know we cannot mass congregate. No one is going to do the adapting for you. That sounds harsh, but the opportunities will be there if you go and search for them. They will not fall into your lap. The question is less about the pandemic and more about socio-economic and the diversity challenge that were faced with. That is what we should be dealing with as an industry and working harder to address.

I was appointed two years ago, and I said to the board we would begin to be an organization that works across three platforms inside, outside and online. What I was able to say to our board is what we are still doing. We are just engaging with the other part of the policy now, which we have never really been able to do because the beast need be fed with the inside work. Now is the moment that we can really work this muscle. This is a real opportunity for us. It is an opportunity to meet international friends, who cannot necessarily get to us for whatever reason, and to be available with more regularity. That is what the pandemic has afforded us. I am risk-averse, but I am risk aware. It is important to take a risk because the only risk is not taking one. We must be really risked aware. Strengthening the relationship with our digital audience can be vital and it can be a beautiful thing. We have to find a way of finding community, which is very hard when we can't be near each other, and when often our most vulnerable are digitally disadvantaged, and disenfranchised because these digital and online platforms are not the platforms that may be able to access.

CS   *What are your hopes and dreams for the field?*

EN   We need to make sure we do not become cynical. Cynicism is the death of imagination. That is my hope. My dream is that as many organizations as possible conserve so that we can get to the other side of this and be able to welcome audiences back, and that the work will be equal to or greater quality than before, and of equal and greater brilliance. Lastly, but most importantly, that the theatre we make and produce will be a reflection – a step closer to being a truly representative reflection of the world that we live in where voices and ideas will be represented that maybe previously have not been before – where a young Asian girl from Bolton will sit in the audience and see herself, where a young Black man in Croydon will sit and see himself, whereby a young person from a low socio-economic background will see themselves, where an older person that has cognitive memory loss can see themselves as well as an older person that does not. The list goes on, but for me that includes all the protected characteristics. The reason why they are protected is because the world that we live in currently is aggressive, and one of the negatives expressed during the pandemic is some people's willingness to expose the most vulnerable. What we need to do as artists is give voice to the most vulnerable because that's how empathy can thrive and survive and that is how actually we grow a world community. If everybody behaved with responsibility and care for our most vulnerable, we wouldn't have to lock our vulnerable people away, because they are in need of more support and more contact and more love and more empathy and more transcendence and more belonging. Theatre, stories, narrative can support that.

Esther Richardson

Esther Richardson is artistic director of Pilot Theatre in York, England. This interview was conducted over email in the week of 16 November 2020.

CS *How has lockdown been for you?*

ER The first lockdown was initially a huge relief, because I'd been so stressed about us being on tour. My anxiety pre-lockdown affected my breathing, resulting in burning sensations in my lungs. I wondered if it was the virus, but it was the weight of it all.

In the weeks ahead of 16 March leaders in the sector absorbed the escalating situation at different paces. Having family around the world, including in Italy, and close colleagues in Hong Kong and Beijing, meant I was being implored daily to stop going to work and to start wearing masks. Outside the UK everyone could see what was obvious that we were in deep trouble, but also in a terrifying denial. I was in the group of people who were emotionally prepared and grateful for theatres closing, but my heart went out to everyone for whom it was a seismic shock.

If lockdown was first a relief, then came the highs and lows. There was the adrenalin rush of making sure everyone we work with was all right financially as well as emotionally. Then adapting to the situation, leaning into our digital skillset at Pilot and relaunching our show based on Alex Wheatle's 2017 novel *Crongton Knights* as a webcast production with wraparound online content made with the company at home. Generally, I deal well with change where I see opportunity, so tried to focus on the positives. The crisis turned old theatre hierarchies upside down and levelled some inequities (certainly for those of us who usually pay for and do most of the travelling). Meetings became a lot more accessible with lots of different people represented. New networks were created. As well as anger, there was a refreshing openness and humility around for a while. Home-schooling and working full-time was tough, and without doubt affected my mental health but most notably, and most troublingly my small daughter's. All year there has obviously been overwhelming loss and huge anxiety as well as rage to navigate.

Overall lockdown has been the opportunity to be at home, both creatively and emotionally; in every sense, the chance to get your own house in order.

CS *What are ways theatre as industry can centre care as one of its core tenets?*

ER People must come first. We can't build theatre back better and stronger without centring values of compassion and care. Yet as well as extending care better to ourselves and one another, how do we then extend compassion to everyone we *could* reach and include in our work?

If the capacity to extend the most far-reaching care starts with looking after ourselves, for most of us the demands of working in theatre means we don't prioritize self-care. This may explain why some of the ways in which we behave towards each other in the industry is not always as caring as it could be. As part of AHRC-funded research I've been doing into the well-being of performing arts leaders during Covid-19, the data shows self-care in theatre is poor; no one holding responsibility I've spoken to has slept properly this year, or taken breaks, and people describe how they have 'aged'. Ironically, this doesn't mean that we are bad at extending care to those we work closest with, and care about most, but it does mean that our efforts may be unsustainable over the longer term and limited in the fullest potential of their reach. We have already lost a lot of people in this crisis, but we risk losing more because of the stress people have been placed under.

I think the expectations we have of ourselves to be perfect in a highly competitive industry can work against our capacity for care between one another. We don't always allow others to be wholehearted and vulnerable human beings who are free to make different choices to us and to make mistakes. Overall, I would like to hear less about being kind and see it more in action. This would be a radical step change in care for the better.

CS *In what ways has theatre industry been forced to reckon with change during the pandemic?*

ER The research I'm doing presents unexpected insights around change. We're very crisis-resilient in the parts of the industry that are often less visible where leaders have simply got on with what they have always done: ensuring people come first, caring for their staff, collaborators and community. These leaders have had to adapt to the situation but haven't had anxiety about the fundamentals. Overall, these are leaders who have navigated, racism, sexism, ableism or the ever-insidious British class system throughout a lot of their life and work. What they've said is: 'For some of us this is *just another crisis*.'

It has been the year where the inequity that has always existed has been laid bare and impossible not to see. In addition to Covid-19, Black Lives Matter, and the murder of George Floyd in the United States, awoke us to our individual and collective responsibilities in respect of anti-racism. Change is a process, but we've already made a shift here on a level I haven't observed before in UK theatre. Being outside so much more, and not in lengthy technical rehearsals in dark rooms, and being in nature, has also awoken again everyone's love for the environment and our deeper understanding of our need to act now to save our planet which makes me optimistic for our work here too.

One of the concerns I have for the mainstream in this second lockdown is that while the first phase was about coming back to care and compassion, with the arrival of recovery funds will we forget all that again ...? Will we remember what we learned and what we felt in summer 2020 and make the most of the opportunity for lasting change? I believe most people who work in theatre are here for the best reasons: for the love of the artform and the powerful sense of community it can foster; to interrogate who they are and grow; to create opportunities for others; to make change in the world. Yet the system is so deeply hierarchical and inequitable it often works against the best of these qualities in us and produces behaviours that breed mistrust, misunderstanding, separation and division. Added to which mainstream funded theatre has been operating in a context for at least twelve years, since the financial crash of 2008, where it is not a given that what we do is regarded as more valuable than economic impact. The political context we live and work in is mostly not about people first and it is not about care.

How do we continue to collectively navigate this, holding tight to the best of who we are and who we can be? I think we need start at home. Everyone can work to communicate better, listen better, consider an alternative perspective better, think better before firing off a tweet, collaborate better, acknowledge the work of others better and work on unlearning racism, sexism and ableism better – those things cost nothing and are choices all of us can make every day. We can even make those choices in a crisis and under stress because there is nothing quite like a crisis to show us the change that is possible in us, as well as in the system.

CS   *What are your thoughts on digital theatre?*

ER   We've all complained of Zoom fatigue, but how fortunate we have been to have had all this technology to connect us, sustain us and to subvert hierarchies and change the rules of the game in this crisis. Nothing will ever be as precious to us after this as in person events, conversations and living breathing theatre performances, but I hope we also never forget the time when our magical screens granted us so much access, gave us modes for survival, enabled the making of new friendships and showered us with opportunities to explore the borders of theatre, technology and storytelling. Until we can beam our physical selves across the world nothing will erase borders like this technology – because it does make it possible to work all over the world and with new people. I hope we keep innovating in this space and keep in mind the positive change it has fostered and its vast creative potential.

CS   *What are your hopes and dreams for theatre's future?*

ER   I want to see a fairer distribution of cultural funding geographically and away from the biggest cities, most particularly away from London. It's wrong that so many people still have no access to something like funded theatre and perhaps so many of our present wider societal problems and divisions stem from these forms of historic injustice.

In my future theatre sector, there would be at least a collective of funded artists in every community, and arts would be reinstated on the curriculum up to at least GCSE. There would be more than a handful of companies dedicated to work with children and young people distributed around the country and they would be funded equitably to the same level as other organizations. In every region there would be a dedicated children's theatre building and a theatre for teens. There would be deeper connections with libraries and theatres; digital productions online would be fully accessible and as far as possible, free. Anyone who wants to develop theatre skills should access these for free. We need a system where anyone who wants to can access the benefits of funded theatre. That's the dream.

Dámaso Rodríguez

Dámaso Rodríguez is a Cuban-American director and producer, and artistic director of Artists Repertory Theatre in Portland, Oregon. This interview was conducted via email on 1 November 2020.

CS *How has lockdown been for you?*

DR Today is day 232 of the lockdown. I have measured time this way since Artists Rep cancelled our fundraising gala on 14 March 2020, our 2020–21 season announcement on 3 April, and the final play of the 2019–20 season (the world premiere of Anthony Hudson's *Looking for Tiger Lily*, which had been scheduled to begin rehearsal on 28 April 2020). I also measure time in 'days until the election'. At this moment, we are two days away from the US presidential election. As the pandemic stretched, and the Trump administration shifted from magical thinking to Orwellian doublethink, the only way for me to envision how much time is left in lockdown is based on which way the world tilts on Election Day.

There have been many somewhat unimaginable logistical challenges to making theatre, but the biggest struggle of the lockdown is proving to be the unknowable duration. For the first few months we did everything we could to keep the theatre intact, and prepared multiple scenarios for returning to a pre-pandemic normal, but all that changed for me by June 2020. Theatres around the United States made plans for a summer reopening, then fall, then late-fall, then just in time for the Holiday show (as so many large US theatre companies are disproportionately funded by the box office of the annual production of *A Christmas Carol*), and now the fall of 2021 is becoming the target on production calendars. At Artists Rep, we were amid a two-year stint producing 'On Tour' while undertaking a $32 million capital campaign to redesign our facility. Producing under these conditions was difficult already, without adding an ever-shifting date for 'returning to safe public assembly'. We made the decision not to announce any productions until we knew we could return to the theatre, with a full house safely breathing the same air. This meant cutting our budget by nearly half, and laying off fourteen full-time employees, including our entire scene shop. We shifted our focus entirely to expanding education programmes online, post-pandemic play development on Zoom and the investment in equipment and processes for adapting stage plays into audio dramas. We also began experimenting with video and short film projects.

CS *What advice do you have for people entering the field right now?*

DR I advise students to use this time to train as best they can in the remote classroom, and to read memoirs, biographies, theatrical history and the books behind the techniques or methods they think they know. Learn all you can during this disruption. Find collaborators. Learn other mediums. Work to better understand the business as it was – both commercial and non-profit. Reach out to leaders like me, who might be more open than ever to meet via Zoom. Write. The task in front of us is likely the best tool we have to comfort ourselves. Bring energy to the task in front of us.

CS *What are the hopes and dreams you have for theatre's future?*

DR Rebuilding (or remaking) the theatre I lead for a new existence post-pandemic is my responsibility and I have an opportunity to reconceive how we do what we do, and how we talk to funders and audiences about what it truly takes to support, empower and listen to the artists around which theatre is made. The US Regional Theatre model was founded under no longer viable assumptions (e.g. large subscriber bases, pre-internet, with long-lost civic, corporate and large-scale investment from national foundations). It stopped working for us – for artists – long ago, but we have done everything we can to keep it stumbling along without the resources it takes to support the work, and to make it accessible to anyone. I want to pay artists as much as possible – for the artists have always been the field's greatest patrons because they subsidize their own work via sacrifice and self-exploitation in the name of their calling. I want to eradicate for-profit 'commercial' thinking in the non-profit sphere. I want to make tickets inexpensive and tell foundations and corporations to discard old standards for 'support'. I want to test ways of creating and producing that are not 'the way it's usually been done'.

CS *During a time of global collective trauma, what are theatre's healing properties?*

DR The theatres and individual artists need the funding from local and national governments to weather the fiscal and emotional trauma of being prevented from doing our work for the safety of the community. Give us the support to prepare for our return and we will become highly energized catalysts for healing. Perhaps theatre's relevance will be made undeniably clear – after two years of streaming a limitless catalogue of content – that the theatre was never in competition with the digital mediums; that we were always about the ritual of gathering, shoulder to shoulder, heartbeats synchronized, breathing the same air and witnessing our stories together.

CS *How did you pivot your working modes during lockdown?*

DR In May 2020, Artists Rep was finally approved for the US Federal Payroll Protection Loan/Grant programme, allowing us to pay our staff, rents and other overhead. We discovered we were eligible for $100,000 beyond these basic expenses, but we needed to use the funds within six weeks, or the funding would go to waste.

We had to move quickly. While Zoom live-streaming performances were of little inspiration to me, I was excited by the audio drama format, and particularly to the idea of working with writers to adapt scripts that might thrive, or even be enhanced, as a listening experience. We identified two plays by two of our resident playwrights. We were able to quickly get Screen Actors Guild agreements to adapt the five-hour, five-part epic 2018 play *Magellanica* by E. M. Lewis, which I had directed and produced in 2018, along with the 2017 play *The Berlin Diaries* by Andrea Stolowitz (a ninety-minute, two-actor play). Each play employed direct address and were invitations for sound designers and composers to create something exhilarating for listeners. We budgeted the projects and realized we could bring more artists and projects onto the payroll to utilize the unexpected PPP funds. The result was several weeks of creative abundance in June 2020, an entirely unanticipated turn of events.

In all we were able to invest in twelve projects simultaneously. Over fifty writers, directors, educators, actors, technicians, designers and producers (including several ART staff) were hired to collaboratively create theatre-inspired work that moved beyond the traditional form. Individuals were involved in a multitude of projects, forming a rapidly assembled repertory company dubbed the ART: Mercury Company. It became a transformative experience during a time of uncertainty.

We then set out to find funding to assemble Mercury 2.0, to further the work on projects in Mercury 1, and to continue to employ local theatre artists. To my great shock, the idea resonated with a funder, and we quickly raised several hundred thousand dollars toward this work. We are amid Mercury 2.0, with twenty-two projects in development or production (e.g. more audio dramas are being recorded, three short films are being shot or edited, several plays in workshop or early script development). Mercury 3.0 is funded and planned for April/May of 2021, and Mercury 4.0 in the fall of 2021 (hopefully, the final Mercury before we return to public assembly in our new facility as the pandemic becomes under control).

CS *The United States has been not only in the grip of the pandemic but in midst of the Black Lives Matter uprising. What actionable steps can theatre take to respond and listen deeply?*

DR During the June 2020 Mercury Company, the protests in response to the murder of George Floyd began around the country, but Portland became a focal point for the national news cycle, and a tool of propaganda by the Trump administration. We set aside some funds to invite nine Black artists in the company to meet and consider how or if they wanted to respond creatively or otherwise to the moment. They reported from their creative discussions with several specific and extraordinary ideas. First, the group wished to make a short film called *See Me*, which would be a slice of life of several Black people interwoven with animated fantastical dreamscapes (currently being filmed in Mercury 2.0). They then proposed what I consider to be an incredibly generous gift to Artists Rep, the demand for a new programme called 'DNA: Oxygen at ART'. As originally conceived, the programme would (1) utilize restricted funding to develop and produce new work generated by, led by and featuring Black, Indigenous and People of Colour (BIPOC) artists; (2) create a long-lasting mentor/mentee programme in which at least one mainstage production each season is staffed entirely with BIPOC artists behind the scenes, each with a paid, BIPOC mentee in their area of specialty; (3) establish an affinity/working group of BIPOC theatre makers at ART. In July 2020, we secured a $600,000 gift to ensure the work of DNA: Oxygen through the 2023 fiscal year. We have created a three-year, full-time position of Artistic Directing Fellow to launch and build the programme, while they themselves are mentored by me on all areas of theatre leadership.

Let us move past the traumatic narrative, and if we must go there to tell our necessary stories, let us couple that narrative always with joy, or at least insist that gravity without levity is insufficient and may be perpetuating the harm caused in predominantly white institutions. Ask those who have been historically marginalized to tell only the stories they wish to tell. Listen, trust, accept the gift of unanticipated ideas. Let us use the pandemic disruption as the unwanted event that forced, or gave the breath needed for, unpredictable transformation, and may the world tilt towards change.

Anthony Simpson-Pike

Anthony Simpson-Pike is a Black British director and dramaturg. He previously worked at the Gate Theatre in London and is currently associate director at the Yard Theatre. This interview was conducted via email on 18 October 2020.

CS *How has lockdown been for you?*

ASP Lockdown has been up and down. My uncle Colin got Covid-19 and died from the virus. He was a care worker in Wales, and he wasn't given sufficient PPE, so the virus has hit close to home for my family. Uncle Colin came from Zimbabwe and, like many other immigrants, was on the frontline in working in a care home. This time has shown clearly that the people who form the backbone of this country, that keep the country going, are often the most vilified or ignored. That needs to change. But it will only change if we make it happen. This government has proven that aside from clapping for our carers, it has no interest in caring for them.

As a theatre-maker there have been other challenges. I am lucky to work part-time at a theatre (the Yard Theatre) that has provided me with some small level of stability over this period but that is not the case for most people in our industry. The pandemic has made it clear how precarious the working conditions are for freelancers. Many people have been faced with impossible choices and pushed out of the industry altogether. It is incumbent on institutions to stop this from happening and change working conditions now so it can never happen again. I started working at The Yard in February 2020 and weeks after that we went into lockdown so, as you can imagine, my new job as Associate Director there has necessarily been different from what I expected. It has been a real journey in adapting an organization to a time of global crisis. There has been a lot of work on reimagining the theatre and how it works in order to make sure it can work better for everyone.

There have also been some creative bright points. I curated and led an online festival, Yard Online, which gave me the opportunity to commission some incredible artists from around the world who were mainly queer artists and/or artists of colour. It felt important to push back against the idea of 'safe' programming in response to the pandemic. We must challenge what people mean by that. Who is it safe for? If the lesson that theatre takes from all of this is that it needs to do more of the same, then something has gone wrong. It was hard to make the case for theatre to the government and to people who don't often go. Lots of people felt it wasn't one of their priorities because it hadn't ever represented or welcomed them. This moment needs to be about reimagining how and what we do. Theatre needs to feel relevant to the people whose taxes fund it.

One community that theatre has not treated well enough is people of colour. It has been a draining time for Black artists as the health crisis has met the ongoing crisis of anti-Blackness and thrust that conversation to the forefront of people's minds for the brief time that it did. Black people, already at the sharp end of the destruction this virus has waged, have also had to contend with the violence that continues to be done to us by white supremacy. There is a third crisis that Black and brown people are most affected by, despite having contributed the least towards it historically, the climate emergency. It is a time of crisis. Every crisis is a source of transformation for the good or the bad. Which way it will go is up to all of us.

CS *What advice do you have for people entering the field right now?*

ASP Know your worth. Know your voice is valuable, and that this industry needs you, especially if you do not see yourself in it already. Do not be scared to get in touch with people who you think can answer your questions, or to ask them in the first place.

CS *What are your hopes and dreams for theatre's future?*

ASP I hope that we can start to put care at the centre of everything we do as an industry and as a society; care for Black and brown people, for freelancers, for the climate and natural world and for each other. I hope we can sew care into the dramaturgy we practice and the words we utter on stage, in the way companies are run and how everyone is treated audience and theatre workers alike.

I want us to make theatre in the way we would like to live life. As multiple crises converge, I hope that we can use the theatre to rehearse for the kind of society we would like to be now and in the future. We spend more time writing versions of the apocalypse than we do post-capitalist societies. We are experiencing a crisis of the imagination as a political culture.

Theatre is uniquely equipped to imagine new ways of being and rehearse them together.

I would also like to see more collaboration and less competition across the sector. The pandemic has magnified the cracks in capitalism and offers us a chance to take another look at how theatre fits into that. Should theatre replicate capitalist modes of production or can it be a space of imaginative power to carve out another, more sustainable, future? As we face up to the fact that limitless growth on a limited planet is impossible, theatre will need to look inwards at how it is contributing to the much bigger crisis of climate breakdown, and how to move towards a circular economy. What is the fundamental purpose and culture of theatre in the context of the crisis? We need to think beyond the politics of content and consider process and form in the way we make theatre. It is possible to make work *about* ecological breakdown while running a process that adds to it. It is possible to make work *about* Black liberation while running a process that marginalizes Black people. We need to consider *how* we make plays not just *what* we are saying with them.

CS *At a time of global collective trauma, what are theatre's healing properties, if any?*

ASP We need to start by examining the assumption that theatre has ever been a healing place for *everyone*. Who has theatre served in that way historically? Because that tells us something about who it is for in its current form. As a Black artist and audience member, the majority of times I have seen people who look like me on stage has been in moments of suffering. We do not see ourselves experiencing joy or love, absent a relationship to racism or trauma, onstage very often. There are very few plays about Blackness where the Blackness is not the problem of the play. Let's start from there. If theatre is going to locate its healing powers, let's ask who it has always felt healing for and for whom it has felt like a site of pain on too many occasions. This goes back to the question of care. If you have a dramaturgical anchor of care for the audience, and you imagine that audience includes people of different backgrounds, then the theatre you make will truly allow all the audience to heal. But if the work comes at the expense of one community only seeing themselves represented in trauma, or not at all, then theatre will not ever begin to locate its healing powers. Marginalized communities deserve joy too. That's the more radical path to healing.

CS *What have you been working on during lockdown?*

ASP I have been working as Associate Director at The Yard primarily and as an associate at The Gate over this period. I have also made two audio plays over lockdown with Tamasha Arts, by Hassan Abdulrazzak and Satinder Chohan, and been working with students at Royal Central on the writing MA. I am now working on a film never having worked on one before, which has been a transformative process for me.

In a personal capacity, I have been thinking a lot about the gaps in the industry. What support is missing? And how do we need to transform to care for everyone in the recovery? One of those gaps is in the way we practice dramaturgy. As I said earlier, there is too shallow a representation of Black stories on UK stages. That is partly because we lack Black dramaturgs and literary managers. I did a call out for Black people who are interested in dramaturgy to organize an introductory session with Ola Animashawun, Louise Stephens and myself to give the opportunity for Black people interested in knowing more about dramaturgy to ask questions. I found that really galvanizing and I am planning to do more work on this.

The other work I have been doing has been thinking about the place of migrants in the country and industry at a time of rising xenophobia. I convened and co-chaired a digital town hall with Migrants in Theatre about how theatre can support migrants but also not replicate the hostile environment that is animating a dangerous politics right now. Theatre and society would be poorer without the contribution of people from around the world. I hope that as the UK leaves the EU, culture might be a meeting point for exchange and a site or resistance to far-right exclusionary ideas. The town hall very much felt like the start of a something. It felt like a coming together at a time when we need it more than ever.

Roy Alexander Weise

R oy Alexander Weise is a Black British theatre director and co-artistic director of Royal Exchange Theatre in Manchester, England. He directed Natasha Gordon's debut play *Nine Night* (2018) at the National Theatre. It became the first play by a Black British female author to transfer to the West End. This interview was conducted on Zoom on 9 December 9.

CS *Alan Lane in the goodaftercovid19 online YouTube panel on rebooting arts futures on 9 December 2020 said that theatre should stop thinking of audiences as customers and more as friends and citizens. Thoughts?*

RW As a director, I have always had an eye on the audience. This comes from my own personal identity, my political and racial identity as well. In my work. I've always wanted to see myself and I've always wanted audiences who look like me and who might also experience things similar to me to be seen and know they are visible and valued.

I've always been fighting to find ways to make it so that the conversations that I have with the theatres that I'm working with are broader than just me coming to direct to show. It was also about what are you going to do to support people that look like me to know that they feel safe in these spaces as well. As a Black man I was going into theatres encouraging them to do innovative things and hopefully engage with people that they don't engage with, but also I was also becoming conscious and a bit paranoid about the fact that that would sometimes mean that the organization might not view the piece as a success, because the lens that a lot of theatres work with culturally is often about finance and about selling tickets.

When I was directing *Nine Night* at the National Theatre, I was very blunt with the administration there that they had to pack the house with people that reflected the family that was on stage or else the play wouldn't hold up because the language and situations in the play were culturally and ethnically specific, and the language needed to crackle and resonate for the play to have its best shot. I'd love if anyone reading this as an artist like would feel inspired to also do the same because sometimes the power imbalance between a producing theatre and an artist can mean that the artist doesn't always feel empowered to ask for those things that are deeply rooted in the practice that the director or the artist carries.

As a Black artist I have struggled to communicate the value of my ideas to people that don't have the same lived experience as me and therefore found that I was having a harder time getting the work that I wanted programmed because it didn't reflect what people understood. After *Nine Night* was a success and went to the West End, I had many meetings with producers and they would ask me to direct plays about slaves, for example, and I kept telling them that Black people don't need to see that because they've seen and lived those narratives their whole lives. We are entering a time when the lens by which work is made needs to be accurate to redress the power imbalance and systemic racism in the field.

When I became co-artistic director at the Royal Exchange (with Bryony Shanahan), I started to see how monies are apportioned and the relationship between box office targets and selling tickets, and how that defines the work that gets commissioned and its relationship to the audience. The Royal Exchange is a theatre in the round, which means that the audience need always look at one another in that space.

I really believe that when theatre happens, and the lights go down as a show begins, everyone in that space becomes a community for that moment. Everyone becomes neighbours, and we are all there to witness this thing in front of our eyes, and hopefully leave being challenged in the way in which we see the world and other people and how we view ourselves and negotiate our own emotional narratives. It's clear to me that there is a disconnect in the way in which theatres approach commissioning artists and also in the invitations we make to people that are receiving the work. If a theatre is subsidized, it exists on taxpayers' monies. Theatre and its storytelling need reflect the community it serves. Too many theatres are working on an old model. The world has been changing. Important political endeavours have and are occurring and those conversations need be at the centre, not at the margins of our theatres.

Bryony (Shanahan) and I are committed to thinking about our theatre as a metaphorical campfire where people can sit around and feel its warmth and recognize lived experiences in order to have a more nuanced and granular relationship with audiences. The other metaphor we have is that of a magnifying glass. Every production is a bunch of artists holding this magnifying glass looking closely at something and asking questions and then inviting the audience to come and look at the work from where the artist is standing.

Director Marianne Elliott's father was one of the founders of the Royal Exchange and we spoke with her about her experience growing up with this theatre in her life, and what its legacy means in terms of accessibility and inclusivity while remaining a pillar of excellence in the community. She told us that one of the important things about this theatre is that everyone – the kings, the porters – need to walk in through the same portal. There's true democracy in crossing the threshold of this magical space. On equal footing.

CS *You streamed a Zoom reading of Katori Hall's* The Mountaintop *(2011) during the first half of lockdown. How did that experience make you think about the possibilities of digital theatre?*

RW This pandemic has taught us that the one thing that we all want is to share the same space, but it's also taught us what is unique and powerful about our art form. There are audiences that have been able to stay connected to our work through digital means, but others for whom this is not possible. Yet, there have been audiences from all over that are connecting with us, which has been gratifying. Our reading of *The Mountaintop* had a lot to do with it. In the preface to our reading of the play, Katori spoke about the fact that Martin Luther King talked about the long arc of revolution bends towards justice, but that it takes time. We did the reading during the height of the Black Lives Matter protests against the murder of George Floyd, and thus, this meant we could contribute creatively to the global conversation. We preferred to do this rather than posting an anti-racism statement on our website. I have spent the entirety of my life being woke. I've been living this experience and fighting for survival every time I tell a story. But making work and being able to contribute financially to support people who were putting their own lives at real risk matters. Because we put our lives at risk as storytellers when we're fighting politically for something. When women talk about the inequalities, when women talk about the violence against their bodies, they're fighting for survival. When Black people and ethnically diverse people talk about the experiences of racism, they're not just telling you that story because it's interesting and people need to know, it's about social justice and it's about fighting for survival.

CS *What are your hopes and dreams for theatre's future? We know the system is broken, but what do we want to see?*

RW One of the things that has been challenging during this time has been that the sector has had to fight for its currency in the world possibly due to the ephemeral nature of the art form. The world is good at showing you what is impossible right now. So, we must be fiercely optimistic. What this historical moment has done is made the world pay attention to the nuance of a variety of lived experiences that they haven't before, and it means that we are all questioning what this art form is and what it's for and why we all miss it.

I would like to see a broader range of experiences and stories told on our stages, and auditoriums full of people that look like the people on stage, and artists having the full range of their creative expressions honoured. I would like to see better equity in terms of the connection that artists and communities have with theatres and a greater sense of ownership from both. I would love to see more work made with non-professionals because this allows people to access a world of creative expression that they haven't been able to access before. We don't exist as subsidized theatres for financial capital. Otherwise, we wouldn't be subsidized theatres. It's about how we reach people's hearts and minds. I want more theatres listening to their communities and asking them what they want to see, which doesn't mean a specific play but a commitment to learn what they value and need in their lives. Taxpayers' monies have bailed the arts sector out. We have to give back.

CS *It's crucial to consider how caring is at the heart of making theatre.*

RW We help people navigate what they think they know and who they think they know and how they think they've known them. It helps us unpick so much of the messiness of life that bureaucracy doesn't have the capacity to navigate or facilitate for people. Art is a great way to measure and understand what and who a society values. We need to find ways to work better with local governments to innovate the ways in which our societies engage with creativity.

People's understanding of their position and their value in society is different when they have access to creativity and when they have opportunities to be heard. Creativity allows people to dig into all those things that democracy and bureaucracy can't touch.

Laurie Woolery

Laurie Woolery is a Latinx theatre director and director of the Public Works programme at the Public Theatre in New York City. This interview was conducted over email between November and mid-December 2020.

CS *How has lockdown been for you as a director and director of Public Works?*

LW Lockdown has been both busy and lonely. How to be of service and help keep people's jobs. How to be a better partner? Partnership is key to everything I do and create. Its central to life both personal and professional. In these times when the very art form we participate in is literally unsafe for people to gather is where we need to innovate and meet the moment. This is what has preoccupied my thoughts and actions in lockdown. Damn, that very word is connected to punishment and isolation. Prisons go into lockdown. Schools are locked down in moments of crises. Can we reclaim lockdown as a space to dive deep and pay attention to what our previous hustle might have been silencing? Listening. Empathy for self and others. In working with community, it is easy to lose yourself or place your needs at the end of the list. How do you address the needs of all those you have committed to? Then what happens when your best does not align with others wants or needs? What do you hold on to and what do you reinvent? Clearly, questions lots of questions have been my constant companion. Solace has come in the form of New York's collective 7 pm applause for the essential workers. Living alone, it's been a daily reminder that I am a part of something so much bigger than myself and clears space to be thankful – for my life, my health, to honour those that have past – both my loved ones and those souls I did not know – but acknowledging we all exist on this planet, at the same time, sharing this experience. It's been both beautiful and heartbreaking. It's been a moment to truly acknowledge our humanity. I miss the 7 pm collected community call.

The gift of this moment has been an invitation to re-examine what it means to be a partner. As director of Public Works at The Public Theater, we work with eight community partner organizations and hundreds of individual New Yorkers from all around the city. We are committed to a mutual investment in one another and that partnership is deep and eight years strong. Gathering together is our love language so how do you show up when you can't physically show up? In the very beginning of this quarantine, we did what we always do – make art. When our summer Delacorte pageant was postponed, we saw our Public Works National Cohorts experiencing that same loss. We turned that moment into a call to action and made a national video of our global community singing 'Still I Will Love' by Shaina Taub. The video was an offering of radical joy in the face of the unknown.

Then, The Public was asked if we could salvage Free Shakespeare in the Park, so we decided to make a Public Works documentary. *Under the Greenwood Tree* tells the story of the making of the 2017 Public Works production of *As You Like It* that was scheduled as part of the 2020 summer season. In the documentary, we explored how the production was created in real time against the backdrop of the 2016 election and the first year of a Trump administration. LGBTQA, immigrant and women's rights were under assault. Now, here we were in 2020, another election year with a global pandemic, antiracist uprising, thousands of lives lost and we saw was our partner organizations rise to the occasion. Despite losing funding earmarked for summer programming, our partners made miracles happen. Once again, the themes of that production resonated directly with the moment we were living in. The documentary was a shared opportunity to spotlight the inspiring work our partners do and how our relations with community directly shapes the art we create. Lastly, we wanted to create an ambitious work of participatory art that could hold the voices of our community in this historic moment.

In this rare moment of intense shared experience, we wanted to collaborate with our national cohort, so *The Seed Project* was born. We created a shared prompt that each organization would turn into public art. Inviting community members to complete the sentence *'Today I'm planting a seed of ...'* these offerings became an expression of hope for the kind of city we want to live in. Collaborating with projection designer Lucy MacKinnon and photographer Jennifer Young, we projected the community responses as well as their portraits on the front façade of our downtown theatre an incredible manifestation of our mission of theatre of, by and for the people.

CS *What advice you have for people entering the field right now?*

LW Stay awake. Pay attention. Listen. Start with a beginner's mind. Be curious to not know the answer. Empathy. And try to see each other's humanity especially with those you disagree with. I try to practice these ideals moment to moment with some varied degree of success, so I don't think it's just a practice for young people. I think it's a daily practice for *all* people. It's hard. I fail but I keep trying.

CS *What are your hopes and dreams for theatre's future?*

LW I have always believed in community. The power of it. The wisdom of it. The heart of it. Community has been my greatest teacher mentoring me through all the work I have done. I believe that community is our future in the American theatre. Once cultural palaces turn to their community and not just offer free tickets or one culturally specific production a year but truly build longitudinal partnerships with their communities as they do with funders and board members, only then will we have cultural centres that are meaningful and a part of every citizens life. Like food, shelter, health, I believe that access to both participate and witness art is a human birthright and is essential to creating empathic and healthy communities.

CS *During a time of global collective trauma, what are theatre's healing properties, if any?*

LW We heal one another by meeting the moment. I come from poor theatre, and by that, I mean, theatre without large budgets or even theatre spaces. We learned to be creative in cafetoriums, parking lots, community centres, working sawmills and prison gymnasiums. These are a few of the site-specific locations that have been the fertile ground to my creative practice. And I loved it. Still do. Being in unconventional performance spaces takes us back to our roots where storytelling happened around the fire, on the riverbanks, at the watering hole, around the dinner table. The origins of storytelling go as far back as human existence and it's how we learned to communicate with one another, share stories to help educate, guide, liberate and heal. Can we liberate ourselves from returning to 'what was' and envision 'what can be' in terms of production? I know we can still make ambitious and excellent art if we focus on access, training, opportunity and extend true invitations to all to feast at the abundant cultural table and not return to relegate anyone to the sidelines.

CS   *How is theatre going to address the wealth gap, which makes freelancers gig workers, often paid or living in the starving class?*

LW   This haunts my mind and heart. Truly. For months I have felt like an elephant is standing with one foot on my chest. I was taught early on that no one is left behind. It's a combo mentality from my military father and Catholic immigrant mother. It's as simple as loaves and fish – everyone gets fed. It must be that way. There is enough to go around. I truly believe that. We all need to adopt both that belief and activate that practice. What we are up against is the perception of what it means to be successful. Yes, we all need to pay bills and want to make a living being an artist. I want that for everyone who wants to choose this life. But the field is set up with every theatre producing the same play by the same playwrights directed by the same directors with the same actors because they are 'proven' or have 'artistic cred'.

CS   *Can you talk about your work currently as director and artivist?*

LW   The two greatest tensions that exist for me are both my love for directing and wanting to be in the rehearsal room with my passion for creating programming and artistic opportunities for community and other artists. Both these desires feed and inform one another. Every opportunity that presents itself automatically goes into the mixer of how it serves community, speaks to the world we are living in right now, tells the story in the most compellingly authentic way and is ambitiously excellent. How do I personally bring my best work to the room and how to I create a space for others to do the same? By meeting the moment with these goals and expectations held central to the work, the audience will experience a collective moment that hopefully challenges, transforms and heals us all.

3

Virtuality

Eleanor Bishop

Eleanor Bishop is a director working across theatre and opera. She works between Aotearoa-New Zealand and the United States. This interview was conducted via email in October 2020.

CS *How has lockdown been for you?*

EB Probably a similar story to many – all work cancelled, tremendous uncertainty. I really questioned whether theatre could continue, and it made me recognize how utterly dedicated to the artform I am.

In Aotearoa-New Zealand we have had a couple of lockdowns. The first one was when we made *The Seagull* in May 2020 with Auckland Theatre Company. We started in a very restrictive lockdown – no take-away coffee or fast food even. Aotearoa-New Zealand pursued an elimination strategy (we had the border closed), so after a few months with no community transmission, the theatres opened again. Then in August, the virus recurred in Auckland and we had to lock down again. That was heartbreaking. Theatre's back as at the time of writing (October 2020) but I think we are all operating cautiously with the knowledge that things could change again at any time again.

CS *What advice do you have for people entering the field right now?*

EB The most exciting thing is that there are no rules. If you want to do something new and innovative, whether it is online, or a drive in or one-on-one performance, we need it. Performance is essential and spiritual. Start making and let the field/industry catch up to you.

It is the same advice I was once given, and I give to all the young people I teach – do not wait for someone to give you permission to be an artist.

CS *You, along with playwright Eli Kent, developed and staged Chekhov's* The Seagull *– a new online version for Auckland Theatre Company over four weeks from 8 May 2020, delivered in thirty-minute instalments, and it is now available to watch on the company's YouTube channel in perpetuity. Would you discuss how this unique project came to be, and your thoughts on digital theatre's potential?*

EB Eli and I began working together in 2007 when we formed a theatre company called The PlayGround Collective, with another theatre maker Robin Kerr. We were all in Wellington and still studying and hanging around BATS Theatre, which is where Flight of the Conchords and Taika Waititi got started. I directed a 2012 play of Eli's called *The Intricate Art of Actually Caring*, which was about two young men going on a road trip through New Zealand after the death of their friend. We first did it in Eli's bedroom at the Fringe festival for ten people at a time, and then subsequently toured it all through NZ, we played opera houses and pubs and community halls.

I also work as an associate director for the NYC-based multimedia theatre company The Builders Association led by Marianne Weems. They have been pioneering the use of media in theatre for twenty-five years. When the lockdown started in the United States, they began an online project, and I was waking up at 6 am New Zealand time to join their Zoom rehearsals. They got me started dreaming about how the form could be used innovatively – beyond bedroom monologues and play readings. I began thinking about Zoom – could it be genuinely theatrically interesting and what material would work? I was interested in seeing characters who were on Zoom in the reality of the play (our time), but I was also drawn to approach classical material (timeless). My brain thinks this way from my background in directing Shakespeare adaptations and deconstructing classical plays.

When the lockdown started here, I reread Chekhov's *The Seagull* (1896) again and it spoke so directly to me. My friends and colleagues were young and ambitious but now we were questioning everything. Could we continue to do this? Were we failures? Had we achieved anything? Just like Nina and Konstantin. And the longing, longing for connection. And then of course, I was attending birthday parties on Zoom, and like the play – there was that sense of tedium, of languidness, of nothing happening – except of course these deep fundamental shifts in the characters and the relationships. I thought – this can work!

Eli and I started work on it with Auckland Theatre Company. In Aotearoa-New Zealand we had a level system for lockdown – the highest was level four. That is when the first act of *Seagull* is set, because that is when we started working on it. We kind of knew that we might go down through the levels – we were watching the news updates and predictions. We wanted to get the first episode out while the bars were not open, cos we knew that we could get the biggest audience, so we had to work fast. We had one week of preproduction and we made an episode each week for four weeks. The week before we started 'rehearsals', we did a treatment for the overall play – trying to solve the bigger problems of how the play would work in a contemporary period and on Zoom. We really wanted to elevate beyond a straight Zoom and our media designer Owen McCarthy had the idea of including an element set inside a desktop. I had recently been in Germany observing Katie Mitchell work, so was utterly obsessed with thinking about how to stage subjectivity and this felt like such a great way to do point of view. Plus, I was particularly pleased that we could subtly give focus to the young female characters (Masha and Nina) by having the first two episodes set inside their respective desktops.

Rehearsals were tremendously playful. We were all high on the joy of being able to create something currently. The actors started turning up to the Monday morning reading with location, costume and prop offers, which were not revealed until we started the read through. We all gasped when the actor playing Konstantin popped up on Zoom with a stand in dead seagull on a stump and said off camera 'I shot this seagull' and then slid into shot with the gun. We kept it obviously! It was all incredibly live and surprising – as a group we just got so excited about the possibilities and particularly how the characters would use their cameras. And the designers and technicians were amazing, figuring out headphones and mics and tripods extremely quickly. I liken it to when you do something site specific (like *Intricate Art*) or when you rehearse in a theatre, with the tech (like with the Builders Association) – the stakes and creativity can be raised because *you're actually doing the thing*.

As for the ongoing future for the digital stage, I am interested to see theatre that is critically engaging with digital space and the way we live our digital lives and exist as our digital selves. That way the digital form will truly be something new, necessary and beyond a poor replacement for live theatre. I think there is a space for digital theatre that engages in this way but does so almost in direct opposition to the corporate platforms that heighten the importance of pace and opinion. My students at Carnegie Mellon having been making beautiful meditative works this semester – from various sources: plays, documentary, poetry. They are internal works that I want to watch privately and intimately. They are refreshing to watch on the internet because they use the form, but they disrupt the form, they are a break from the form.

CS *What are your hopes and dreams for theatre's future?*

EB I hope that the field will become more democratic, flexible and diverse. More relevant, more responsive, more rooted in community and more reflective of the world.

CS *In a time of global collective trauma, what are theatre's healing properties, if any?*

EB It must respond quickly to the current moment. The ancient roots of theatre are not in buildings. To invoke Peter Brook, all theatre needs is an empty space, someone to walk across it and for someone to be watching. It is that simple.

Theatre can and should be lean and local. I am reminded of Bruce Mason who in 1959, unable to earn a living in a country without a professional theatre, performed his solo play *The End of the Golden Weather*, all through New Zealand, nearly a thousand times. After years of watching British plays, it was the first time many New Zealanders saw themselves reflected onstage. My mum remembers seeing it and being breathless. He did it because at that time, there was 'no theatrical framework' in New Zealand. So, Mason said, 'I would create my own. Touring a play is expensive? Then cut to the minimum, table, and chair. Scenery is costly to make and cumbersome to cart around? Do it all with words: appeal directly to the audience's imagination. Casts are expensive? Be your own. Do all forty parts. Play anywhere, in any circumstances, to any audience.'[1]

Maybe this moment warrants a return to essentialness and simplicity, and an opportunity for a theatre that is more democratic.

---

[1]Bruce Mason, 'Note to the Second Edition', *End of the Golden Weather*, 2nd edn (Wellington: Victoria University Press, 1970), pp. 7–27.

Jason Crouch

Jason Crouch is a UK-based artist, researcher and technology specialist with a particular interest in live performance. This interview was conducted over email between October and December 2020.

CS *How has lockdown been for you?*

JC Like many arts freelancers my entire calendar of work disappeared in March, and with the anxious background hum of the unknown permeating through life and work, I've found it hard to concentrate on self-directed creative projects or wider strategic thinking. This anxiety stems from many sources: government policy made on the fly, the vagaries of lockdown rules, and management of personal health risks. It confounds any forward planning in a sector so demanding of face-to-face contact.

I'm at home almost all the time, and it makes me feel like I'm a background player in my own life, running through a set of pre-programmed tasks which could be work or play. Here we are again. Same place, different time. Yet this is in sharp contrast to the joy and fulfilment I've had working on specific projects where I'm asked to focus on particular technical or dramaturgical elements.

My background is in what had been a niche world of online and streamed performance, and of course this expertise was suddenly in demand. Inquiries grew into huge Twitter threads, online articles and invited talks. These conversations led to rich collaborations with arts organizations, venues and individual artists, and a strong desire to build a more concrete home for online and hybrid practice.

I've discovered that working online with artists, makers, festival teams and audiences somehow seems to occupy a similar space to the temporary community that appears around any live event. There is a buoyancy to be had working alongside co-collaborators, even remotely. We're all still driving towards something that will connect performers and audiences for a single live moment, together.

Although online is certainly not without its downsides; when the meeting is ended everyone flickers out of existence, and each of us are once more alone.

I'm reminded of how much of the making of theatre, performance and festival is a collaboration between embodied skills and new situations and spaces. Yet in the online spaces we've discovered or made, these things are out of balance. When performers and participants are remote from each other, it surfaces the lie that the audience is one homogeneous bloc. The myriad different ways work can be accessed means that the grasp we think we have on how our work is experienced is exposed in all its fragility.

CS *What advice do you have for people entering the field right now?*

JC Dare to dream and throw yourself into your practice.

Don't overthink, but value reflection.

Prototype, scratch and play.

Learning through doing is a hugely rich way of gaining experience and knowledge.

Value your work on your own terms, not those of others.

There's nothing cut and dried about success or failure, you'll find useful things from both.

Try not to be overwhelmed by making new work with new technologies and remember to centre your own practice. It is too easy to find the work framed and moulded by technology or platform, you must wrest control back.

CS *What are your hopes and dreams for theatre's future?*

JC Art and culture offers us a unique way to understand ourselves and the world we live in. It opens our eyes to difference, widens our perspectives on ideas of society and community and inspires new thinking on how we can change ourselves and the world around us. There is a freedom gifted by arts practice to transport ourselves into different lives and to shrug off our ingrained social constructs, for a while at least.

Throughout this pandemic an unexpected vitality has been realized of culture. We've engaged through virtual museum tours, watching live-streamed performances, and taking part in online theatre. This ability of culture and technology to create moments of joy and connection in a difficult time serves as a launch pad for future possibilities.

I feel it is our duty as art makers to embrace this as a civic responsibility: to create encounters in which imaginations soar, to create moments that challenge us, to question our past and present and to imagine possible, preferable futures.

In the current crisis we turned to digital and online tools through necessity. Pivoting to all digital all the time. This means more artists and cultural organizations have engaged with digital and online platforms than at any time in our history. Not only is this an incredible creative success, but it also means that platforms and systems are at the pointed end of an inquisitive scrutiny. By disassembling and repurposing commercial and open-source tools of communication for the making of art, the biases and assumptions (of gender, class and race) baked into our online and digital experience become more and more apparent.

The cultural sector must grasp the opportunities of digital without cementing dependence on commercial platforms that create space for the arts by accident rather than design.

Remote working has helped to remove inertia around access. Bringing BSL interpretation or captioning to streamed and archive work has never been easier, nor has its lack been more apparent. Artists working creatively with remote presence and audiences lapping up interactive experiences from home have allowed us access to creative works without the need for carbon-fuelled travel to inaccessible venues. The sector must hold on tight to these advances and work towards securing a regular budget line for these practices in every project.

It is vital that this is not lost in a rush to get back to the real world, the old world with its own demands, where access is the first budget line to be cut. It's worth reiterating, a budget is a moral and political document.

Artists, audiences and participants have been on a rich learning journey within digital and immersive spaces. It's past time to establish an online, networked community of art and artists that evolves current practice. One that provides many of the services of a building but without being tied to one. To be a cradle and an archive, to provide administrative support, commissioning opportunities, a place for skill sharing and a space to hold learning.

It will also allow us to scrutinize the power structures present in our current institutions as we try to fashion new ones that defy the inequalities found there.

CS *During a time of global collective trauma, can theatre heal?*

JC There persists the idea of culture being for and by the middle and upper classes (despite evidence), and this is used to simultaneously decimate funding and reinforce existing power structures. Yet, through choices of where support is given and who might qualify, this persistent fallacy is being made into reality, and those without guaranteed wages or support may no longer be able to pursue careers in this ravaged sector.

The pandemic crisis has brought to the surface the precarity of all of us in the sector, whether artists, freelancers, cultural organizations or buildings.

Yet culture at its most activist and engaged survives and is reinvigorated by crisis. Take Holbeck-based theatre company Slung Low, who responded to the current crisis by taking stock of what their values are, and who they serve. During the pandemic they provided support and food distribution to the people of Holbeck and were still able to put on plays outside their building and via live stream.

The late John McGrath suggested that (a national) theatre asks the question: 'who are we in this place at this time, together?' Perhaps theatre relocates its healing powers by rediscovering what it stands for and who it serves. By supporting its community, it becomes intertwined with it, opening up space for childcare, civic engagement, political action, thinking big thoughts and doing things that matter. Theatre can't afford to be insular, serving an imagined theatre crowd, when the community on the doorstep are its artists, audiences, participants. They demand and deserve a space for themselves.

CS *What are you working on now?*

JC At the start of the crisis there was a huge desire to move work online, unearthing old recordings or racing to make a new streaming-friendly version of an existing piece. I think of this as the Pandemic Rush, and during this time I was an enthusiastic enabler, helping create websites and social media groups, writing how-to articles and twitter threads.

Over time this resistance spirit began to fade with the realization
that I'd been ignoring lessons from research and experience in favour
of Doing Something Now. I stepped back and decided to take a
wider view: rather than throwing all manner of digital works online
in the name of content (and survival), creating space to engage with
the art of theatre making in new online places.

Right now, I spend my time helping artists to consider and
reconfigure their practice for a remote audience, or I work
with festivals to recreate their visceral buzz online. Often these
conversations begin with talk of platforms and internet bandwidth,
cameras and green screens. But making technology a starting point is
often restricting and can detract from the heart of the work. Instead,
we'd talk about what the work really is: what beats are important,
what will survive or thrive in the shift to an online version and what
has to go or find another way to be told.

After this conceptual and dramaturgical chatter, it's vital there
is a process of playtesting. Tests will cross platforms, use video or
audio or neither. This generally inclines the work to a particular
platform or format. Material is worked, refined, tested, rebuilt, fed
back on and tested again. Equipment is borrowed and exchanged,
the wrong cables bought and new ones substituted.

As part of this pattern new parameters become available. What
once was a ninety-minute small-scale theatre show becomes an
episodic video game. An unexpected phone call whispers intimate
possibility into your ear. An escape room is reimagined as an Escape
Zoom, participants shouting instructions at something that feel like
the same time, together in the nearly now.

Dante or Die: Daphna Attias and Terry O'Donovan

Daphna Attias and Terry O'Donovan are co-artistic directors of Dante or Die, a London-based company that makes bold and ambitious site-specific performances, gently transforming ordinary spaces to create unique and intimate theatrical experiences. This interview was conducted over Zoom on 15 October 2020.

CS *How has lockdown been for you?*

DA We had a major tour cancelled and four projects that were cancelled or postponed. We were working on a piece with the Tower of London and another project with a company in Sheffield. We do not know if any of this work will return. At first there was a panic about cancellations and the anxiety of not being able to pay people and then grieving the lost work. But recently it has started to become a creative time, and it is good to be able to think differently about things. Even if you are forced to do so through a lockdown.

CS *What was it like to reconfigure your 2018 piece* User Not Found *from a site-specific piece to be performed in cafes to this new version, which streamed on YouTube?*

DA We had been planning to reconfigure it already. In some ways, we had had a lot of time to tinker with every decision we made. What has been amazing is that the piece has gotten a lot of attention and more exposure than we would have ever had had we been performing it live. The *Guardian* came on board as a partner, and so did Brooklyn Academy of Music (BAM) and the Traverse Theatre in Scotland and so many venues have supported it.

When we were making this version of *User Not Found*, it took a while to decide the form or to know what to call it. It is not a podcast because podcasts do not have visuals. It is not a video because it does not have visuals all the time. It took a little while to get confidence and say, 'this is an immersive video podcast.' We had a lot of conversations about whether we should ever see Terry in this version but I'm really glad we stuck to our guns and you don't see him, because it feels like he's in your head.

TOD You have my voice, but you get to imagine what I look like and what I'm wearing and where I am. Whereas when the live performance of *User Not Found* occurs I'm in the space with you and you see me, and you also have me in your ears. But I am right amongst you and I am sitting next to you. That was always important because the piece was inspired by looking at people in cafes on their headphones, working on their laptops or on their phones – in all these individual worlds at the same time. During Covid-19 time, we are individualized all the time. Even at home I have my headphones on and so does my husband, and we are doing separate things, creating these little bubbles for ourselves. That is important to the storytelling.

CS *How you are thinking about making work now in this climate when there is such a different relationship to the digital body and the physical body?*

TOD We're working on two projects right now. One is a live piece about touch. It is called *Skin Hunger*, and it is for an audience of three people at a time that experience three one-on-one monologues. During these monologues they will be invited to either touch, hold hands, touch faces or hug a performer through plastic. It is exactly about that sense of lack of touch and what we have all experienced to do with skin hunger and touch hunger and not being able to have that. [Note: After this interview, *Skin Hunger* was postponed due to a second lockdown.]

DA The other piece is a digital piece. We are working with the tech designers that built *User Not Found* with us. This piece is about online gambling and how it can become addictive very quickly. At first we thought we might build it for a website, but it's become clear that we are going to build it to be seen and experienced on a phone, as the reconfigured version of *User Not Found* was.

TOD   We have found that the phone is a site people know how to use and understand, and it is a space that we can disrupt in some way and that is interesting to us. In our practice we always think about rethinking existing spaces, and how to reimagine the known. We've rethought physical spaces like hotel rooms. So, why not digital spaces? One of the things that interests us is to think about what people get out of going to such spaces. So, we interrogate, for example, a specific quite vibrant colourful noisy online space like a slot machine website app that feels like an exciting place to visit.

CS   *Where is* Skin Hunger *taking place?*

DA   In Stone Church Chapel in central London. We have always wanted to make a show here, but now feels like a good time to make something local.

TOD   It is going to run for two weeks from 1 pm in the afternoon till 10 pm at night.
　　We have never made a show this quickly. But we've built this very lightly because we wanted to do something live now while we can that does respond to what's going on and offer opportunities that the audience has to experience something. It will be very intimate and there will be an opportunity to just be with one person, but three people over the space of an hour and I think that will feel joyous.

CS   *For children growing up during Covid-19 time, their earliest memories will be around no touch, wash your hands, and social distance. These behaviours will be in their body as memory. How can we take care of our audiences, but especially the children?*

DA   I've been thinking a lot about this not just because I'm a mom but also because I run a children's theatre company called Peut-Être Theatre and I am finding that process of transitioning to the new world is much harder for making work for children than the work we do with Dante or Die. When lockdown hit, we took a moment to grieve about all the projects that got cancelled, but as we moved forward, we knew we were talking to audiences who already have references and can reflect on the things they know and bring this new experience intellectually into it and who can balance their own screen consumption. Whereas with children the liveness of the interactive encounter is important between performers and children in a room together. I found it hard to replace that and letting go of that as well. I genuinely do not want any more screen time in my children's life, especially when they are homeschooling and spend from 9 am to 3 pm every day in front of the screen doing Google classroom. Children say they have a headache from screen time and their back hurts. Their bodies are not used to this kind of routine. My only answer right now is to provide audio projects for children that are focused on movement. It is a much harder field because we are genuinely competing against Disney and *Minecraft*. I cannot imagine my son saying, 'Oh, I'd like to see a filmed production and not play *Minecraft*.'

CS *What are your hopes and dreams for theatre's future?*

DA It is an exciting opportunity right now to be able to really interrogate what other forms could we work in. It feels like a good opportunity to completely throw away habits and find new forms. It is a natural transition for us because we work with small audiences. We also integrate technology in our work. What we do is work with audiences in unusual ways. We think about how their bodies move in space and we recreate quite intimate experiences.

TOD There's way more people considering what the form is and that is exciting. Work on screen for us however is not that interesting. I do not want to spend my night watching an archive footage of a play, because that is not what it was made for. It was made for people being in the room with you. Theatre-makers have a distinctive way of telling stories different from how filmmakers approach their art forms.

CS *At a time of global collective trauma, though, how to hold space for this in your work?*

DA We really try not to make work about what is currently burning. *User Not Found* is resonating right now because of its themes, but the story is not about living during a pandemic. *Skin Hunger* is also not about Covid-19 time. It is about people experiencing lack of touch. We are interested in inviting the audience into an experience that reflects on a current social drama. Like we are doing with the gambling project. But even this project is not about Covid-19 time.

It is about vulnerable people who found themselves in front of the screens with lots of time to kill and they have been really targeted by online casinos. We will not be ready for a play about these times until maybe five years from now. It is a little too soon to have an interesting opinion about this time because we do not know what is going on. We can kind of reflect on an element of it, but we are not yet in the expanded moment – the moment beyond.

Tim Etchells

Tim Etchells is a British artist, performer and writer. He is artistic director of Forced Entertainment, the world-renowned performance collective based in Sheffield, England. During the lockdown of summer 2020, the collective made a theatre piece for Zoom entitled *End Meeting for All*. This interview was conducted via email between 6 August and 21 August 2020.

CS *How has lockdown been for you?*

TE Lockdown has been a strange mix. I am lucky enough to have income that continues for the moment and work that can be done from home. I don't take this position for granted – people on the front line are obliged to risk their lives through this whole thing (from health workers to shop assistants and bus drivers) and I'm really sensitive to the inequality and the violence of that. At the same time, it is challenging personally. I have health complications since birth. So, I am isolating seriously. Workwise things are hard. Forced Entertainment lost all its upcoming work and associated income, and all the planning is out of the window. The first months were crisis management – thinking about saving the organization, the employees, the financial situation, the FE projects as well as about my own solo stuff that was also thrown into chaos. The later months we have switched focus to figuring out new things we can do trying to do projects and collaborations remotely.

The main thing I am thinking about is division. The way that class and economic separation has been such a factor, the way that race has been such a factor – the disproportionate impact of Covid-19 on communities of colour. The BLM protests in the middle of all this were so inspiring and heartbreaking in their way – the overlapping of urgencies (health protection and political necessity).

CS *How did* End Meeting for All *come to be?*

TE *End Meeting for All* came about relatively early. I was on Zoom a lot – company meetings, crisis, planning and, socially, seeing friends. I started to think about the grid of screens as a space, an environment, with a particular set of properties and possibilities. Around the same time one of the German partners asked if we would show something in their online season, to mark the dates when we would, under normal circumstances, have been presenting the new live work there. We proposed a series of three episodes, made on Zoom, with the initial conception that it was a kind of meeting-gone-wrong. I had the title right away, taken straight from the Zoom interface – *End Meeting for All*.

The process was, in some ways, like our other projects. We spend a long time deconstructing, complaining, deciding that things do not work, cannot work. Through that process we are slowly figuring things that are interesting to us. For *EMFA* we were gripped by the simultaneous sense of being connected and being disconnected, sharing space online but at the same time being in our separate physical spaces. We focused on an idea of porousness and disconnection. We were – as is typical of our projects – trying to understand and make sense of the 'fundamental' properties and dynamics of the space. You can see us invoking tropes from online communication – people not hearing, or not understanding, people talking at cross purposes, disconnected conversations, people 'freezing', people being distracted or interrupted by events in their own real environments – noise from off, distractions in the room and from outside. All these things – most of them recognizable instantly – are useful for us. It's often in the theatre work that we like to play with the signal to noise ratio – the idea of an activity that's happening (a story being told, a conversation, an explanation) but which is being intercut by other events. Compositionally the grid of screens was a perfect space for us.

CS *What does time mean in a virtual space?*

TE We have always divided our live works into two categories with regards to the claim they make on time. There are the theatre shows intended to be experienced from start to finish – you take people through the dramaturgy together and let them out at the end. And there are the durational works built for people arriving, departing and even returning, any time they like. In that latter case one surrenders control of the dramaturgy as well as control over the length/s of time people are spending engaged with the work. These two modes we use for the work present vastly different contracts with audience, and they create rather different demands challenges and opportunities for us as makers.

Working online adds even more layers. In theory people can focus on things online, but there is a sense the audience will duck in and out, especially as work gets longer. There is just not the kind of ethical bind of the performance space. Another thing we lose online is a sense of immediate direct contact with people watching. The sense of public gathering, 'here and nowness' or co-presence and triangulation in the digital sphere – even for livestreamed events – is constructed very differently and has something of its own frailty built in.

Working on *End Meeting for All* came at an interesting moment for us. We have done so many stage performances over the years that have used direct address, and been concerned with this process of triangulation, dynamically activating the line between the stage and the auditorium. Shows like *Speak Bitterness* (1994), *First Night* (2001) and *Bloody Mess* (2003) were obsessed with the live and dynamic edge of that relation. But more recently, in works like *The Notebook* (2014), *Real Magic* (2016) and *Out of Order* (2018), we've become rather more insular – creating these worlds which spectators are peering into, to an extent, worlds which appear to be (and know themselves as) performances but which also appear to be dream-spaces, locked in their own temporalities and logics. *Out of Order*, and the new work that was still in process when the pandemic hit (*Under Bright Light*), take this approach quite far – they're performances without spoken text, in which the performers are locked in cycles of doing – busy with their own activities and behaviours. As spectators we are peering in, and the event unfolds in a kind of tension with the situation of being watched, a dynamic tension between private and public. The *End Meeting for All* work slotted in well to this line – we frame the grid of six screens (the Zoom meeting) as a space into which the spectator is peering, not quite addressed. And in it, substituting or ghosting the feedback process of audience we are in different ways and at different moments, audience to each other. It's a drama of connection and disconnection, of contact and isolation, in which as performers we are sometimes 'doing things' and at other times witnessing each other. It mirrors, also, the state of the world at the time of its making, and the isolated-but-connected-although-isolated situation in which we were working.

CS   *What advice do you have for people in the field right now?*

TE   It is hard now, not least with the added complications around gathering and travelling which the pandemic has produced. The squeeze on resources and austerity that the pandemic will bring in its aftermath (whenever or whatever that is) will not be easy either, especially given the propensity for larger institutions to monopolize stability funds.

If I had to advise, though, I would only say be resourceful, be pragmatic, be tough, find ways to do your work and to support each other, band together, follow your noses. That is all any of us ever has done, all anyone can do.

It's been important to me to understand and underscore a sense of connection and separation – to think of oneself as an artist in conversation with communities, funders and other artists and – at the same time – as distinct from them, making decisions (such as one can!) in relation to an agenda that is only emerging bit-by-bit from the work itself. There is, in this respect, a sense that you are following the work rather than it following you and your intention.

CS   *What are your hopes and dreams for live performance's future?*

TE   We are all gripped, very rightly, by the importance of diversity. There are so many voices that are not heard, so many experiences, so many communities that do not get to speak or participate, or which are not represented – as makers and as audiences. A dream would be a much more diverse and open sector. It is something we all need to focus on, in the different ways that we can (including just making space), so that the landscape can be changed.

I am a fan of the artist-led independent sector. The work with Forced Entertainment is in that zone but most of the work that has changed my life, my way of thinking, my sense of artistic and other horizons has come from artists, independent players, collectives, collaborative groups on the edges of theatre, performance, and dance. That's where the passion, the invention and the ability to think and do things in a different way often lies and I would like a future where more of that work is possible and where it is better supported, where the plurality of approaches it produces is celebrated and properly resourced. We are far from that right now.

Finally – I support the broadening out of creative opportunity that we are seeing moves towards the emphasis on participation and on everyday creativity. I also want to see support for artists who dedicate their lives and energies over long time to art making. To be an artist in this way is a privileged position, but to be an artist in these terms is also a matter of obsession and of lifework, the pursuit of a particular interest, form or question with a dedication that goes beyond obvious logic. The work that's changed my life and my thinking – challenged, inspired, even torn me to pieces – has come from artists who have worked over long periods and pushed deep into their forms and their questions, to find results that transform the arena, the sense of what's even possible.

CS *During a time of global collective trauma, what are theatre's healing properties, if any?*

TE Healing may not be my favourite metaphor – something too final, too resolving about it. I do not expect to be healed. Perhaps what performance, theatre, art, can do is create the conditions in which we see better who we are, and who we are sharing space (immediately and metaphorically, on the larger scale) with. It is a confrontation, a journey to see or find something on the edge of knowing. Discomfort is a part of that experience for me, an understanding of one's complex connection to others and one's separation from them, a miniature mapping of the structures that shape and define us. In the broader social and political context of lies and silence – a step towards healing could well be speaking and truth. Performance plays a part in that.

We certainly have lost something in the present situation – when performance cannot physically gather us, bringing us into the same space to feel each other, our interconnectedness and our separation. Perhaps that is what I miss most of all. The opportunity to sit with 300 other people, or 30, or 900 and not know where we are going, or what we will figure, together and alone, in relation to a performance that unfolds before us.

Morgan Green

Morgan Green is an American theatre director and is co-artistic director of the Wilma Theatre in Philadelphia. This interview was conducted over email on 26 October 2020.

CS *How has lockdown been for you?*

MG I encountered heavy sadness and plentiful anxiety, and insomnia which was new for me, and then when I did sleep, extremely vivid dreams. I realized early on that all of my work, every single project I am involved with, relies on being in a room with other people. I don't actually have a solo practice besides consuming art that other people make and doing research. So, I've been trying to shift that mostly by trying to write for the first time, mostly screenplays because I'm in film school at the Fierstein School of Cinema at Brooklyn College. I'm getting ready to shoot a short film that I wrote for some actors who are my friends who I know from theatre. It feels like I'm learning a new language, which is mostly visual. I'm not the first person to say this but a film is the closest art form to the experience of a dream, in terms of mechanics and aesthetics, and I've been having some trippy and vivid dreams in quarantine and I'm interested in translating them to film.

Besides studying film, I am also a Co-Artistic Director at the Wilma Theater. Just before lockdown, the Wilma announced the 'Next Chapter' which involves a shared leadership team of four Artistic Directors: Blanka Zizka, Yury Urnov, James Ijames and me. We work collaboratively, and each year for the next four years there is one 'lead Artistic Director' who the rest of us support. This was Blanka's generous and radical idea and it's a really exciting experiment to be a part of. The bummer is that the Next Chapter was announced in January 2020, I went to Philly a handful of times for meetings and openings, and then we went remote in March. So, we've been working together intensely and getting to know each other, build trust, improve communication, assess the organization, find a vision for the future, collaboratively curate and manage crises all via Google Meets. I didn't even get to meet everyone who works on the staff before this happened.

The four of us really like each other and get along beautifully. We don't always agree with each other and we all have egos, of course, we're directors. So, it has been interesting to navigate those sticking points and learn where to push and where to shut up. But there is genuine openness in the group, and I have already learned so much from them since we started. It's a pretty big learning curve going from being a freelance director with a small self-producing theatre company of four people (New Saloon), to being part of a leadership team for a midsize theatre.

CS *The Wilma has had a robust series of digital/audio productions and/or streamed events between March and August 2020.*

MG Despite the unprecedented challenges associated with Covid-19 and working remotely, the Wilma has continued producing digital work at a rapid pace. With the support of the PPP loans, we were able to keep working without having to furlough anyone, and even commission digital work from Hot House artists.

Wilma's radio play of *Is God Is* (2016) by Aleshea Harris went through at least five iterations to land where it did. James Ijames, the director, details all this in a great short documentary Wilma put out with the piece. Essentially it went from an in-person production with full design and live audience, to a filmed version of that production with no audience, to a filmed version of that production with no design and completely socially distant, to a remotely executed radio play. Each decision was made collectively, as a leadership team, and discussed with the cast. The radio play was the way to continue producing art, therefore keeping staff and artists employed, and it made everyone working on it feel safe from Covid-19. The equipment for recording was delivered to each actor's home and rehearsals happened on Zoom.

The first show this fall-winter 2020 season, *Heroes of the Fourth Turning* (2019) by Will Arbery and directed by Blanka Zizka, is going to be a digital capture with no live audience. The second show, *Fat Ham* by James Ijames, which I am directing, will incorporate a virtual live feed component. We are bringing on a film team to help us do that.

I am thinking about how to maintain that feeling in film/theatre hybrid, something that maintains the feeling of a live performance, but is mediated through a screen in a way that goes beyond simply capturing an event to actual cinematography. It would live somewhere in the family of a live-edited sporting event, a jumbotron at a big concert and a highly intimate home video. We're hoping to experiment with this hybrid art form for *Fat Ham* and I'll be working with a filmmaker to help storyboard, capture and edit the live event.

We are at the tip of what will be possible with digital work. New technologies and vocabularies will enter a brand-new performance landscape. I feel the worst for the dancers right now or any artist that relies on bodies touching. It doesn't seem like we'll get that back for a while.

CS   *The field is going through a massive reckoning on multiple fronts. What are ways we can listen to one another?*

MG   The incredibly detailed and specific *We See You White American Theater* demands, released in June 2020, created a seismic shift in the way I think about my work, both at the institutional level and as a freelance director. The Wilma Theater released a public response to the WSYWAT demands, and I am simultaneously reflecting on my past work and thinking about how to proceed. I am trying to deeply understand my role as a white cis female director in a systemically racist theatre industry. What does it actually mean to decentre myself as a white artist? How can I create a safe working environment as the director, knowing that means different things for different people?

More immediately and concretely, I am applying some of the WSYWAT demands directly to the next production I am directing, which is *Fat Ham* by James Ijames at the Wilma. We'll hire an EDI Officer to support the process, which is something new that I'm looking forward to. And we are going to experiment with a five-day rehearsal week and eliminate 10/12 tech rehearsals.

My biggest philosophical revelation has been around time and dismantling the 'The Show Must Go On' mentality in my own directing style. This is a truism I grew up with, and until recently, adored. It is not until these past few months that I realized how harmful it is, linked to white supremacy and capitalism. I now see how the result of this thinking is a brutal and aggressive push towards product rather than tender and flexible care towards artists and process. Art should centre the artists. My love for productivity will be coupled with a deeper appreciation for deliberate and unrushed process, and acknowledgement that we each have a different relationship with time.

CS *What are your dreams for the field?*

MG I'm dreaming of radical change! I don't know how much theatre is going to be able to do when some of the issues we are facing are much larger than us: Covid-19, health care, childcare and racism. But I still think we can shift habits of thought, re-examine our practices and do things differently going forward. Do we have to rely on galas to raise money? Can we shift the relationship between the staff and the artists, the artists and the audience? Can we dedicate resources to anti-racist work in an ongoing and sustainable way? Can we truly shift the culture for how we work? I am learning *a lot* and pushing to be an agent of change at the same time. We need to be able to do more than one thing at a time.

Peter J. Kuo

Peter J. Kuo is a theatre director and is associate conservatory director at American Conservatory Theatre in San Francisco. This interview was conducted over Zoom on 17 October 2020.

CS *How has lockdown been for you?*

PK   I do not think it has been as bad as it has been for everyone else. I think because of all the successful work that I have been doing on transferring a lot of our form into this digital medium and frankly because I have also just had that experience already prior working in video performance and entertainment. This time feels like things merged for me. But overall, I feel the way our industry has been functioning in this pandemic has been really disheartening. Theatre in general, specifically regional theatre and Broadway, is incredibly elitist and has been for a very long time. The industry's refusal to lean into something new has been awful. YouTube, Twitch, TikTok and Vine have taken off and we have completely missed the boat by not latching onto those working in these mediums and interacting with them and at the same time preserving liveness. Synchronistic observership and interaction is key to our form, but also playing with what that means. We will spend $34,000 on a set piece, whereas if we invest in the tech, there will be more opportunities for all of us. Theatre has always been about Innovation. It has always been about exploration and to look at how we exist now. People hold their noses up at TikTok and other online platforms, but they are vital and there is a huge audience there. So many theatres are deciding to 'take a pause' but by saying so they are slandering digital theatre. It's easy to take a pause if you're still getting a pay cheque. What about your artists and artisans?

CS *What are your hopes and dreams for theatre's future?*

PK I will start with the challenges. We must adapt. We cannot just stop doing theatre for a couple of years and come back to a 'normal'. It's going to take decades to get over what we've lost both in terms of production modes and gaining the trust of audiences and their desire and ability to return to see work in person without a sense of fear. So, why turtle up and wait until the next big thing? Why not find something that bridges us between now and then? The younger generation is doing it already on YouTube and Twitch and so on.

My hope is to make the whole process a little bit more equitable, but that requires an entire re-envisioning of our field and our society. The wealth gap is so huge and not just here but in many other countries. But our field specifically has a huge problem with this. Because it means changing what the funding streams are and how those funding streams operate.

We could see a complete demise of our traditional theatre system. And if that is the case, where are people getting this form of entertainment? It is already in the Twitches and the YouTube, but where is the live component?

What's going to happen is we're going to build a field of theatre and filmmakers who took advantage of the social capitalism and creativeness of the digital theatre world that may not have the skill and athleticism, but they will be more popular because of celebrity and cache that we've built around them.

I say all this because I know I am a product of this system. I watch YouTube videos.

I find them very enjoyable. There is one of this guy who eats the entire menu from a fast-food place. I find it entertaining just as much as I find Lynn Nottage's *Sweat* (2015) entertaining. But that generation is disappearing because we have not tapped into that relationship. So, eventually we are going to watch some guy eating an entire menu live on stage and that is going to be acceptable entertainment. We are kind of in a losing battle right now. The best thing we can do as an industry is embrace this other form and allow it to shift our storytelling. To be more inclusive in so many ways. Because otherwise, and I hate to say this, maybe we deserve to become extinct.

Hamilton (2016) is now on-demand streaming on Disney Plus. But how many people have seen it compared to the box office numbers of the run of the show on Broadway? When I was making YouTube videos, my highest peak of subscribers was 5,000 people. That is more subscribers than certain theatre companies. The numbers are telling. We put so much work into getting a few thousand people to see a show and then I go online and watch a YouTube video and the video has been up for eight hours and it's already got 100,000 views.

We're never going to get that with theatre in the same way, but there's definitely an audience out there that we're not tapping that would love and embrace some of the forms of art that we are creating as a theatre industry. Theatre does not serve a lot of people.

The accessibility conversation around theatre has changed as well. Previously it was: are you near a theatre? Can you get to a theatre? Can you afford to go and are you socially accepted at this theatre? A lot of those limitations are gone. Now the accessibility conversation is: do you have the broadband access and is the piece of interest to you? The difference is now having the tech. Tech equals access.

The live space that must change to accommodate a different way of experiencing and viewing. What is the culture that we embrace and what is the culture that we want to teach? If your show cannot sustain someone tweeting during the show, then you are not allowing someone in. In Shakespeare's time, the groundlings were talking, and Shakespeare knew he had to repeat things over and over and over again because he knew people were distracted, but he also knew that there were certain parts of it that were compelling enough. If your show is not engaging in every single moment, whose fault is that?

You could say to yourself, 'I know this part isn't the best, but this one moment is so nice.' The point is that every moment matters. Some people are going to tune in; some people can tune out. The work needs to have multiple dynamics. It's a matter of attention.

I am going to say really something controversial. I think theatre artists to a degree have gotten lazy in the sense that they know the audience is stuck in their seats and cannot leave. The play is not demanding of attention. It is not asking the audience to draw into the material. It is assuming that the audience will listen and be attentive. As a director, when I was younger, I felt that I had to make everything compelling and interesting, but at some point in my career, I realized that what's exciting about this medium is watching people being human. People doing their thing living in the moment. What is interesting to explore is how this pays off in the digital medium. It requires something else from a performer, but also from the audience, because the space is virtual.

CS *Theatre, however, is tied to market value systems. How to change that paradigm?*

PK One of the biggest problems in our world right now is a wealth gap. TikTok, YouTube, Twitch are not any better at not perpetuating this because these mediums are about influence and power. Several things must go through a massive change for us to really survive as an industry and to take advantage of all these new things and truly become a more equitable society and culture. Amazon, for example, is a behemoth and thrives on increasing the wealth gap and yet people use it, and some people rely on it. The system is built for certain underprivileged folks to have to need Amazon to get the things that they need to survive in life.

The massive change must be structural and systemic and must be wide and everyone must buy into it. I would love to say 'fuck you' to the wealth gap and just participate in a society and create change. But I know that without funds, I do not have the influence and resources to be able to do that. Unless I can get that influential sphere, it is going to be difficult to have access to resources and power to change things from within. Most of my actions must be about a greater good at the cost of others because there is no way you can do good. No good deed goes unpunished right now. The wealth gap is so great I do not know how it is achievable. At the same time there is a cultural gap between live and digital theatre, and until we get huge, massive agreement to bring those together, nothing's going to happen, and frankly, I wonder if we lost the battle five years ago.

Eve Leigh

Eve Leigh is an American playwright based in London, England. Her piece *Midnight Movie* was scheduled for presentation at the Berliner Theatertreffen in Germany when lockdown hit. Her digital piece *Invisible Summer*, transmitted via email, was produced by the Royal Court in autumn 2020. This interview was conducted via email on 1 September 2020.

CS *How has lockdown been for you?*

EV It has been gut-wrenching from a mental health perspective. And totally infuriating. I feel that Universal Basic Income is just staring us in the face, and it cannot happen in the UK and the United States for purely ideological reasons. Unnecessary suffering is being inflicted on a massive scale. I can hardly speak about the cultural vandalism taking place in the UK right now. In addition, technically speaking, every single one of my nearest and dearest is in a vulnerable group, and I have been frankly terrified for them. A number of my friends are now suffering with long Covid-19, and I have to say, as someone with a chronic pain disorder, I cannot imagine trying to manage long Covid-19 on top of that and have any kind of a life. My medical care has understandably gone haywire with everything happening. As a result, I have a migraine about half the time. But also: although I have had commissions postponed, I have also had other work come up (usually smaller and shorter-term, but I am hanging in there).

CS *What advice do you have for those entering the field now?*

EV Endurance strengthens the heart. Please do not give up. We need you, even if it feels like gatekeepers do not know it yet. Create for the joy of it. Create because you are a human being.

CS *What are your hopes and dreams for theatre's future?*

EV   My dream is that there is a future, that the difficulties of these last years inspire us to live and make art in ways that support life on Earth.

CS   *What are theatre's healing properties, if any?*

EV   When I have experienced the healing power of theatre, it has been unexpectedly, by stealth. I feel about the healing power of theatre, now, the way I feel about the dead. I do not know where it is, but it is somewhere. And unlike the dead, I do expect it to return and surprise me!

CS   *What are you working on now?*

EV   I feel in some way that there is something very pure about the creative work I am doing now. Continuing to create in the face of all these unknowns feels like it can only happen for the joy of it. I feel that my best work is closest to joy, and that part of my job as a teacher of playwriting is to instruct people on finding regular routes to their own creative joy. I have practiced Buddhism for the last eleven years – I chant and study every day – and there is a passage of Nichiren Daishonin's writings from *The Writings of Nichiren Daishonin*, Volume 1, page 1097 of the Nichiren Buddhism Library that begins with the phrase 'This is a mountainous place' and ends with the phrase 'where they attain enlightenment' that I return to daily, because in the passage Daishonin refers to the place of remoteness as one where a person can look within and locate their strength, or better put, find yourself in an unknown realm. It is always the case when you write that you do not know who your readers will be. All writing is an act of faith.

CS   *What are your thoughts on digital theatre?*

EV   My prediction, if you can call it that, is that the more finesse we acquire around the difficulties and limitations of digital theatre, the more we will fetishize and aestheticize them.

So much of middlebrow performance aesthetics is perceived 'difficulty' – not too difficult, or it's elitist, and not too pleasurable, or it's suspicious, just a nice round of Daniel Day-Lewis doing some really effortful acting, so we know we're watching something that matters. Google writer Aaron Sorkin on 'degree of difficulty' in performance (his phrase), if you would like to see exactly what I mean.

What this means for institutional digital theatre, in the future, is that the tropes of technical difficulty will be made to stand in for narrative mystery, perplexity, the holy. It will be harder and harder to stick to the indeterminacy of space and time that are the hallmarks of the form at present. The genuine risk of failure the new digital theatre offers will be gone before you know it.

CS   *What is a digital body, and what is the point of a digital body?*

EV   A low moment of 2020 came when I tried to explain it to the UK Jewish Theatre Practitioners' WhatsApp group (yes), and someone responded by saying 'so ... a digital body is just emails?' Well, maybe. The thing is, of course, not everything that lands in your inbox is what it seems. I started thinking about digital bodies when I was writing my play *Midnight Movie*. The dramaturg, Matilda Ibini, and I had talked a lot about our relationship with the internet, how we both use it to try and distract ourselves from chronic pain, especially when it strikes at antisocial hours of the night. I began to recognize the night-time internet (although of course it is always the night-time internet somewhere) as a powerful aesthetic force, and perhaps one which disabled people are uniquely equipped to understand. Our presence on the internet constitutes its own body, I began to feel – a digital body, both more and less reliable than flesh. As the mostly disabled cast and creative team continued to develop *Midnight Movie*, we realized that the show needed to have its own digital body, if only because a lot of the people who could relate to the show most directly, people in chronic pain, would be unable to access it if it only existed in the Royal Court Theatre Upstairs from 19.45 to 21.00. But what is the digital body of a play – or more correctly, a production since the whole creative team was involved?   We hit on the form of email because we enjoyed how mundane it was, and at the same time how intimate. We felt that there was something meaningful about our narrative showing up on your own turf, not asking you to go anywhere else to experience it. We also liked the way the timing of the messages made it feel like a conversation, but a one-sided one – like drunk-texting, or something, how inappropriate and silly it felt to be sending three messages a night to hundreds of strangers. The original series had writing by me, music by Nwando Ebizie and visuals by Josh Pharo, Sarah Readman and Cécile Trémolieres. It is rare to find something in your inbox which is visual, and rich, and not trying to sell you anything? There was something else about the timing – sending three emails a night, and then nothing for three days, and then starting again. It felt like a crystallization of the problems of the attention economy in theatre. If I am writing for the stage, I want to draw your attention in specific ways, but I can never fully be in control of it. Director Katie Mitchell has often spoken about a constant struggle for the audience's attention, that always you are either winning them or losing them. In some way, sending these intimate, crafted messages out into the void of your inbox, hoping your spam filter doesn't take them out, deciding deliberately to send them out at 3 am but never knowing when or if you'll read them, is the experience of wrestling for the audience's attention turned all the way up. That in-your-face vulnerability, and how easily you could ignore it, felt thirsty to us in a very internet-appropriate way. The form felt like a funhouse-mirror version of disabled trauma porn. A digital body is a multimedia play for your inbox, an access tool and an online spectre. You could say that the point of a digital body is to bring people who cannot always access theatre into the conversation. The point of it is that it is fun, and sexy, and gross, and taking up space where it does not belong. And yeah, you know. At one level, it is emails.

CS   *How is poetry connected to resistance?*

EV   When I think of the role poetry is currently playing in my life, I think of strands of broken DNA. There are little bits of it sticking around, divorced from the larger forms that make it make sense, and my little brain is like an RNA molecule, running along the tracks, trying to fix it or make it make sense. 'Every time the time was right. Every time the time was right. Every time the time was right the words just came out wrong.' Something about that repetition of the word time feels like a weird gift. Another weird gift: there's a poem of Federico Garcia Lorca's entitled 'Balada de la Placeta' that begins with the phrase 'My heart of silk' and ends with the phrase 'with a feathered cap and wooden sword', which I apparently know by heart and which has been with me all summer. Yes. I think the function of poetry in my life right now is that of a spell I have not yet figured out how to cast. Which gives me hope.

Walter Meierjohann

Walter Meierjohann is a Dutch theatre director based in England. He directed the sound and light installation *Blindness*, based on Jose Saramago's 1995 novel, adapted by Simon Stephens at the Donmar Warehouse in London. It was the first indoor theatre installation that was programmed by a live art venue, attended by a live audience, since England's first lockdown. This interview was conducted over Zoom on 30 October 2020.

CS *How has lockdown been for you?*

WM It was a busy period. This sound and light installation of *Blindness* started to materialize during like the second part of our lockdown. I spoke to Michael Longhurst (artistic director of the Donmar Warehouse). I was fortunate to have been able to do this production. And it has an afterlife, and it is touring. I am grateful for that, especially because I had spent twenty years trying to find a way to get an adaptation of Saramago's *Blindness* on stage.

In 2016 I commissioned Simon Stephens, when I was artistic director of HOME in Manchester. He wrote a version with a full cast and 100 people on stage. We did a workshop of the piece at the National Theatre Studio in 2019 and actor Juliet Stevenson came on board. After the workshop Simon said he wanted to turn the piece into a monologue. I distilled the piece to thirty-five pages – and in November 2019 I sent the script to five artistic directors.

For a while I did not hear from anyone. Then Covid-19 hit. About six weeks into lockdown, Michael Longhurst called me expressing his interest in doing the piece given that it is about a pandemic, though of blindness (which is both real and a metaphor that Saramago uses in the novel). We knew that we couldn't do it as a live performance because of Covid-19 restrictions, so we had to come up with this more technological idea, which was the headset, and limiting the audience at the Donmar to fifty-two people, all socially distanced. The audience was on stage and there were no live actors. Only Juliet's voice as the Witness/Narrator on the headsets, and the sound design by the Ringham Brothers (Ben and Max Ringham), which used binaural technology, and made the piece feel intimate.

In terms of the process itself, we had one week of rehearsal and one week of recording and then we had to edit and mix and everything, and then we had a tech, except it was a tech with no actors. I had Juliet Stevenson giving me notes after previews, which has never happened to me before my life! We were all working very democratically, and far less hierarchically than I had ever worked before.

CS *What was it like to walk into the Donmar during lockdown to do tech?*

WM It was really moving. Just to be on a stage again in any capacity and stand there and see the potential. We had been rehearsing in a studio about 100 yards away from the theatre in Soho, and the city was deserted. The rehearsal room still had newspapers lying about from 13 March and props lying around. People must have been rehearsing and told to leave immediately when full lockdown was announced. There's a passage in the original book that talks about the effects of this epidemic of blindness on society, and one of the key moments is about the empty theatres, cinemas and museums and the effect this has on the soul of a nation. When we created this sound and light installation of *Blindness*, we wanted that feeling to resonate. The audience was on stage, but they looked out onto the empty auditorium. The book and this play have a sci-fi horror scenario but inside of it is something we all experience daily: this sense of emptiness and lost purpose.

CS *Any advice for people entering the field right now?*

WM This may be terrible advice to give, as it is harsh, but I would say you have to make sure that you have something else which can support you. I do not believe that great art comes from suffering. You must protect yourself, because the pandemic and the effects of it will go on for another year or maybe two. People will have to do other things to survive.

CS *What are your hopes and dreams for theatre's future?*

WM Art will become more politicized. We are all angrier and that is a good thing. Secondly, I think art will serve a purpose again.

Theatres will be more embedded in society, and community work will be prised more.

The Arts Council gave £1.57 billion to the arts here, which is nearly unheard of compared to, say, Germany. But looking at this from the other side metaphorically: if the house is leaking, you must protect the roof. But so much energy has gone to protect buildings rather than making art. I see someone like Michael Longhurst spending more time firefighting right now instead of having conversations about art. Because the focus has shifted entirely to maintaining the organizations. Suddenly all these artistic directors are in a position where they are trying desperately to save the buildings.

When Longhurst approached me about *Blindness*, I said to him: You do realize that this material is very bleak, but he said he felt it was absolutely the right piece to share with an audience. Simon has always said that for him the story of *Blindness* is a hopeful one because it's a story about survival – a story about a woman who takes us through this journey and is responsible for this group and without her these people would have died. It is about trauma. My main concern for the show was how to create a release in it. There is this cathartic moment in the piece where the audience has been listening to the play and they know it is coming to an end, and we opened the dock doors of the theatre and suddenly let natural light in, and it is a really beautiful moment. Some audience members cried because they had been sitting in this terrible situation and then at the very end, there was this release of emotions. We are all craving for some light. But what we are not trying to do is to put on the happy show, because during this pandemic, we have seen sides to ourselves which we had not wanted to show to other people. What this piece does is ask these questions. What is it to be human? Who are you? The piece is a reflection on darkness. I always saw this piece functioning like an ancient Greek tragedy. There is a catharsis. It is about a city and a reflection on community in an abstract way. We staged it so that the audience never has their back to one another but are always looking across into another stranger's eyes. The audience members became the protagonist of the story.

This virus is like an X-ray of society and all structures. Everything that was bad before is even worse in a way because the virus is like a magnifying glass on all the inequalities. I was born in Holland but grew up partly in America and then in Germany as well. I have been critical of Germany with its horrible past, but now the shining lights of democracy – the United States and the UK – have turned into sick patients. This was true even before Covid-19. Ever since Ronald Reagan and Margaret Thatcher, which started the period of mass privatisations. The ripple effects of all that is still felt, and now has reached its extreme.

This country has turned into a complete monster, especially since Brexit. How do we live together after experiencing everything we have experienced? When Trump is gone, what does it mean for America? How will it recover? How can people reach out and talk to each other in a reasonable way? It is the same the UK. It is a complete split society. The last few years have been dark but maybe it must go even further for people to really be shaken up because maintaining this capitalist system is impossible. It does not work anymore.

I was very hopeful at the beginning of the lockdown because I felt like we could see that nature was coming back into the cities. Suddenly they were no planes. You had a glimpse of an alternative utopia in a way and very quickly, it was all gone again. I think everyone had a glimmer of saw something that was an alternative. There was a short window, as it were, near the top of lockdown, which pointed toward a different kind of future.

CS *Related to darkness and doing a show that occurs in the dark puts me in mind of the act of deep listening, because it is something society needs.*

WM Our piece was all about listening and the work of the imagination. To go into a space to hear words and imagine what a sentence can mean and let the image occur in your brain is very old-fashioned. But it is also the source of who we are. I love the tool of just listening. We are overfed visually, and do not exercise the muscles of our imagination. It would be fascinating to sit in a room with Brexit or Trump voter and see how much tolerance I would have to not shout but just listen. Bringing together two factions that are in opposition and doing the kind of listening necessary is the opposite of drama, but it may be a way forward.

Ralph Peña

Ralph Peña is artistic director of Ma-Yi Theatre Company in New York City. This interview was conducted over email between mid-September and 1 October 2020.

CS *How has lockdown been for you?*

RP Most of my days are spent thinking of ways to overcome the challenges brought by this pandemic, and how we can seize this opportunity to give artists more agency in the creative process, especially artists of colour. I chased every grant opportunity that came up and pitched this idea for a digital platform that can safely capture live performances. I knew this lockdown was not like any other, that it would last for a while and devastate the theatre community. My first instinct was to preserve our ability to create, so in that sense, it felt like the early years of Ma-Yi Theatre, which to me was very energizing. Here was a chance to rethink how we make art and connect with audiences. As a small theatre in New York City, we are constantly bumping against the constraints of space and money. In a digital world, some of those barriers are less of a hindrance.

CS *What advice do you have for people entering the field right now?*

RP Young people have a huge role in shaping post-pandemic theatre. Now is the time to break barriers and upend hierarchies, and challenge how things are done. I am telling young people to sharpen their ideas and to pitch them to their local theatres. I am not talking about Zoom readings. I mean outside-the-margin ideas that rethink modalities of performance. This is the time to do these things before American theatre returns to its rigid ways.

CS *What are your hopes and dreams for theatre's future?*

RP The first is giving BIPOC theatres the respect they deserve. They have been doing the heavy lifting for many years and cultivating their communities to think of art and theatre as part of their lives. These are the communities that are not on the radar of large institutions because they require real work and sustained engagement with little to no dollar upside. For decades, the government and private foundations have thought of these organizations as second-tier, special interest groups that do not merit the same level of support that larger institutions deserve. This is a kind of social engineering, reinforcing the barriers between the haves and have nots, and supporting a white-centred theatre landscape. This needs to change if we are ever going to have cultural equity in this country.

The second thing I hope to see a rejiggering of the standard patterns of making theatre. A producer picks a play, assembles a team, stages a production and hopes for a hit. It is a cycle with built-in filters and gatekeepers built around the idea of 'excellence'. Who defines excellence, and who picks the play? How much agency do the artists have in deciding what is important to them? Where is the community in this process? The pause brought on by the pandemic is a chance to rethink how we can return power to the artists. What if we removed most (if not all) of the filters and gatekeepers between the first creative impulse and production of the work? This is what a digital platform has made possible. We can give artists control over every aspect of the process, including how they make money. It is a model we want to take with us when we move back into a theatre.

CS *Could you walk readers through the decision and implementation of the Ma-Yi studio?*

RP We assembled artists and commissioned them as a group, instead of just the playwright, so we can get money to more people faster. We partnered with Culture Hub to get smarter on live broadcasts and we hired our usual production crew to build us a new studio. The animating principle here is to provide employment to artists. Making art comes second.

Culturally specific organizations need to have deep conversations with their constituents to ask how they can be most useful during this crisis. Art and theatre may not be what is needed most at this time. We must find ways to adapt and be of service to our communities. It might take a while to figure out how to marry theatre-making with what the community needs, but it can be done. Knowing the essential: why and for whom we create – will help us find the answers. We cannot discount activism. Speak up, speak loudly and often.

CS *Do you think it will be crucial for artists in the United States, given that there is no government subsidy, to move into other fields to support their artistry?*

RP My father drilled into my head that if I wanted to be an artist, I needed to first secure my financial independence. I did try to go into theatre with no safety net. I lasted about a year, eating spaghetti out of a can, and hocking my small thirteen-inch television so I could pay rent. After that experience, I vowed never to starve again and I took a job at a finance firm, thinking I would do it for a year or two. Twenty-two years later, I was still working in finance. Somehow, I found a way to balance a full-time job with theatre work. It came at a cost. I had to give up performing and directing to focus on growing Ma-Yi. I finally left my Wall Street job in 2015 to work full-time as an artist.

CS *Ma-Yi often co-produces with companies that are not focused on works made by Asian-American artists. Can you speak to this?*

RP The instigating desire to work with other 'non-Asian' companies was probably driven by a need for greater visibility. I remember bringing the *The Square* to The Public Theatre in 2001, just a month after 9/11. It was the biggest stage we had ever performed in, and we were all stoked going into it. And then the anthrax scare hit, and few people showed up. It would take another seventeen years before we were invited to come back to The Public in 2018 for Mike Lew's *Teenage Dick*. For both of these productions, Ma-Yi bore all the production costs and paid for The Public's staff. The Public provided the space for free, but it was still a substantial cost for a small company like Ma-Yi. We made this deal with our eyes open and knew it was an opportunity to reach one of the most coveted audience bases in New York City. We had a sold out run and got more press than we have ever received in the past. For about six weeks, we were a 'visible' part of mainstream New York theatre. Then, we went back to the ghetto – to that specialized field of ethnic specific theatre.

I have always rebelled against that label, an othering classification that sets us apart from what is considered legit theatre-making. It is a type of condescension that grates. It also has real consequences. We are never seen as having broad appeal or making a significant impact on our field. It affects funding and our ability to attract bigger donors. We struggle to get press, even after decades of making work. The constant need to prove ourselves is very tiring, so on the rare occasions we get to swim with the bigger fish, it feels like a respite, however brief.

CS   *What are your thoughts on digital theatre?*

RP   The pandemic has likely changed how our field looks at digital work which many purists will say is not really theatre. In transitioning, it became clear that this kind of work needs to become part of our vocabulary, not just as a business continuity strategy, but also a way to nudge creativity. We are only now investigating ways for live performance and technology to coexist in the same space, without diminishing each other. I have been talking to a couple of artists in Asia about creating a digital realm where audience and actors interact – a virtual reality world – that is theatrical in its construct. This technology is not new, but how can we use it to tell our stories?

   There is also the matter of reach. We can bring our work to places and communities we have never been to. Our streaming content is now seen on six continents by viewers numbering in the millions. There is the thorny issue of how to monetize digital content. This is something the field is still grappling with, but I am confident we will find a way.

CS   *How do you see Ma-Yi's work from a historical perspective?*

RP   I have not had much occasion to consider Ma-Yi's historical significance. What consumes me is the daily task of survival that institutional racism has and continues to make a very heavy lift. Our work today is focused on supporting the creation of new plays by Asian American playwrights as a rebuttal to the perception (still prevalent among large regional theatres) that 'there are no Asian American plays' – which is really code for 'there are no Asian American plays that are good enough'. We have made some progress in this area with writers like Lloyd Suh, Mike Lew and

Lauren Yee – but there are still many obstacles in the way for most Asian American playwrights, and my hope is that our work can help break them down. We are part of a long thread of struggle that began in the 1960s and 1970s with the founding of East West Players, NWAAT and Pan Asian Rep. The animating reasons that gave birth to these companies are still present. Ma-Yi is now thirty years old, and I do not think we have made it past the metaphorical hallway. I want my gravestone to read: 'He tried.'

Marike Splint

Marike Splint is a Dutch-French-Tunisian theatre maker based in Los Angeles, specializing in creating work in public space that explores the relationship between people, places and identity. This interview took place over Zoom on 27 August 2020. Special thanks to Gabriel Greene at La Jolla Playhouse.

CS *How has lockdown been for you?*

MS I've dealt with, of course, many anxieties and issues that I'm sure a lot of people have had, from worrying about those who are most vulnerable to the virus and about the social and economic consequences of the pandemic, to missing loved ones and missing the freedom of moving around.

Maybe two or three days into the lockdown in March 2020 I felt we were in a new paradigm and the world, as we had conceived it before, was just not going to come back. I remember realizing that the time before this, is what we will eventually consider the strange part of our lives, the not normal. That we had turned a corner and would not return.

My piece *You Are Here: A Homebound Travelogue*, commissioned by La Jolla Playhouse for their 2020 Without Walls Digital Programming, is a reflection of this: going from very immediate changes in our daily lives, to reflections on what is happening on a global level and on a longer timeline. How do we conceive of the world? How do we conceive of time? And sort of oscillating between that, the very concrete and very abstract.

CS *How did* You Are Here *come to be?*

MS I knew from the beginning that I wanted to do something with Google Earth. I am a site-specific theatre director, so I usually conceive from sites – the site is the given structure that I work with and around. I had been fascinated for a while by Google and how its virtual map relates to our physical world. When I began talking to La Jolla Playhouse, the virus was still very much spreading across the globe, and people were figuring out where it came from and where it was headed. Part of me was also just impressed with this little invisible virus that was traveling so quickly through to all these places through our bodies. The first research I did was looking on Google Earth at various places where there had been super spreader events. I went to this village in Northern Italy that was the first community to go into lockdown, and to this church in rural America which doubled as the rehearsal place for the local choir. China does not have Google Earth, but they have their own version called Baidu. So, I virtually walked around the Wuhan seafood market.

As I began working on the piece, I kept bumping into the question what I could really say artistically about this moment beyond what we were seeing on the news. We were still so much in the middle of it, and our reality was changing so fast. I did not feel in a position to reflect on anything yet. I realized that the only honest way for me to talk about this moment that was to put myself in it, to depart from a very subjective and personal perspective. I needed to zoom out, to not fixate on the nowness of it all. What is interesting about Google Earth is that it is a memory of the world. We are looking at captured images of a world that has passed and is also still constantly being overwritten. That quality also makes us look past this moment in time. It makes us consider that the world is in constant movement, but also that there will be something beyond this moment.

With *You Are Here*, I knew from the beginning that I wanted to try to find ways to keep audience awareness within the piece, to what extent that is even possible, virtually. One part of it was integrating the image of the full audience, in the form of forty-nine Zoom tiles, into the visual fabric of the piece. Zoom allows you to look at others in such a satisfying way. In all the Zoom work meetings I have had since the pandemic I have loved looking at people's living rooms or kitchens. All these people in their homes, like small moving paintings. For the performance I wanted to find a zone where people felt included and invited to see each other, but not necessarily made to feel self-conscious about their environment. When you are sitting in a theatre, you hear the audience breathing, you are aware that people are around you. So, what could be the virtual equivalent of that?

You Are Here also integrates the diasporic history of my family. That heritage has left me with the ability to adapt almost everywhere, but not really feeling rooted anywhere. A reoccurring question in my work is what is our relationship to place and how does it form our identity? How do we inhabit places and how do they inhabit us? In *You Are Here* these questions are explored in a virtual world. I see the virtual as a site that many of us spend an increasing amount of time in, and I often wonder what that does to our sense of self and community.

Google Earth is in a way the ultimate metaphor for that. It becomes this parallel, elusive world that seems complete and immediate. Yet it also affects our present – it tells us what detours to take when streets are busy, what time we need to leave our home to get somewhere or what businesses are currently open or closed. Our physical world is affected by the way that Google Map records the world.

What I attempt to do in my work is redirect the gaze of the audience. I consider the eyes of the audience as a camera and try to edit their gaze it into a sequence that disrupts how you normally, if you quickly pass a place, categorize it. So, what I am working on is the perception of the audience. That is the focal point of my work. I like playing in a space that combines subjective fantasy and empirical reality so you can look at something and be part of something at the same time.

CS *What are your hopes and dreams for the field, and do you have any advice for those entering it now?*

MS I am hopeful for the next generation of artists because we are living in a moment where we are questioning some essences of the art form. We are asking ourselves: what constitutes theatre? What constitutes performance? Historically, these moments have been catalysts for innovation in the art form. Radical questioning is also a welcome necessity because, in many ways, the field was ossified. I am hopeful this crisis will make space for new ways of seeing and making. As much as the theatre is in crisis now, it was in a crisis before the pandemic, albeit a different one. It was a crisis of complacency. The established cultural field in the United States did not tackle social issues at all. But now we are living in a moment where we must look at the bigger picture. We cannot look away anymore. It is a moment to think radically about form and content.

If we do not do it now, then when else are we going to do it? It is the younger generation that will have the response to the big questions about the future of the artform. Not the establishment.

CS *In what ways is theatre a healing practice?*

MS Your choice for the word 'healing' in your question made me realize that I encounter that word a lot in the United States in relationship to art. But in Europe, where I have lived and work too, they seem more focused on showing the pain – the uncomfortable truth. We have this Dutch saying: gentle healers make for smelling wounds. It basically means that you are not served by a doctor who is not willing to look at the truth. As an artist I am probably informed by that. Healing means diving deep into the places where it hurts. We live in a moment where that is required. It is heartening to see that people are doing that right now and that it is leading immediately to vibrant expressions of culture. The Black Lives Matter movement is an incredible example of that. What we are seeing with the protests – the reclaiming of the streets, the making of new culture and really the reimagining of what it means to be coming together – gives me hope.

Healing also comes from looking at systemic issues and the potential for systemic changes rather than individual narratives in the creation of art. Our current events force us to think about the collective and to think about societal issues beyond our own lives. It is not a gentle invitation. It is a surge, and we cannot move against it. We must move with it. We must let go of old narratives about who we are.

When I lived in Amsterdam, I remember a friend from graduate school coming to visit me. We walked past this square in the city centre. There was a street performer who was beating a drum. The rhythm was infectious. It made everyone in the square adjust their step to the beat. There was this vibration going on all over the square and bouncing of the buildings. My friend turned to me and said: I want the work I make to be like the beating of that drum.

Tassos Stevens

Tassos Stevens is a British playmaker. He is co-runner and director of Coney, a London-headquartered company dedicated to creating games, adventures and play where people can choose to take a meaningful part. This interview was conducted on Zoom on 20 August 2020. England and New York City. Audio transcription by Emily Ezzo.

CS *What have you been working on during lockdown?*

TS Coney has seventeen Associate Artists, but most of those are on a freelance basis. Quite a big part of my first response to the pandemic was from the point of view of running the company and looking after everybody within Coney HQ, including freelancers and our extended family. At Coney, we are relatively privileged. We are an NPO (National Portfolio Organization of Arts Council England). I am lucky to be salaried. I've a position of relative security. As it happened [at the start of the pandemic], most of Coney HQ was furloughed for at least three months – I was not. A lot of what I was doing was trying to keep things afloat. We promised that we would honour every commitment we made to freelancers. General management was where most of my energy was spent. But I carved out a little space. I suggested we work on devising rapid-fire experiments – which we called 'remote socials' – somehow, live online. The first three were designed around what would be fun for people and what might give people a sense of connection with each other. It gave us a chance to learn how to play on these [online] platforms. Quickly, we had an audience, and a regular audience emerged, which was somewhat new for us, given that the last piece Coney had that was public facing was two years ago, because much of our work is made for specific audiences or contexts.

Those first three pieces were made at the top of lockdown were all game shows of some form. They were easy to conceive. Then, we took a break, after which we decided to dig in a little more deeply and to choose some new formats. We chose a murder mystery and an escape room because these are commonly understood formats, so we could describe them to a wider audience, but we could do more interesting spins on both. *Telephone* was conceived with the notion of figuring out what live storytelling is like online and thinking very much about connection. It is important to say that both *Telephone* and *Escape Zoom* were made in less than two days each. We also had another opportunity to create a piece called *The Delegation* with a Russian theatre company. Initially, they wanted me to do *Telephone* as part of a festival, but I was interested to make something with the gesture of a UK audience meeting a Russian audience and what that meeting and encounter could be across the language barrier, as well the geographical barrier, and the cultural barrier.

CS   *Mid-pandemic and post-pandemic, what are your hopes and dreams for the theatre? For interactive and digital theatre?*

TS   Broadly, I hope everybody is going to be okay. It still feels so uncertain. The economic impact and what that will do. The fact that we are still not clear yet, in terms of a vaccine. It is going to be unpredictable. I am in a more secure position than most – in theatre, certainly. But I have concerns. I hope that we can break things up enough that we can make it better, even if it is a little bit. And [to think], what has been opening around the anti-racism work that needs to happen everywhere. And here in the UK, the legacy of empire. That is of paramount importance. It is also a clear example of something broader, systemically: recognizing that things are a bit fucked. There is opportunity, as much as this is a crisis. I fear/I know that also what we are facing and what we are going through, and what we are suffering from is a crisis of capitalism. And the climate crisis and the ecological crisis has not done anything to go away, and how that is also very much a product of capitalism, of empire. So where do we, what do we, how do we topple that?

As far as theatre goes, I am not wedded to things happening digitally. I never use the word 'digital' if I possibly can. I prefer to call them 'remote socials', because they are socials for remote audiences. We kind of call them 'remote programs'. *Telephone* is a piece I am thinking about that as an architecture, where we are just all in our rooms conjuring a theatre together. More than it happens through Zoom. [Zoom] is just the platform that enables that. Think about the tech without thinking about the tech. Think about what it enables, in terms of the connections of the people, in the places where it has the most impact. Coney was already a weird fish. Even though we are a theatre company, we are less and less bothered about making things inside theatre spaces. We are much more about going to whatever location has the most impact for who the people we are making it for – with a real variety and agility to make new formats of work and new events. More of that will be needed. I have found that we can bypass gatekeepers, and I have a lot of hope around that. Did you ever make it over to the Shunt Vaults in London? Basically, it was pay £5 entry to the best bar in London and once inside we will invite you to come see a performance for free. They did that themselves and I wish for something like that again. I just fear that so many people have been crushed in spirit and in income.

CS *Any advice for people entering the field right now?*

TS What I benefited from was being immersed inside a scratch culture, and I ran a venue for a while that was kind of a scratch platform. I think it is about understanding that you can just do it and bypass the gatekeepers. You might not be able to make a full living that way. People for whom theatre becomes a full, one-stream income is so few. You should be unashamed about having a side hustle. I was a medical secretary for three years while I was transitioning into Coney. Also, experimental theatre makers have incredible creative skills and resourcefulness that should be of great interest to the corporate sector. Coney made a living as a company before it was an NPO. We have values that we can make a living from. I do think there is something about letting go of expectations of the industry and the industrial model.

CS *Thoughts on making work post-pandemic?*

TS Coney's ambition is not to be in a 400-strong auditorium. We have some things to figure out: What kind of constraints? What kind of communities do we want to be making work for by and with? That is sort of the process that we were always doing. And a lot of the time, the collaborative process is via lots of screens, at different times. You cannot rehearse it till you have an audience. But how much do you have to build it till you have the right to call in an audience? You can make all the plans, but you really do not know till there is an audience there.

Playing audiences are the smartest creatures on the planet. They are predictably unpredictable. You can never be sure of what they are going to do. An audience is infinitely complex, in an emergent way. People are different and play differently. And again, there is a weird consistency. But how and who is a bit of a mystery. Do you know of Bertie De Koven? I consider him a Jedi Master. In his posthumous book called *The Infinite Playground* (2020), he is mostly talking about imagination. There is something [about] the material: as a carpenter works with wood, the play designer works with people and imagination. Because you must imagine how people will respond to things.

CS *While we make work during this time, we know that audiences are handling trauma in different ways.*

TS Simultaneously, we are going through this experience. Coney has been doing a collaboration with Kathryn Beaumont-Evans, who is a theatre-maker and a psychotherapist. Coney very much considers impact, figuring out how to design for impact. Frameworks to better understand, to design better. And finally, how to measure the impact. And any measures of impact are too often for the organization or the stakeholders. But they must be far more meaningful and relevant for the people. The work I am concerned with is figuring out how that design for impact works. And the work I have been doing with Kathryn has been fascinating! We did a sharing from a recent piece in development, which is a show about Brexit. In it, Kathryn led a guided dream reflection: thinking about the dreams you have had during lockdown. Then we asked everyone to renamed themselves as 'X' in the Zoom chat, so everybody was anonymous. Then, whenever they wanted, people would write a line or an image from one of the dreams they had. And it became a montage – a kind of collective dream, through trauma – which felt cathartic to do. That is an awfully specific tangent. But more broadly, as citizens, we should consider what we can do to take better care of each other through this. That is the primary imperative: The real impact of going to the theatre is the experience of going to the theatre together; it is less about the play on stage. It is about being in the theatre with other people. If we could figure out how that plays, we can figure out more ways to take care of each other.

4

Resistance and faith

Leila Buck

Leila Buck is a Lebanese American playwright, performer, facilitator and educator. Her pieces *American Dreams* sustained a seven-state digital tour in autumn 2020. This interview was conducted over email between 25 November and 4 December 2020.

CS *How has lockdown been for you?*

LB Like most people I am filled with many questions, uncertainties and unknowns, in our lives, our field and nation. It's been remarkable to be sharing such a huge experience with my family in Lebanon and friends and loved ones all over the nation and world. I feel that even if we're not reading the same news or seeing the same images or experiencing things the same way, on a national and global level many are more aware of our connectedness, of a shared experience along with all the things that divide us. So overall I feel there is a power and possibility in that collective consciousness.

CS *What advice do you have for people entering the field now?*

LB Don't work for free. Question anyone who asks you to about why they are doing so. Listen to their answer. See if it feels fair to you. Take the work if you need to. Ask yourself where you can challenge asks that don't feel right, band together with others to do so or make sure you create another opportunity for someone who can't afford to work for free. If you are able to take internships or work without pay, ask yourself if that means what you are doing is not accessible to someone who doesn't have the financial means to do that – or the physical or emotional ability to work the three jobs you're working to make it possible. Recognize that these often seemingly small asks for work without any or adequate pay perpetuate classism, racism, ableism and more in our field. Stick together. Find the people who bring you joy – who challenge you with respect the way a good friend calls you out when you need it, because they care. The people who are willing to go to the mat with you about an idea or a piece of work – but always about the *work*, not their, or your, ego.

AND: dream big. Demand systemic change.

Remember that our work is to collectively, collaboratively imagine, envision, create – and dismantle – worlds. We have the power to impact, and change, ours. And to invite and inspire others to do so.

CS   *During a time of global collective trauma, what are theatre's healing properties, if any?*

LB   I have felt healing through the process of connection, which is still very possible in this virtual/online work. I've felt it in audience engagement, in laughter and connection with individual friends/colleagues during and after shows ... I've seen it and heard it from audience participants who felt the connective power of theatre through the screen, in some ways more intimately than in a physical theatre. There is healing in connecting with people from all over the country and the world in ways that would be impossible in a physical space – and in being reminded that we can still be together in real time for collective imagination and connection.

As a field, this time has brought out so much grace in so many of us – for childcare, elder care, self-care – in ways we are normally expected to fit in on the side around our insane working hours. For me there is healing in allowing ourselves and each other time and space *away* from the work – encouraging respect for and prioritization of health, self-care, connection with family and loved ones, caregiving of ourselves and each other as not only things we fit in outside the work but deeply necessary *to* the work and our own sustainability in it. Theatre is often such a culture of expecting superhuman efforts and sacrifices of time and energy, 24/7, 365 days a year. I believe there is healing in challenging and changing this culture which connects deeply to white supremacy, colonialism, Western/Northern cultural domination, capitalism and patriarchy in so many ways. There is healing in redefining the entire field, dismantling power structures that were and are not just or sustainable, and opening possibilities for imagining new ways of creating, working and being that support personal and collective care.

CS   *Can you talk about your work currently as a theatre-maker?*

LB Necessity sparks innovation – and collaboration. That is something that has been highlighted by this time for me. Working Theater's model for our recent seven-state online 'tour' in the fall of 2020 of our piece *American Dreams* was really inspiring to me. It began with director Tamilla Woodard and our team reaching out to people with whom they/we had relationships – not transactional, short-term relationships, but deep, long-term ones based in creative collaboration and shared values around the work, and why we do it – how we believe it can impact people in meaningful ways.

The team that Tamilla gathered for us really inspired me. Their commitment to collaboration and innovation went above and beyond anything I've experienced in the theatre. The ask was to make it possible for us to engage directly with audiences all over the country and the world – to invite them to interact fully, playfully and deeply with the experience on multiple levels – and our designers, actors, stage management, production manager, line producer and Tamilla made that possible. Through painstaking, often ridiculously frustrating and mystifying trial and error, ingenuity and resourcefulness, they invented whole new ways of connecting platforms and ideas that made a level of design, performance and audience engagement and interaction possible in ways that amazed me and our audiences. Our team and the way they collaborated and created through and beyond every obstacle was emblematic of how this time can push us to reimagine what is possible, inventing new ways of working and creating, collaboration and connection in the process.

CS *In what ways do you instigate joy in your work processes?*

LB For me joy is in connection, and laughter, and discovery – those moments of creative collaboration when we recognize that we make something so much better together than we could separately – and feel heard, respected, cared for in the process. Joy is in choosing, wherever possible, to work with people we respect, and even come to love in various ways. Finding – or creating – time for spontaneity, flexibility, connections that are not solely focused on the work, both during rehearsal or performance and beyond it, is so essential to the process for me – as is celebrating small discoveries and milestones in the process, even and especially when there are many challenges still to come. Laughing at everything possible in the process. And remembering to keep the *play* in playmaking! I have needed these reminders often, and still do sometimes, and am so grateful to have collaborators who are friends and loved ones that remind me consistently of how essential joy is to the process.

CS *What are your hopes and dreams for theatre's future?*

LB   I make theatre because it requires us to be in shared space together. Even the most traditional proscenium-staged non-interactive play is a shared experience with the people on and off the stage. If you cough, or laugh, we hear it. If you are moved, we feel it – the 'we' on stage and the 'we' in the house.

It's interesting we call it a house. Right now, many of us are truly making, and sharing, and experiencing theatre – in our homes. As the wonderful Arab American scholar Zeina Salame asked me and Tamilla in response to the experience of our piece *American Dreams* recently: what does it mean to bring the theatre home? To invite someone into your home, as performer and audience member?

My hope is that as a field we listen to the voices inside us and in our field demanding that we commit to making theatre sustainable and accessible – physically, emotionally, financially, creatively, environmentally – for those who make it, and those who engage in it. That we centre and fund ideas and people instead of buildings; that we commit to the real, long-term, personal and institutional work of challenging and dismantling all the oppressive and unjust systems in our field and beyond it. That we share resources in new ways and create an ecosystem in our field that is sustainable for all.

My dream is that we remember that we are people who know how to create – and dismantle – worlds. And that we create a world in our field that is as just, joyful, beautiful and inspiring as the best of the worlds we create on our stages and beyond them.

Rachel Chavkin and Alexandra Lalonde

Rachel Chavkin is a Tony Award-winning theatre director, writer and dramaturg and founding artistic director of the Brooklyn-based company the TEAM. Alexandra Lalonde is the producing director of the TEAM. This interview was conducted on Zoom on 5 November 2020.

CS *How has lockdown been for you?*

AL It has been challenging. But also, not nearly as challenging as it's been for many others. We are a touring company, but we were not in the middle of touring our work. We were not planning anything for the pandemic period thus far that was revenue-generating. This year was supposed to be an investment year into new play development. So, we are going to be extending that development period.

RC Because of the success of *Hadestown* (2016), I was fortunate to have a solid cushion of savings, and thus am doing alright – financially speaking – even amidst the Broadway shutdown. I am incredibly lucky. I am also working on my first film and developing some film and television projects I've long needed space to work on.

AL What was the most disappointing part for us was that we were supposed to spend three weeks in Montgomery, Alabama, in June 2020 for research and development work at Alabama Shakespeare Festival on our new piece *Reconstruction*, which has twenty-four writers. Lockdown prohibited travel or the ability for us to do work engaging with communities there. So, we pivoted a bit of the work to the Zoom environment as best we could. But given that our practice is rooted in place-based research, we are eager to be able to move forward with the Alabama residency when it is logistically possible. In addition to a bit of work on Zoom, it has been nice to be able to step back a little bit and clarify our values as a company in the interim.

RC   We initially began the project in 2018 to look at race, particularly between Black-identifying and white-identifying Americans, and to examine *Gone with the Wind* (1936) as a Confederate monument. But by the third day of work, we no longer had any interest in the latter because it felt that we were just perpetuating this racist novel by a racist woman in Atlanta in 1936. One of our writer creators, a Black feminist academic and writer-performer, Jillian Walker, brought the work of Professor Hortense Spillers into the room, particularly a lecture she gave about intimacy between white and Black people within the context of an anti-Black America, and specifically the relationship between Sally Hemmings and Thomas Jefferson. This gave sharp new focus to the room, which is evenly divided between Black-identifying artists, several Artists of Colour and white-identifying artists. We are now almost entirely focused on intimacy: *if* it's possible – and if so, *how* – in the present day, and in the context of our past.

The work has been quite personal and quite deep, including having a process chaplain embedded in our rehearsal room; her name is Milta Vega-Cardona, a self-described recovering social worker, and an anti-racism facilitator with the People's Institute for Survival and Beyond. And this work has impacted, in turn, the company's work at the board level. We want to make sure that the board reflects the values that we have been nurturing in the *Reconstruction* room.

CS   *At a time of global collective trauma, what is theatre's role, if any, towards healing?*

RC   The heart of our work in *Reconstruction* is healing. I want to be clear I can only speak from my singular vantage point as co-director and co-facilitator of the project, and as a white woman in a room that is examining both whiteness and Blackness. But I would say healing is being cultivated through honest conversation among people of different races, steeped in both personal histories and historical research. Sometimes the process has been ugly, and a lot of ancestors and demons have come up in the work. But everything is driven by a need for self-healing and self-discovery, and in pursuit of finding shared intimacy, which we hope will then translate to our audience.

AL   On an institutional level, it felt essential to support the mental and spiritual health of our artists in this deep work – particularly our Artists of Colour. And so, to Rachel's point earlier, we have called on a process chaplain to be in the room with us. She has been in the room any time we are gathered as an entire company to help facilitate and hold space for both interpersonal and one-on-one conversations. We know that everyone's healing is going to be and look different.

CS   *What kind of relationship do you see between artmaking and resistance?*

RC   Again, I can only answer for myself because I suspect every member of the TEAM might feel differently about this. I certainly remember us talking about resistance before the 2016 election, but significantly more so since then. That said, I don't personally start with the idea of 'resisting' or being in reaction to something. There is certainly an awareness of the present – of where we *are* – and the focus is on trying to manifest where we might *be*, and then dramatizing all the points of conflict or obstacle that arise on that journey. We're in pursuit of collective liberation, and I would say *Reconstruction* is quite consumed with the nuances that arise in that pursuit when you really consider the vicious inequities both past and present.

AL   I am Canadian and was brought up to see art as a public good that should be supported by the government. I think there is something very American about making art in rebellion to something rather than embracing culture.

CS   *What advice do you have for people entering the field right now?*

RC   I generally don't believe in giving advice because I think it is presumptuous and inequitable, in that it assumes my given circumstances looked anything like someone else's. Again, I can only speak to my journey as an early career artist: I never waited for anyone to hire me because I assumed no one would ever hire me as a young director. No one trusts a young director with money. I also only wanted to do experimental work at that time, so I just began making my own shit. I think there's enormous merit to making work in a basement. So perhaps, thinking about the present pandemic circumstances, I will offer that it's tricky for an early career artist to *ever* rely on the 'industry' for work. All that said, it was essential to me to have health insurance (which I got through Barnes and Noble) and pay rent and meet financial obligations (I worked a variety of odd jobs). And back to today, industry-wise people are still reading shit, and still having lots of Zoom meetings. So, it might actually be a good time to reach out to people.

AL Before I worked with the TEAM, I was working at SITI Company. While there, I saw *vast* numbers of early-career artists come through our doors and start making their own work – looking to cultivate their own artistic agency. I do not think this is unique to pandemic time. But I do think there is a conversation to be had about how expensive training programs have become and whether that investment is worth it in the long term.

CS *In what ways do you activate joy in your work process?*

AL We think about joy all the time. There is so much joy in my life that comes from art making and experiencing art, and I have been missing that a lot. In August, as part of our Petri Projects lab program, we produced *Quince*, a show by Camilo Quiroz-Vazquez and directed by Ellpetha Tsivicos, in a community garden in Bushwick. Just the act of being present with other people making art for each other was such a beautiful, generous act. We also did a Zoom benefit reading of our piece *RoosevElvis* (2013), and there is so much joy and celebration in that show that I found myself completely transformed every time we were rehearsing it.

CS *What are your hopes and dreams for theatre and a more equitable future?*

RC I've just joined the board of New York Theatre Workshop as an Artist Member, and we have been using this time to do a lot of self-education about racial equity and are deeply examining the work of NYTW to ensure anti-racism is at the forefront in every conversation. The same is happening with *Hadestown* – for instance there has been a long pressing conversation about racial and gender diversity in our band (which has been both white and male dominated, in comparison to the acting ensemble), and that work has been able to get both deeper and more practical (towards policy change) during this pause. I do not think there is a project that I am involved with right now that is not talking about anti-racism training becoming a core and ongoing part of the work. My union – Stage Directors and Choreographers Society – has been developing anti-racist practices, including recently releasing a major study about the financial realities of mid-career directors and choreographers, and the profound racial and gender inequity in earning potential for both directors of Colour and female directors (including white-identifying) in comparison to white male directors. The inequity is appalling. And the study, as well as the larger national movement for racial justice, has spurred on some important grant and leadership opportunities for the field, including from the Stage Directors and Choreographers (SDC) Foundation.

AL I would echo everything that Rachel has been saying about equity and anti-oppression work. On a personal level, in this time without theatre as we have known theatre, it's been clarifying to think about what are the things that I love about theatre and what are the things I miss about it? In our Petri Project program, which is a lab program for our artistic community that supports new projects (including radio plays, oratorios, films, etc.), the artists themselves decide how to distribute the funds that we have for the year. The goal is to take away decision-making from Rachel and me, and to decentralize it in order to expand both opportunities for artists and new ways of thinking about the TEAM's mission of looking at America from as many different vantage points as possible. So, there was the project *Quince* performed in The People's Garden, and it was beautiful to watch artists rethinking how work could be made during the pandemic. The pandemic, alongside the uprisings against racial violence, have released us in many ways from a lot of status quos, and we want to use that release to manifest a better theatrical practice that is more generous and more equitable.

Kia Corthron

K ia Corthron is an American playwright, activist, television writer and novelist. Her plays include *Breath, Boom* (2000) and *Force Continuum* (2002). Her novel *The Castle Cross the Magnet Carter* received the 2016 Center for Fiction First Novel Prize. This email was conducted via email on 6 November 2020.

CS *How has lockdown been for you?*

KC I was workshopping a new play at Washington DC's Arena Stage the week of 9 March. When I met the cast on Tuesday the 10th, the theatre had provided Purell but, other than that, the virus only seemed to affect us in deciding whether or not to hug – and for every actor who wanted to embrace, which I think were most (it was a big cast), I complied without reservations. By the time of the reading two days later, the nation had undergone a sea change. When I took Amtrak home to New York that Friday, the train was like being in a ghost town.

I had seen my last production the night before, a revival of James Baldwin's 1954 play *Amen Corner* at Washington's Shakespeare Theatre Company with an audience that socially distanced itself naturally by the enormous number of cancellations. That same evening, Broadway closed. And still I don't think the seriousness really hit home until a week and a half later when I saw a news report that Terrence McNally had died from complications due to Covid-19. I was never close to Terrence, but I'd known him personally a very long time. Another week, and as we moved into April, I think it began to sink into all of us that this isn't going to be a brief quiet time wherein we could catch up on work, but rather something protracted and grim. I began to hear estimates projected for American deaths: upwards of 100,000. I was shook.

Six and a half months after the original lockdown, wanderlust me had not spent a night away from her apartment in Harlem,

Manhattan. My feelings about isolation evolved. In the initial weeks, I waxed nostalgic and sentimental: *is this the end of human touch?* But I got used to it and, because I can be antisocial anyway, half a year later I'm shrugging: eh, who cares if it is? Which I find funny. Or maybe it's denial?

It is now early November 2020, and there have been well over 200,000 American corona fatalities, with the death count from the South and Midwest continuing to click in fast and furious. It doesn't have to be, as wiser nations have shown us. But mask-wearing has proved inconvenient for the president, and his dismissiveness of the simple life-saving device has been catastrophically imitated by his base.

CS *What advice do you have for people entering the field right now?*

KC At the risk of generalization, I've been very excited by the younger generation since the founding of the Black Lives Matter and Occupy movements of the last decade, not to mention their enthusiasm for left-progressive political candidates. My advice comes less from my own experience than from my observations of theirs: bring that same activist passion and energy to the arts!

In 2014, I won the Windham Campbell Prize for Drama, an annual award presented to no more than nine international writers working in the English language: playwrights, fiction and non-fiction writers (and, more recently, poets). There was an awards week with presentations, and I read a monologue from a play inspired by the 2008 financial crisis and addressing economic disparities. One of the non-fiction winners confided to me later that he felt arts were the true way to reach people. I replied, 'Arts, activism, journalism, electoral politics – whatever works to bring about change' – which I firmly believe. But, as that non-fiction writer witnessed, we artists have a unique opportunity to affect the public. The world could be made a better place if we take that privilege as a responsibility.

CS *What are the hopes and dreams you have for the field?*

KC I have many times hoped that when we come out on the other side of this pandemic – assuming we do – that we will have learned something. But being asked directly, I felt rather stumped.

And then I reread the question: *dreams*. A radical rethinking of theatre.

In 2016, I wrote an article that was published in the July/August issue of *The Dramatist* entitled 'The Price of the Ticket', a phrase borrowed from James Baldwin. I began the piece by citing a musical revue on stage that season, *After Midnight*, celebrating Ellington-era jazz and dance. As a Tony voter, I am granted two orchestra seats for every Broadway show. All the performers were African American, and when my sister and I entered the lobby, there were loads of Black patrons. But by the time we reached our orchestra seats, they had all vanished. There we were, surrounded by a sea of white. The Black folks had all climbed the stairs to the balconies. This phenomenon of segregation in the theatre, if you haven't already guessed, comes down to economics.

I interviewed composer Stephen Schwartz for the article, who spoke of being terrified when, in 1973, the producer of *Pippin* wanted to go for a whopping $12 top ticket price. Until then, no one would pay more than $10 for Broadway. Even adjusting for inflation, Schwartz goes on to say, today's top price should be around $75 – which is now the bottom-tier price of some Manhattan *off-*Broadway venues. In 2017, *Hamilton* premium tickets hit $1,150 at the box office – the legit price *before* scalpers. The entire system then segregates the audience racially as well as economically, and the latter trend also tends to discriminate against the young, who often scrape by on minimum wage or less. So, this dreaming I have been asked to do – I imagine an American theatre for *the people*: made affordable so that a patron may sit in the orchestra of any venue, commercial or fringe, and observe a microcosm of the city – the dazzling variety of ethnicities, ages, classes.

As I write this, we in the United States are in the post-election days, awaiting confirmation of the next president, with most artists and people of colour desperately praying it will be a *new* president. If that prayer is answered, then I will be among those pushing the incomer toward Medicare For All, something that should be a no-brainer in the midst of a global pandemic. This godsend for the country would allow artists to spend less time working a soul-crushing day job for the sake of the benefits, or spending their days worrying about having no health insurance at all. Easing that burden, I believe, will be astronomically beneficial in the creation of American art.

CS *Can you talk about your work currently as a playwright and novelist?*

KC The Arena Stage workshop I'd mentioned at the beginning of this Q&A was for a work commissioned through their 'Power Plays' history project. The subject matter of my new play, *Tempestuous Elements*, is Anna Julia Cooper, a legendary educator who worked as teacher and principal at DC's renowned M Street School, a public preparatory institution for African American students, from the latter nineteenth century into the early twentieth. At that time, the education of Black students was at the centre of national debate: classical, college-bound studies or, as many white donors favoured, vocational training? In addition, my second novel, *Moon and the Mars*, will be published fall 2021. The setting is New York City in the years leading up to and into the Civil War, the protagonist a girl born of a Black father and Irish mother. The book addresses the relationship between the two communities.

Decades ago, I read Augusto Boal's *Theatre of the Oppressed* (1974). What has stayed with me all these years is the notion that if audience members leave the theatre so devastated by their experience that they can't do anything but throw up their hands in despair, that's exactly what they'll do. But if they are left with even a sliver of hope – *not* a fake Hollywood happy ending but truth in the resilience of the human spirit – then someone in that audience might actually do something to try to make a better world. I try to find that hopeful ending, and my novel certainly has that. But completing the first draft to show to readers on 15 April 2020 – a month into the pandemic shutdown, with the American public literally gagged while ultraconservative political operatives were instigating every dirty deal they could to push through devastating legislation – I wondered if my optimism was naïve, if not downright silly.

Then, on 25 May Minneapolis resident George Floyd was killed by the police. And suddenly the streets were filled with mask-wearing, enraged Americans, and the Republican law-grab scheme decelerated. Statues of historic racists began to be toppled, professional athletes across the board started taking a knee during the national anthem if not refusing to play altogether, a few white political conservatives incredibly began to publicly utter 'Black Lives Matter' and as of this writing the DC professional football franchise is being called simply 'Washington Football Team' until a name is decided upon to replace its decades-long moniker denigrating Native Americans. The fury over Floyd's death rekindled an outrage concerning another police killing that occurred at the start of the shutdown: the shooting of Breonna Taylor in Louisville, Kentucky, in the early hours of 13 March. The outcry over that tragedy and subsequent questionable court proceedings continues. Which all goes back to the 'resilience of the human spirit' of the aforementioned paragraph.

But, as I said, my second novel *Moon and the Mars* was given to first readers several weeks before the uprisings began, when my own resilience was at its lowest. Yet I kept the ending, optimism and all. As prison abolitionist Mariame Kaba has said, 'Hope is a discipline.' To put it more pointedly: we have to see the dream to be the dream.

Kristoffer Diaz

Kristoffer Diaz is a Latinx playwright, screenwriter and librettist, and teaches at NYU's Gallatin School of Individualized Study and in the Tisch Dramatic Writing Program. His play *The Elaborate Entrance of Chad Deity* was a finalist for the Pulitzer Prize. This interview was conducted over email in early September 2020.

CS *How has lockdown been for you?*

KD On the work side of things, it has not been terrible. I keep writing, messing with new pieces, revisiting old ones, trying to figure out what is still relevant, what is maybe more relevant, what is no longer speaking to my values and concerns. The writing does not end.

As a citizen, I am less sure. My dealings with real people are wonderful. Folks have rallied. They are taking care of themselves and others. Yet, everything I read about the rest of the world is brutal. People are sick. People are out of work or in danger of losing their jobs. People are fed up and protesting and fighting for new lives, all of which is wonderful and important, but all of which is daunting. There is so much to rail against, so much to try and fix, we are diffuse in our efforts. We are becoming a society based on being *against* things instead of being *for* things. We are steeped in anger, in conflict, in tearing down. It is exhausting and self-perpetuating. When I listen to that side of the world, I do not have much hope. When I speak to individuals one on one, I feel a lot better.

CS *Any advice for people entering the field?*

KD The world is not going to look like it did before all this. It is possible that we lived through the 'good old days' and did not realize it. We probably did not realize it because it wasn't good for everyone and it wasn't perfect even for those for whom it was good, but there's a non-zero chance that it was better than what lies ahead. Theatres are going to be different. There may not be as much opportunity to make even as decent a living/life out of the arts as there once was. Maybe that is a good thing! Maybe we find new ways to make our art, to divorce it from the profit-driven philosophy that has impacted so much of what we call 'the American theatre'. This may be the time to make new things – new institutions, new art forms. There may be spaces available in big cities for once. There may be openings at large theatre companies or, better yet, ways to repurpose their spaces to better serve more communities. I think working local is the next big thing: make art for the people around you, share it with them, make it with them. That kind of work often turns out deeper and truer anyway. If you are good with the internet, you may find digital ways to take that local art and spread it globally.

CS   *What are your hopes and dreams for theatre's future?*

KD   Going local. Finding room for a multiplicity of voices. Celebrating folks of different identities not only for those identities but realizing that having a different story to tell is as important as telling the same story 'well'. Listening to what people today are into, not just adhering blindly to old ideas of what 'theatre' is. Louder plays. Messier plays. Work that matters to the people making and the people watching it. More honesty from producers and institutions. Less cowardice. I try to stay positive and lift folks up, but I hope some 'leaders' fall and fall hard.

CS   *At a time of global collective trauma, what are theatre's healing properties, if any?*

KD   I hope that the act of making the art is healing. I talk to my students about 'the churn', that thing that's living in your heart that you can't stop thinking about, the thing about your identity or your soul or this world that you're nonstop turning over and over in your brain, the big issue or idea or problem that follows you around all day every day. That is the thing I want them to write about, because it is messy, and it is unsolved, and it is rich and full and fertile. If they investigate that, their work feels true and unique. It becomes your therapy, and then you work on it with others – actors and directors and designers – and you process together, and you find community and hopefully, you heal. I am not a big believer in setting healing as a primary goal or even the stated subject of the piece. I think the whole thing – the job of writing, of making art – is a quest for finding yourself and settling yourself down. We have got to go into the work, and we have got to go into the community.

Doubling back: the people who I want to see fall are the ones who preach community, who preach a dedication to each other in the process of creation, and then sell that out for ticket sales and other financial concerns. I get it. You run a theatre, you have fiduciary responsibility to make money and keep the lights on. But the decisions that are made in the name of 'business' in the theatre world are almost invariably *awful* business decisions and *awful* artistic decisions, and they often come at the expense of the building of community, which is really the only thing that matters in all this.

Maybe we need to bring back the rep company? Maybe we need to build deeper relationships with audiences in real, palpable ways?

CS   *What are you working on currently?*

KD   The theatre industry feels unloving as a partner. It moves too slowly and too unresponsively. Now that the theatres are closed, it may be time to take most of this stuff into different media and seize the means of production on my own. I am not sure I can trust this business with my best stuff anymore.

Maybe I keep making certain things for the theatre in new ways. Musicals seem to still be worth shooting for – something about the overtly commercial nature of that world makes the heartbreak a little less heartbreaking. Maybe my plays become faster and messier and more *I-don't-give-a-fuck*, which honestly is the attitude that has produced my best work. And maybe we give the plays away. I tried this a few years ago, offering productions of *Chad Deity* for free to theatre companies that also produced plays by Matt Barbot and Monet Hurst-Mendoza. Maybe I follow playwright Chuck Mee's example more than anything. Maybe plays become gifts.

CS   *What are your thoughts on the art, given the volatile state of the country?*

KD   We are in bad shape. Things are going to get so much worse before they get better. As cold as this may sound, I believe the bad stuff has not happened yet. There is no good outcome to the election this year. Violence is on its way. Cities and states are in huge financial trouble. Whole industries (including ours!) will not recover for a generation. Is theatre the way out of all/any of this? I am not sure it is.

Part of what I am grappling with is the idea that we need more playwrights who are not *only* playwrights. I make my living through writing (and writing-adjacent work), and I have for my whole adult life! Still, I dream of folks who fight the good fight by day and develop art by night. Plays by nurses! Plays by schoolteachers! Plays by soldiers and bankers and business owners and politicians! I know some of those sound like stranger bedfellows than others, but that's kind of the point. How do we break down the silos? How do we put 'artists' back in touch with 'real folks' and show that, hey, artists are real folks too and real folks are artists too? The biggest, scariest thing I see in the United States today is division. Theatre is about collaboration. How do we bring our skills to bear to help get over the divides?

Common ground is 100 per cent what we need. I do not have a lot of hope right now because I do not feel like the loudest voices have interest in finding/creating common ground with the other loudest voices. We've got to find ways to support folks doing their own things – the things they need to find their voices, to improve their lives, to seek out stability, to feed their families – while understanding that we've got tons of common cause that we need to support. There were lots of stories about the profound loneliness of this generation of Americans, even before the pandemic. There is a weird interconnectedness and ease of finding things you want that paradoxically are leaving young people (but not just young people) cut off and alone. Theoretically, theatre is a space to overcome that! But theatre is siloed like everything else. We are making shows for people who like theatre, who increasingly are people who *do* theatre, who are people who do not have money to *pay* for theatre, which is an unsustainable business plan. And the theatres that do find audiences to pay hundreds of dollars for tickets are catering to the wealthy, which is not a recipe for great art or building of community.

Soraya Nadia McDonald

Soraya Nadia McDonald is an American writer and culture critic. She was previously a reporter at *The Washington Post* and has been the culture critic for *The Undefeated*, ESPN's arts and culture desk, since 2016. She was a finalist for the 2020 Pulitzer Prize for criticism. This interview was conducted on Zoom on 4 December 2020.

CS *How has lockdown been for you?*

SND It's been weird in part because I did not realize how much I missed live theatre and it's not just like because I enjoy it but also because it gets me out of my house. The *Undefeated*'s offices are in DC and I live in Brooklyn. So, I normally spend my days at home working. I spent the first weeks of lockdown looking at my schedule from last year and wondering how in the world I got anything done. I was seeing five to six shows a week then. I also realized that much of my social life revolved around theatre-going. Seeing shows was also how I saw friends and hung out after and so forth. I took it granted. The beauty of having meandering conversations and going to unexpected places and passing time allows for a different kind of thinking and approach to life and sparks creativity in a very different way. It also affects my writing, because often writing reviews also come from drawing upon conversations I have had with friends about the work. Now, all that is gone. And it's just me. It's very lonely.

I know I'm very lucky compared to most people. I have a home that's safe and comforting. I'm not worried about keeping a roof over my head or feeding myself. Across the street from me is a school that is open to give out like free meals every day. So, I have felt guilty for feeling bad about my loneliness because it feels like such a trivial problem compared to what others are going through.

Most people in the arts sector have lost their livelihoods overnight and have no idea when those jobs or work opportunities are going to return. There hasn't been relief for the arts sector at all. It's been frustrating. Nobody's talking about the arts on the floor of the House or Senate as if the arts are not vital to the economy. Right now, I am working on a story about the Federal Theatre Project and what a new FTP would look like and why do we need it. They could be such a vast array of opportunities if money were reinvested in public education and arts education, for example. Many brilliant artists like Chadwick Boseman supplemented their income as actors by teaching, and that's really important because teaching artists become ambassadors for the art form. Also, there needs to be a sense of ownership for people who historically have felt shut out and have been disenfranchised from the arts sector. I live a block away from an amphitheatre in a public park that would be a perfect place for community to come together to see a show but also simply be together grilling and cooking. I remember when I was growing up that my parents would take me to an event at Meredith College for the Fourth of July and the Boston Pops would play and people from all walks of life would sit outside with their picnic blankets and spend time together. That's what I think about when I think about a new deal for the arts – spaces where people can gather for free and share through art.

The arts need to find different funders as well rather than relying on a small group of extremely wealthy benefactors who often have dubious sources for their wealth. The Sackler Gallery in DC, for instance, is beautiful but it is basically being funded by the opioid epidemic. Surely there is another way like that we can do this that isn't morally disgusting. I would like to see funding Solutions that are more egalitarian as well.

CS   *The field is undergoing much change right now, but I worry that as we move through the pandemic, it may become an even more siloed rather than more equitable and open.*

SND   I was filing a story for *National Geographic* early during lockdown and comedian Wyatt Cenac said a similar thing: that he felt that when the arts sector comes out of this it will be even more unequal than before. I am not sure. With subscription streaming services like Disney Plus and HBO Max, audiences are getting lots of content for far less price than, say, going to a movie and buying a movie ticket and snacks for their whole family. They can see *Hamilton* for far less than the cost of a Broadway ticket. For minority communities especially these services are cost-effective forms of entertainment. Ironically, I don't know anybody in the arts that can afford to have five or six subscription services. I think a bigger factor in terms of the field's recovery is how to make space for arts education because teaching children how to watch and think about art is an important tool of critical thinking instead of training them to be passive consumers.

CS *What are your hopes and dreams for the future of the field?*

SND I wish we think more about making it easier for people to see and access things whether the work is online or in a live venue. When I was growing up in North Carolina, Public Television was my gateway to the arts and being able to see recorded performances. That's how I saw Audra McDonald and so many more artists! I want audiences to be able to access works from companies all across the United States and not just New York City. Also, live spaces need be made fully accessible for disabled people as opposed to thinking of them as an afterthought. Jeremy O. Harris as a producer of Fake Friends' *Circle Jerk* (2020) had sliding scale tickets. Why can't everyone do this? I also hope that theatre companies engaged more with theatre students at historically Black colleges instead of interfacing only with theatre programs at Yale, NYU and Juilliard. Theatre has been too niche in its ways of operations. It needs people who are passionate about it and are better evangelists for the performing arts. Everything takes time. Organizing voters in Georgia to produce the results in 2020 did not happen overnight. Black women had to work for years to make it happen. I think it's imperative as well for arts organizations to think beyond the arts in order to connect with their communities, forming coalitions with institutions that also serve communities in different ways around issues of sustainability and resiliency, for instance. Banding together with non-arts orgs can yield amazing results and give audiences/ community members a feeling of ownership about organizations dedicated to their well-being and basic needs, rather than just being seen as ticket buyers.

CS *How to strengthen the field of arts criticism and its training?*

SND This comes down to the way newsrooms have been structured for a really long time. The pathways for critics have never been smooth. Unless you go to a college where there's a criticism program, you basically have to learn on the job. News orgs haven't done a very good job of surveying or reporting on minority communities which leads to a depletion in the field and a crisis of credibility for reporters trying to make their way. Journalism is supposed to be a public service, but most communities are not being served. They are not represented. There are also major financial pressures on news orgs because there are fewer and fewer resources. After the market crash of 2008, there were massive layoffs and buyouts that disproportionately affected minority journalists and they were sort of the first ones sacrificed and pushed out the door, which makes the problem even worse, because the population of folks that remain is so narrow that there's no room for critics of colour to thrive. Training is virtually non-existent. The National Critics Institute at the O'Neill is one of the few places, and it is free, thankfully. I would like to see an overhaul of how newsrooms understand their place within communities so that you have folks that are invested in the places where they live and also consider themselves to be part of those places. You cannot suspend your race, for instance, and leave it outside the newsroom when you walk in. Being cognizant of the role you play within your local community and in the newsroom is important for the sustainability of journalism.

Gregory Mozgala

Gregory Mozgala is an American actor and artistic director of the Apothetae, a theatre company, arts incubator and service organization founded in 2012 devoted to producing works that explore and illuminate the 'Disabled Experience'. This interview was conducted over email on 29 October 2020.

CS *How has lockdown been for you?*

GM The first few weeks were filled with great stress and anxiety. I was actually in rehearsals for a show at a regional theatre in the Washington, DC area, and the production got cancelled/postponed at the end of the second week of rehearsals. I raced back home on a bus and made it back to New York City a few days before the lockdown orders went into place. My wife was teaching her first year at La Guardia High School for the Performing Arts. Schools were scheduled to close, and we had no childcare lined up for our son. Thankfully, I have a day job that is simpatico with my lifestyle as an actor; a disaster restoration company classified as an 'essential business'. So, I had a job to return to – one that was flexible and would let me work from home and provide for childcare – as all teaching for NYC schools transitioned to remote learning.

I had a year's worth of acting work lined up, something it has taken me two decades of working professionally to achieve, and a Theatre for Young Audiences (TYA) play I had co-written was in production with La Jolla Playhouse. As the quarantine stretched on longer and longer, and as the virus continued to spread, the phone calls from Artistic Directors, and so on, which had a tone of hopeful optimism about being back in the rehearsal room or the theatre soon stopped all together. Theatre stopped all together.

For the first few months, I was extremely happy to have the time with my wife and son. As primary caregiver, I enjoyed daily trips to city parks and a quieter, slower-paced version of the city I called home. I started using a stationary bike for the first time with regularity to keep fit. I realized that if I bike backwards the neurological triggers associated with my cerebral palsy that regularly brutalize my body with spasms and incredible amounts of tension are greatly reduced by this non-habitual approach. I encourage everyone to try to this.

I also devoured the news during this time. I called my elected officials almost every day, sometimes multiple times a day, at all hours of the day. Their offices were closed but they were still taking messages from constituents, and I found leaving a sixty- to ninety-second voicemail expressing my unadulterated opinion a much-needed release and extremely cathartic.

September seemed to bring with it a 'back to school' mentality and a desire for a return to normalcy. Ultimately, I don't think this is helpful. Nothing about this is normal. I find that I am not as emotionally or psychologically prepared for the next six months of these active measures. I am extremely frustrated by what appears to be a colossal failure of leadership from our elected leaders and decision makers and power brokers in the Cultural Sector on a local, state and national level. Nearly eight months later it's abundantly clear: There is no guidance. We are rudderless. There appears to be no end in sight. This is unacceptable. We can't go on. We must go on.

CS   *What are your hopes and dreams for theatre's future?*

GM   There is a lot of discussion online and in disability circles about how everyone to some extent these days is having a 'Disabled Experience'. So many of the adaptations the majority of people have made as a result of the pandemic (Zoom, working from home, etc.) are things the deaf/disabled communities have been asking for, for years now. As performances transitioned to Zoom and other platforms, geographical and structural barriers were removed. I find this heartening. The work of groups and initiatives like We See You W.A.T. and AAPAC NYC are essential to calling out and correcting structural inequities in the industry. If 'experience is what you get when you don't get what you want', then I have that in spades. That is the nature of this business. However, I also believe in hope over experience. My hope is that the lessons learned during this time will carry through to when things return to a sense of normality and that the 'new normal' will be more reflective and inclusive of everyone regardless of race, colour, creed, background and ability.

CS   *During a time of global collective trauma, what are theatre's healing properties, if any?*

GM For an industry and profession that professes to do so much good for society it has also inflicted much harm on historically marginalized communities. Change is needed and I believe it is coming.

Last year (2019) I was nominated for a Drama League Award for my performance in *Teenage Dick* by Michael Lew. The awards ceremony takes place in a hotel ballroom where all the nominees sit on a tiered dais and awkwardly eat chicken in front of the assembled audience. Name celebrities are on the top level and everyone else is on the lower tiers in descending order based on notoriety, etc. On the top level were stars like John Lithgow, Bryan Cranston and Laurie Metcalf. The only person of colour was Andre De Shields (*Hadestown*). On the next level down, the only person of colour was B. D. Wong (*The Great Leap*), but all the remaining rows showed an increasing level of diversity encompassing age, race, gender, sexual orientation and ability. The incoming cohort of Drama League Directing fellows was also one of the most diverse I have ever seen. This stuck me as illustrative of the change foreshadowed by those in attendance being honoured at the event. I could literally see and envision the day when the people on the bottom row would be at the top level, and how the paradigm was shifting. Those participating and in control of the narratives told on our stages would no longer be predominantly white, cis, straight men.

CS *Can you talk about your work currently as an actor and artistic director?*

GM My background is as an actor and I have become an Artistic Director and Arts Administrator out of some combination of accident and necessity. People here in the states love to talk about 'Accessibility'. For most people this means installing ramps. I am working to shift the focus towards *artistry*. In my experience programmatic accessibility (the creation and production of work and content) is as important – if not more so – than structural access.

Any progress that I have seen in my own career and any change I have been fortunate enough to precipitate in the field has come because I have had plays to be in or created projects that can support the casting and employment of Deaf/Disabled theatre professionals. Talk is in fact cheap; I am much more interested in Action. It may sound reductive, but just make work. Then make some more.

CS *What are ways to parse through these times as artists to perhaps address the volatile state the United States is in?*

GM   There's a line in the last scene of the Pulitzer Prize-winning play *The Cost of Living* (2016) by Martyna Majok that I keep thinking about and is resonating with me more than ever these days, 'So, we're neighbors.'
We are suffering from a deficit of decency, dignity and empathy. To speak to the political moment, in a Republic empathy is essential because a Republic runs on our seeing each other not as adversaries but as neighbours. That is a core element to how not only Theatre, but America, has survived and thrived.

CS *The disability arts movement and its people have been triply hard by the fallout of the arts sector due to Covid-19 and, in many ways, are less visible voices in the field. Are there ways through this?*

GM   Making connections in key. Since 2015, I have helped organize five national convenings to discuss issues at the Nexus of Disability and Theatre. I have launched the first ever national playwrighting fellowship for Deaf/Disabled playwrights and have helped develop acting training programs specifically tailored to Deaf/Disabled actors. Since 2017 I have been directly involved in three new plays that deal directly with the 'Disabled Experience': *Cost of Living* (Williamstown Theatre Festival/Manhattan Theatre Club), *Teenage Dick* (The Public), Emily Driver's *Great Race Through Time & Space* (La Jolla Playhouse). I may be an 'army of one' but I haven't done this alone. We live in an age of global networks; we should be creating locally but sharing on a bigger scale. By doing so our art becomes a vehicle for social change by challenging perceived perceptions of our cultural landscape, and by more accurately reflecting our day-to-day reality on the stage; one where people with disabilities not only participate but also thrive.

CS *In what ways do you instigate joy in your work processes?*

GM   Theatre has changed my life for the better. That's not hyperbole. I believe in the transformative power of theatre. Through the collaborative experience of the artistic process, I believe the 'Disabled Experience' can be more sincerely and accurately reflected on stage, that new communities can be forged, perceptions changed and barriers to understanding and empathy can be shattered. Conversely, I also find myself constantly repeating something an actor friend of mine told me years ago about the craft which we love so much: 'Theatre is a small group of people trying to keep a larger group of people from coughing.' This helps keep things in perspective for me. It reminds me to proceed, in all things, with a sense of humbleness and gratitude.

Kaite O'Reilly

Kaite O'Reilly is a UK-based playwright and screenwriter of Irish descent. She works extensively with disability arts and culture and wrote the ground-breaking play *peeling* for Graeae Theatre in 2002.

CS *How has lockdown been for you?*

KOR Lockdown has been a time of loss – not just of liberty and the freedom to roam, or the loss of work, livelihood and opportunities – it has been the loss of that life-affirming exchange of energies in a rehearsal room or theatre. It has been a time of solitary confinement, so many of us stripped of the simple essential of being in a real space in real time where another heart beats with our own.

Lockdown has brought actual physical loss with the death of loved ones, collaborators and allies. Within the UK's disabled peoples' movement and disability arts and culture we have lost many of our own – Chris Ledger, Sian Vasey, David Toole and Geof Armstrong to name just a few. Covid-19 has been a brutal lesson in inequalities. Disabled people or those problematically described as having 'underlying health conditions' have been disproportionately affected by the pandemic. According to the UK's Office for National Statistics, 59 per cent of all deaths involving Covid-19 from 2 March to 14 July 2020 were of disabled people; yet according to the 2011 Census, only 16 per cent of the population have disabilities.

Lockdown brought problematic labels of us being 'vulnerable' and needing to 'shield'. With a faulty track and trace system and a vaccination still months in the future, many began to question whether we would be 'left behind', expected to self-isolate as the rest of the country seemingly returned to so-called 'normality'. As life and work moved increasingly online, this offered the opportunity for connection and activism with new disabled-led campaigns like Wales-based #NiChawnEinDileu – 'we shall not be erased' – #ymaohyd – 'we are still here' – and UK-wide

#WeShallNotBeRemoved – a forum to advocate, to campaign, amplify and support Deaf, neurodivergent and disabled creative practitioners and organizations through and after Covid-19.

Moving online has had unexpected benefits – a place where we can meet, support, campaign, skill-share, grieve, have virtual speakeasies and cocktail hours without too much concern about whether we'll physically be able to get into the venue. Although the technology is not always accessible and problems such as 'Zoom fatigue' have emerged, we have been flexible and creative in our willingness to adapt and change. I have attended livestreamed play readings and livestreamed funerals. My year of international projects and theatre productions in Berlin, Cork, Singapore, the United States, Spain and India may have been cancelled, but I have connected more with allies and comrades through this loving, supportive network. We are all facing restrictions, bereavements and hardships. We are all doing the best we can to not just survive but thrive.

CS   *What are your hopes and dreams for theatre's future?*

KOR   I dream of an arts/cultural sector that does not assume one audience, but audience(s) that are diverse and multiple, using many modes of communication to access the work. I hope that the aesthetics of access will be at the heart of the creative process from its conception, and not scaffolded on at the end, as an 'add-on' for a specific stratum of the audience, identified by impairment ('touch tour and audio description for the visually impaired'). This is dehumanizing. I want a holistic experience in our theatres, where human variety is not just expected and respected but celebrated. By changing the stories, we tell, by whom, and how, by changing the characters we create and their outcomes, by expanding the creative use of the theatre languages at play, we change not just the processes, product, dramaturgy and the buildings, but theatre itself.

CS   *Can you talk about your work currently as an activist and playwright?*

KOR   Many years ago I decided to follow Gandhi's advice and be the change I wanted to see. For decades I have been critical of what I called 'cripping up' – non-disabled or hearing actors impersonating disabled or Deaf characters ('Cripping-up is the twenty-first century's answer to "Blacking-up"', one of my actor-characters says in my 2002 play, *peeling*). I have written extensively about systemic ableism not just in our social structures, but the ingrained narratives, assumptions and 'truths' in Western culture regarding the Deaf or disabled 'other'. Almost twenty years ago, I chose to 'answer back' to problematic representations and started creating performance texts specifically for Deaf and disabled actors informed by lived experience and the social model, which sees disability as a social construct – it is the physical and attitudinal barriers which are disabling, not the body. Informed by conversations with over 100 people across the world, I have written fictional plays and monologues published as *Atypical Plays for Atypical Actors* and *The 'd' Monologues* – the 'd' denoting disability, Deaf, diversity, deviance, deliciousness and other delightfully distinct differences. Until we arrive on an equal playing field, I will use the small power I have as a playwright to write engaged, sexy characters who are not identified by diagnosis or 'fault' but are instead the protagonist of their lives. I will refuse to give the rights to these specific plays to those who wish to 'crip up' rather than cast inclusively Deaf and disabled actors.

In the past years I have offered alternative feminist crip alternatives to problematic narratives and characters like Shakespeare's *Richard III* – *richard iii redux OR Sara Beer Is/Not Richard III* (2018–present), co-written with Phillip Zarrilli. I recently reworked Strindberg's *Miss Julie* for Theatr Clwyd, exploring the social Darwinism at the heart of the text through disabled characters. During lockdown performances have increasingly gone online and disabled and Deaf-led productions of my often-radical 'crip' work have recently been streamed in China and Korea for disability arts festivals and provoking discussion. I have been giving talks for international conferences and festivals on the history of the disabled peoples' movement and emergence of disability culture (*Nothing About Us Without Us*) and leading pedagogical projects online involving Disability Equality Training and 'creative enabling'. Also, in defiance of Brexit, I'm working with Disability Arts Cymru as part of the European Culture of Solidarity – a pan-European series of talks, provocations and events online, the material of which will inspire disabled artists and lead to an online gallery of disability art.

Apart from my obvious political and cultural disability arts/activist practice, I am trying to take my 'crip' perspective and integrated aesthetics of access to so-called mainstream theatres and platforms. This is not distinctly disability arts and culture, but it is disabled-led, using the aesthetics of access and 'alternative dramaturgies informed by a Deaf and disability perspective'. Before lockdown (2 March 2020) I wrote and, with Phillip Zarrilli, co-directed *The Beauty Parade* – a mainstream commercially successful story of female spies – but presented in spoken, sung, projected, signed, musical and visual languages, with creative captioning incorporated into the scenography.

For a long time, disability has been considered worthy or educational, belonging to the third sector rather than the main house. In my work, wherever possible, I try to bring inclusion to the mainstream – casting performers and creating characters who just happen to be disabled or Deaf, rather than mounting the narrative about problematic stories of diagnosis or 'overcoming' a condition. I want to incorporate audio description, sign or visual language and creative captioning into the aesthetic texture and material of the performance for all, and to celebrate and welcome all the possibilities of human variation.

CS *What advice do you have for people entering the field right now?*

KOR Have hope.
Be resilient.
Learn stillness and patience.
Dream.
Practice radical self-care.
Breathe. Breathe again.
Learn moving meditations like yoga or tai chi which will help calm anxious nervous systems. You will be anxious. We are all anxious. It makes perfect sense to be anxious. We are in a time of plague, of flood, of war and pestilence – the world is on fire – work to counter the 'fight or flight' induced by elevated cortisol levels. Know that the panic is just a chemical reaction. It will end. Everything, eventually, will end. Try to smile and be present and put some tender playfulness in the world through random acts of kindness.
Keep dreaming.
Be ambitious.
Ask yourself what your goals are and where you would like to be in five years' time. Be precise. Once articulated, start exploring strategies to get yourself there. Skill yourself up. Identify those

whose work you admire and find those who love what you do, then try to collaborate. Be selective. Do not accept everything you are offered because you think you *should* or *must*. Find those who 'get' you and your work. Find your tribe. Find ways to exchange and nourish yourself. Remuneration can take many forms.

Fill in application forms with truth, integrity and passion. It is a skill. It can be learnt. Learn it (I did through practice).

Apply for everything going, especially opportunities that make you tingle. Work against imposter syndrome. Be a contender, throw your hat into the ring. Say yes, yes, YES to offers but no no NO to anything or anyone who makes you feel uneasy, inferior or stupid, or who aggrandizes themselves at the expense of others.

Some of my worst experiences have given me the largest lessons. Try to learn the lessons the first time and not have to repeat them.

Embrace challenges. Creativity comes from problem solving.

Remember: living well is the best revenge.

Taylor Reynolds

Taylor Reynolds is an American theatre director and on the producing team of the Harlem-based theatre company The Movement. This interview was conducted over email on 20 October 2020.

CS *How has lockdown been for you?*

TR The lockdown has been up and down for me. I avoided working too much for the first two months because I was trying to make sure that I was okay as a person first, and that's also what we did at the Movement Theater Company, where I am one of the Producing Artistic leaders. Around April and May I started getting opportunities to work on small projects with playwrights, but I loved, and they were shorter projects that required last time commitment. I have been dealing a lot with my anxiety and my fears around mortality and death and my fears about being in a collapsing democracy. That is where most of my energy has gone.

CS *What advice do you have for people entering the field right now?*

TR The advice I have for people in the field right now is to join in digital theatre if you want. I have found both working on digital content and experiencing digital content that there are still moments for connection, there are still moments to be surprised, to feel the power of 'live' performance. But if it does not feel right to you, then do not feel like you must be pressured to participate. Live theatre will return, at some point, in some new and more radicalized form and be ready to know what your values are as an artist, how are you can name them clearly in the rehearsal room/contract negotiation/whatever.

CS *What are the hopes and dreams you have for the field?*

TR   The dream that I have is that we operate more collaboratively, more collectively, and that they are to receive national funding. I have seen a lot of tweets saying that people are consuming art through Netflix, Hulu and through live streaming and not necessarily acknowledging the work of the artist and the importance of the artists who are creating that work. I hope that in this time and past this time in the future that the work that we do as creators, as generators, as artists are recognized and uplifted just as much as any other essential practice.

CS   *During a time of global collective trauma, what are theatre's healing properties, if any? And how can the industry rebuild and reform itself from long-standing systemic racism and fiscal inequities?*

TR   I have always been drawn to working in theatre because it is a space to process, share and examine trauma. It has been said that theatre as a medium has been dying for years, but it is not dead yet. If something is in bad shape, trauma must occur for it to pull through and reformed into something more sustainable. The art of theatre locates its healing powers in every artist's decision to create, to show up and try again. I have been finding it incredibly difficult to feel inspiration and excitement about the projects I have been working on during the pandemic even though they are projects I love and wanted to work on. I have just been holding onto so much grief and exhaustion. But the decision to show up to Zoom rehearsals, the boldness to make something badass on a platform that was not designed for creativity, those are steps and decisions that will help us keep 'theatre' alive. What will take years to recover is the continuous abuse and neglect communities that are not based in white supremacy must face. White supremacy runs through every thread and foundation of every theatre that is a PWI and the white leaders at these institutions have yet to even really begin to account for the trauma they have caused, are causing and will cause in the future.

Our mission at The Movement Theatre Company is to create an artistic social movement by developing and producing new work by artists of colour. Our work engages audiences in a rich theatrical dialogue, enlightens communities to the important issues affecting our world and empowers artists to celebrate the many sides of their unique voice. We are small and mighty – there are five of us who run the company non-hierarchically, which means we all share the title of Producing Artistic Leader. Equal artistic and administrative weight! Our operating model works well for us because we're based in Harlem, but we don't have our own space, which gives us a lot of flexibility to partner with Harlem organizations and other theatre companies in New York and beyond to really intertwine our workshops and productions and the spaces that fit them best. We view artistic leadership roles as guides for our artists depending on their needs. Between the five of us and our extended community of associates and collaborators, we have a bounty of resources to support the herculean works we produce. We have produced mostly in New York, but two of our productions (*Hope Speaks* and Aleshea Harris's 2017 piece *What to Send Up When It Goes Down*) have toured to theatres and colleges across the east coast.

When theatres shut down in March, we were on track to bring our production of *What to Send Up When It Goes Down*, directed by Whitney White, to Playwrights Horizons Theatre in New York City in June 2020. *What to Send Up ...* provided an essential space for Black people to process trauma and pain caused by the loss of Black life due to racialized violence. The global uprising around racial injustice that occurred shortly after the shutdown began fuelled us to continue the work this play started. We pivoted to create digital spaces of joy, release and healing, and gave artists the opportunity to develop work on digital platforms. We hosted ZOOM DANCE PARTIES for our community to reconnect and feel the joy of being alive in a time of so much turmoil. When the global uprisings peaked, we paired with Aleshea and Whitney to create RESILIENCE, a digital initiative consisting of an online love letter drive called #LoveLetterstoBlackPeople and a video entitled soft light, a meditation on the joys and challenges of Black remembrance. Our artists spoke to the lack of emergency funding for designers. We addressed this through our digital content series 1MOVE: DES19NED BY, commissioning thirty designers to act as lead artists, creating digital content in response to the issues affecting their world, namely anti-Blackness, global uprisings and Covid-19.

CS *The United States is in an especially fraught place socio-politically: deeply divided on multiple levels and suffering from a* *growing white nationalist terrorist movement. What are ways to parse through these times, and perhaps offer some light?*

TR I do not have much of a positive or hopeful outlook to offer right now. There is the desire to press on and create even in the darkest of times, but my creative capacity often feels like a third of what it once was. As an artist and activist, sometimes I try to separate the two because of my emotional needs. My art needs to be a safe space and sometimes that means limiting the amount of 'real-world' issues that make their way into whatever I am working on. It is not the best model by far, but on a day-to-day basis, it helps to keep me on track about what I need to accomplish. White artists need to understand that white supremacy is a white people issue. Racism is a white people issue. Climate change and capitalism are white people issues. The people who benefit most from oppressive structures and whose ancestors created them need to do the hard work to tear them down. BIPOC artists and humans should not have to do the work of rooting out our own internal oppressions and must guide white people through as well.

CS *In what ways do you instigate joy in your work processes?*

TR Whenever possible, I carve out space at the beginning of each rehearsal/meeting/etc. for everyone to be able to check in and touch base about where we all are mentally/physically/emotionally. I have heard theatre practitioners say before 'Leave everything outside the door and be ready to work', which does not work for me at all. Everything that happens to me in a day, everything I am holding onto comes with me into whatever space I am in. I try not to let it affect the work as much as possible, but if I'm feeling anxious or overworked, it helps me exist in the present more if everyone has an understanding of where I am. By opening space to voice how we are all really doing and what is going on with us as humans, it opens space for freedom and play in the work, which ideally leads to joy. Very simply, I will sometimes hold one-minute dance parties (participation is optional), especially if the energy needs to be pepped up or if we have had a particularly difficult conversation. In thinking about current and potential future projects, I am focusing more on projects that give the people of colour in the plays the chance to experience a wide range of emotions, whether the inciting incident is based in trauma or not. Inhabiting a well-rounded character gives such joy because it is often work that is reserved for white characters to experience. At The Movement, we encourage our artists to bring us their most herculean ideas, the projects that are 'difficult' to produce/develop. Feeling artists of colour be freer in a collaborative group primarily made up of people of colour (from artistic leadership to interns) gives everyone involved space to relax and express joy however they want.

Roy Williams

Roy Williams is a Black British playwright. His play *Death of England: Delroy* was the first play to open on the Olivier stage of the National Theatre in London after the end of the first lockdown in autumn 2020. This interview was conducted over Zoom on 3 December 2020.

CS *How has lockdown been for you?*

RW I should disclose that not long after the first lockdown I was stricken with the virus, which took me out of action for about two weeks. I didn't do any writing. I wasn't physically and mentally able to. But in terms of to be more elaborate with your question, lockdown was strange, because although people say that for writers lockdown is not all that different from how we usually go about our days (since so much of our work occurs in isolation), the fact of being in actual lockdown made me realize the little things I simply had taken for granted like being able to go out for a walk and go to a coffee shop, or have a drink in a pub with friends. Suddenly not being entirely in control of one's actions was immensely difficult. As writers, we are stimulated and inspired by other people and what's happening in the world. Every time I turned on the news, it was Covid-19 all the time. And I get it. It's a massive global event. But what's the story? Where's the interaction? Where's the human nature? It's the incidental things in life that often inspire storytelling.

When Dominic Cummings, chief adviser to the Prime Minister of the UK, was caught breaking lockdown rules, suddenly there was an opening into a story within the world of the Covid-19 story – the one of privilege looking after their own. The government were basically going to bend over backwards to protect this guy. Well, that's something we can as a nation talk about and pull apart and dissect.

Then months later the murder of George Floyd occurred, and it too was something else people could talk about and debate. There were marches worldwide. It was inspiring, despite the awfulness of the event that prompted the marches. I felt that – and still do – the galvanizing protests fired me up again as a writer and reminded me that we should be poised and ready whenever something happens to be in a position to respond and reflect.

CS   *Is that how the 846 project came to be?*

RW   Yes. I made myself watch the video of Floyd's murder. All eight minutes and forty-six seconds that Chauvin's knee was on his neck. It was awful to watch but I felt it was also necessary to witness it. Let's face it. There have been many unjust, tragic deaths of Black people especially at the hands of police. In some ways we have become used to the stories. But the thing is, we should not be used to them. The deaths, the injustices, should be shocking. I told myself: No, no Roy, you cannot normalize this. It was shocking and it's okay for us to be shocked and to respond accordingly. We should never ever get used to that. This happens in the UK too. Not only in the United States. What separates our police from yours is that ours don't carry guns. But the antagonism between authority and individuals who are Black is exactly the same as in the United States.

So, I wanted to respond. Somehow. I belong to a writers' group of Black and Asian British writers on Facebook and I asked them if there was any interest in writing five- to ten-minute pieces, rapid response theatre, for a project called *846*. The only stipulation was that the writers respond to the sentence 'What does 846 mean to you?'

I then approached Nadia Falls at Theatre Royal Stratford East, once everyone had written their pieces, and she said she would put them in a podcast and release it on their website. So, June 2020, we were writing and recording and in July the podcasts went live. Fourteen writers responding to what 846 meant to us. The project then had a bit further life with the Docklands Festival where some of the pieces were performed outdoors, live.

CS   *You were working on* Death of England: Delroy *at the same time?*

RW I was multitasking. Clint Dyer was my co-writer and director. We had been commissioned by the National to make the piece after the success of the first play, *Death of England*. So, we had been working for several months already on the Delroy story when lockdown hit. That said, the murder of George Floyd did hit a nerve and resonated with themes and concerns of our piece. In some ways it made us feel that we were striking a chord.

CS *I saw the piece on 27 November 2020 when it was streamed on YouTube from National Theatre Live. Tremendous work. But bittersweet experience. Because after two weeks of previews you opened and had to close on same day, 4 November 2020, because the UK went into a second lockdown.*

RW It hadn't been an easy rehearsal period either because the original actor Giles Terera had to leave after four weeks' rehearsals, because he had appendicitis and required emergency surgery. So, his understudy Michael Balogun stepped in on very short notice. But yes, the show was captured on film and the National has committed to bringing it back in spring of 2021.

CS *What are your hopes and dreams for theatre's future?*

RW In terms of audiences, it's hard to predict how many people will want to come back to live theatre. I think there will always be a hunger for it, but the make-up of the audience is going to change when we are on the other side of this, which could be in itself a good thing. I'm hoping theatre here and the people that run it reflect on what's happening in this moment and have broadened their minds. What they think the audience wants and what the audience wants, and needs are different things. There are stories that need to be told. We need to change. To think that after Covid time, things will be the same is simply not true. I want to see range. Everyone's got a story.

I really do want to see more inclusivity and diversity. I don't really care how politically correct that makes me sound. I really don't give a toss. That's what I want. That's what I want to see in theatre. I want to see a full range. I want to see more organizations and more people in power ceding some of their power. I want to see different worlds reflected on stage.

CS *In the UK there seems to be more support for the arts than in the United States.*

RW Lots of theatres are closing. It's worse than it looks. The big Culture Recovery Fund of $2 billion was announced but the monies have not been distributed. So, theatres are scrambling and barely hanging on. The Arts Council, which gets their money from the Department of Culture, Sport and Media, decides who gets what, and each year, theatres have gotten less and less. Although we always give back to the economy. But getting less has been partly driven by austerity measures. But Brexit is also setting in soon. Times are uncertain, and not just because of Covid. I don't think the country realizes yet how devastating Brexit is going to be once it kicks in next year.

When the first *Death of England* opened on 31 January 2020, it was on the same night as the announcement that we'd be leaving the EU, and I remember walking along the South Bank and on the marquee, in lights, were the words 'Death of England'. And it felt eerie.

Because once Brexit kicks in, no one is going to care about the arts. Artists will still punch above their weight and shout, but many people won't give a damn and it's going to be a battle. Listen, even one of our politicians said not long ago about the arts that 'those fucking ballerinas can get to the back of the queue'. That's how they think about the arts. When you hear shit like that, it makes me realize just how much of a fight we have in front of us.

CS *Yet, you remain hopeful somehow and/or inspired to do your work?*

RW Well, the National has had a lot of faith in me. I have a good relationship with them. I feel lucky. They believed in *Death of England* and asked for the second play and are now asking for a third. So, eventually there will be a trilogy. Can you imagine people coming in for a day of theatre to see all three? It gives me hope that there are theatres that believe in playwrights and are supporting them.

CS *You're not sceptical about these times of change maybe not yielding change?*

RW   There's always that fear. If Trump had won, I think I would be more scared. I mean, I know we're British and what happens in the United States shouldn't affect us but there's that old saying 'if America sneezes Britain gets a cold', so, who is in the White House does matter. But his leaving is reason for celebration. That said, I know that Brexit will be the one that puts us over the edge, which is why I think we need artists more than ever. To tell the stories. And get to work. Our job is to question and never stop doing that. That's all we can do and that's all we should do.

5

Communion

Hassan Abdulrazzak

Hassan Abdulrazzak is a playwright and writer of Iraqi origin, born in Prague and living in London. His plays include *Baghdad Wedding* (2007) and *And Here I Am* (2017). This interview was conducted over email on 30 November 2020.

CS *How has lockdown been for you?*

HA Initially lockdown was very disruptive. In March 2020, I had a play on at the Soho Theatre called *The Special Relationship*, a verbatim piece about British citizens who were deported from the United States. The play was commissioned by Synergy Theatre and directed by Esther Baker. I'm very proud of this piece as it documented the out-of-control immigration control system under Trump and in the UK. Unfortunately, the last week of the production had to be cancelled due to the lockdown. I also lost some commissions that were supposed to take place in 2020.

However, lockdown has also afforded me the chance to reflect on my practice, to go for long walks, to connect with a few friends and relatives on a deeper level. This Corona time has been a time out of the frenzy. A useful detox. Your brain is able to process all you have seen and read. The play I'm writing for the RSC is partially about Sufi philosophy. It's about a man who abandons the hectic world for the solitude of the wilderness. He effectively chooses lockdown. This is not such a mad response to our world as it first seems.

CS *What are your hopes and dreams for theatre's future?*

HA This is an opportunity to embrace technology in our sector in a big way that we haven't done before. Zoom technology can be utilized to create theatre without necessarily needing a stage or a building. Theatre doesn't need a stage. We have known that in the past through site-specific work for example but not through Zoom as we do now. The success of shows like *15 Heroines* at Jermyn Street Theatre in London illustrates that there is an appetite for streaming theatre. The exciting prospect of that is that every show can become international, that you can write a play in Hackney and it could end up being watched in Hanoi and vice versa. This could create an international conversation between artists on a scale we haven't seen before.

CS *During a time of global collective trauma, what are theatre's healing properties, if any?*

HA Theatre has the power to heal communities. In *The Special Relationship*, I had the chance to interview and get to know British people who were deported from the United States. For some they had been waiting a long time for someone to hear their story and give it the space it deserved. The experience was, I believe, incredibly healing for that community. On a much grander scale, when Tony Kushner wrote *Angels in America*, that provided a kind of validation and healing to the gay community that first watched that seminal play. Post Covid-19, we will see work that delves into the specific trauma experienced by various communities as a result of the virus. Our society has just been hit by the equivalent of a bus. Theatre can help us answer the question 'what the f**k just happened?' Theatre will offer healing if it can provide insightful answers to that question, ones that address the inequities that exist in society which the virus has magnified.

CS *2020 has been a year of multiple uprisings and exposed fractures in the capitalist exo-skeleton. Ways to parse through these times?*

HA We need to demand more. The idea of a universal wage was floated seriously for the first time. The freedom from serious financial worry is clearly the next revolution the world is crying out for. Some think this will lead to indolence and a lack of productivity, others, myself included, think it would unleash creativity and help people achieve their potential in ways we can barely imagine right now. Theatre should hold on to these positive ideas that have emerged in the pandemic and help in the dismantling of the worst aspects of the current system.

CS *The artist starving class remains even more so now that the pandemic has shut down work avenues and those making six figures in the arts are carrying on.*

HA It is one of the ironies of theatre that it is sometimes made by the 'starving class' for the benefit of the 'well-fed class'. But by and large, success still comes more easily in theatre, as in other spheres of life, to those with privilege. Something of that inequality will remain as long as the status quo remains.

I am optimistic about the potential of digital theatre to democratize the space further. In the Arab world, there is a culture of watching recorded plays on TV as most people do not have access to the theatre. With NT Live, we have developed a culture of watching plays in the cinema, but this model still favours the middle classes as ticket prices can be prohibitive (though not as expensive as tickets for the live show). But now any theatre can or could record their productions and put them online. *The Special Relationship* is being offered for £4 by Soho Theatre. This has allowed friends of mine who live abroad to see the work.

Breaking down barriers of access to the theatre is an essential step to ensuring that a wider section of society can feel that the art form belongs to them. I think digital theatre can play an essential part in this as long as it doesn't remain in the control of the big players only.

CS *How to regard one another during a time of countless deaths and ongoing illness?*

HA Sontag in her 2003 book *Regarding the Pain of Others* is very suspicious of the power of images. She writes, 'Photographs of the victims of war are themselves a species of rhetoric. They reiterate. They simplify. They agitate. They create the illusion of consensus.'

One of the earliest images of war that I saw as a child were the bloated bodies of the victims of the Sabra and Shatila massacre in 1982. It was in the pages of *Time* magazine or *Newsweek* that my dad subscribed to. They disturbed me greatly but also as a child I did not comprehend them. Who would do such a thing? Why kill people, including children, in this horrific way? The images alone were not enough to tell the story.

Sabra and Shatila is largely forgotten today although I have written an unproduced play inspired by that event where a Middle Eastern woman from an unnamed country tries in vain to convey to her English boyfriend the horror of what she has experienced at the hand of an army backed by Britain. But the boyfriend is uncomprehending. He is concerned for her mental well-being but cannot share her war trauma. It's a play about the limits of empathy, about our inability to truly see the other.

I overheard a conversation on the street post Covid-19 that went something like this: Woman 1: Do you know anyone that died? Woman 2: No, do you? Woman 1: No. And then they both laughed as if to say ... what? The alarm over Covid-19 has been exaggerated? Or phew, we have been spared? How different would their response have been if one of them had answered in the affirmative.

CS *Immigrant and migrant status artists often not centred. How to disrupt this?*

HA I was recently commissioned by Tamasha Arts and the National Archives to write a thirty-minute audio play called *The Fireman* inspired by records of Yemeni sailors who arrived in Britain in the 1920s and 1930s that exist at the Archives. I ended up writing it from the perspective of Sahar, a bipolar sufferer of Yemini heritage who has been charged by her grandmother to find out about the life of her great-grandfather whose letters to the Home Office are at the National Archives. In the play I made a link between the discrimination the great-grandfather faced which was perhaps more overt and the discrimination Sahar faces as someone in whom race and invisible disability intersect in our present time. This intersection of identities that are subject to discrimination is a potentially fruitful way to explore prejudice in society and the impact it has on the victims who may not always readily discern that they are being discriminated against till after the event. It is also a potential way of bringing different groups into the same space and to compare experiences. The play will be available on the National Archives website from 2021 and I hope it will contribute to the conversation about race and disability as well as the history of marginalized communities in Britain.

CS *In what ways are you or not considering distances (spatial and emotional) in your work, process and so on?*

HA I have always been fascinated by plays that did not require much physical interactions or props or sets. For me such work is pure theatre. People just saying words and the words carry the action. They can hurt, heal, instigate desire or hate. Just words uttered changing the charge in the room. I've written numerous short plays and over the years I've learnt to be economic with them as some were staged in non-conventional spaces. Don't have a character telling the other to sit down because you won't be able to guarantee there could be something in the space that would serve the purpose of a chair. Make it all about the words. Going forward I will write thinking this could be on Zoom. This could be under conditions of social distancing. How do I make the action carry through words? How do I embrace these limitations and make them shape the art? Of course, post-pandemic there might be a desire to go the other way. Have a long scene of people embracing which could be exhilarating.

Tanuja Amarasuriya

Tanuja Amarasuriya is British co-artistic director of Bristol-based company Sleepdogs. She is a director, dramaturg and sound designer. This interview was conducted over email between July and August 2020.

CS *How has lockdown been for you?*

TA Workwise, lockdown has been mega busy for me. After a moment of feeling like the ground had dropped away, I found that rather than plummeting, there was lots of unexpected ground there for me to explore jumping between. I feel particularly lucky that I was already working in different creative fields and industries, which had always been driven by me having a sort of undisciplined artistic curiosity, but it had also become the only way I could make a living as an artist. What's most exciting about that is that for the first time, outside of the work I make with Timothy X Atack through Sleepdogs, *every* theatre project I'm working on is asking: what sort of shape can this take? What are the ways we can share these propositions with audiences?

CS *What advice do you have for people in the field right now?*

TA I feel so much for people coming into the field because the noise that the industry is making just sounds like FEAR FEAR FEAR OH SHIT OH SHIT OH SHIT. If I think back over my twenty years of working in theatre, mostly as an independent, I'd say the main thing that's changed is that buildings are suddenly being forced to reconfigure business models that should probably have been re-examined long ago. As independents, we have always had to be agile, entrepreneurial, mischievous and wildly ambitious to get anything made at all. There are many ways to be an artist. Spend time understanding what honestly matters to you. You can be a successful artist even if that is not how you earn your money. Do not be dazzled by status in hierarchy. Find allies who share your values. Remember that 'theatre' is different from 'the theatre industry'. Everyone's career looks different, so invent your own.

CS *What are the hopes and dreams you have for theatre's future?*

TA My favourite theatre experiences are those where we are collectively inhabiting the same dream-space. One distinct opportunity of theatre, as an innately experiential form, is its reliance on make-believe – the recognition that dreaming has value and power. The capacity to dream is a powerful political tool, which is why governments and right-wing media so often peddle the lie that arts are a luxury. But imagination is a superpower and a survival skill for life. All of us should be allowed to cultivate our capacity to dream, to imagine, to invent privately and collectively – because this world and the future desperately needs systems, values, pleasures and new myths that don't just serve the short term and the currently powerful.

But I have found the UK theatre industry to be increasingly instrumentalized, practicalized and literal. It is like there is a fear of doing any actual dreaming – a fear of anything that cannot be immediately explained as a rational, consumable, easy-to-discuss item. Also, because the bubble is so small, with most critics being London-centred, and most venue ADs listening primarily to people in similar treetop positions, the most visible discussion around what should be the gorgeous possibilities of theatre becomes increasingly limited by this recursive feedback loop.

If I met a magic genie and they granted me three wishes for the theatre industry right now, they would be:

1. Make everyone be completely honest for a year and find out what people in this industry want and care about.

2. Find out what power each of us is honestly willing to let go of and redistribute that. Weed out the humble brag bullshit.

3. Treat audiences as intelligent people with their own minds and souls, rather than as ticket buyers or service users.

CS *In a time of global collective trauma, what are theatre's healing properties, if any?*

TA I do not think theatre is necessarily a healing thing. Theatre can be a powerful space to sit with difficulty, complexity and, yes, trauma – whether that is through reflection or ritual or (though it is perhaps uncool to say this) through distraction. The theatre *industry* is in trauma of course, but the industry is not the form. The industry was in poor health on so many fronts way before the pandemic brought lockdown. Much of our huge grief for productions cut short and careers on hold is accentuated by the feeling that an already deeply unequal industry will retreat into even deeper inequality, where those of us who don't conform to mainstream conventions will lose any foothold we ever had in this industry. What does a healthy theatre sector honestly mean? What does a healthy theatre community look like? We need to agree terms first.

CS *How can joy, instead of trauma, be part of theatre's 'narrative' and work processes, especially when centring stories about BIPOC individuals?*

TA The tyranny of a single narrative is so exhausting and diminishing. It is, in effect, the commodification of identity. For me it is less about *instigating* joy and more about inviting it as a possibility and then letting there be space for it when it arises. Joy is really about people. If you invite people – collaborators, audiences – to participate as their own selves, rather than as machines or as a bundle of assumptions you have made, then there will be space for joy. That's why the insistence on trauma narratives as the only narrative of marginalized people is so harmful and feels so joyless – because it leaves no room for us as people on our own terms, and therefore no room for joy.

In a practical sense, it is about knowing why I am doing a project. How do I keep a sense of my soul with this, even if the process treats me like a product delivery machine? Where is the private space for my own joy with it?

CS *The act of listening to the room but also listening to nature and the world, and processing those sounds at a root level, feels key now. As a sound designer, how do you think about sound?*

TA The truth is I do not ever respond as a sound designer – I respond as a director and dramaturg first. When my sound designs work best are when there is room for that. I tend towards score, dynamics and atmosphere. My first responses to a play are usually about dynamic flow – the emotional energy of it. I am less interested in the literal or representational, which is what theatre sound design is most often asked to do. Score can really open up space and time for an audience to feel what they are feeling. It is a more cinematic convention because it suits a more cinematic approach to time.

Sound is a physical and durational thing, and if you know your audience is listening on headphones, you can also create a spatial sense – which can all build towards an embodied immersive experience. I'm happy that lockdown means more theatre-makers are realizing the potential of sound as an experiential tool – because that sense of being *in the space* of what's happening is a big part of what we're missing at the moment. One of my worries when we streamed the archive video of *The Bullet and the Bass Trombone* in late June 2020 was that we had no way to remix the sound for headphones, so you miss a whole level of atmospheric immersion, which is a big part of how the live show has transportive effect.

I am also unafraid of sentimentality. One of the things I love about artists like Björk, ANOHNI, Franko B, Pina Bausch is a fearlessness of speaking directly to and creating space for frank emotions. Score can really make that invitation, because music is abstract and physical – it invites us to feel rather than intellectualize. You cannot be superficial about sentimentality though, which is where it gets a bad rep. You have got to believe the (often uncomfortable or abject) truth of that emotional space, and theatre can be a bit coy about that. This is probably my live art roots coming out, but I find it weird that so much theatre is about *showing* you feelings, rather than inviting you to feel and making space for you to feel. In our current, atomized day-to-day, that space and time to feel stuff is a useful thing to offer people: whether it is to sit with deep grief or effervescent joy.

CS *On your website for Sleepdogs you proudly state that the work you do as a duo (with Tim) is of a 'mongrel heritage'. Going against the tribal. Can you expand?*

TA Is 'tribes speaking to other tribes' the same as 'people speaking to other people'? If we remember that we mean different people talking to each other, then it makes it easier to see routes to connection and allow for times when someone just does not want to talk to you.

That is basically what we are getting at when we question the tribal propriety around artforms.

I do not buy into the utopian notion of a holistic world equilibrium. There is something slightly colonial about that vision – the idea that difference can be managed, or softened, in the service of the commonly understood greater good. There is no such thing as 'common sense'; because those intuitive norms and defaults are only fluid beliefs and social codes. You can see the friction of that at the edge of civil rights movements throughout history. You can see it in our struggle to abandon consumerism despite proven environmental devastation.

The history of the universe is about change. I was reading about gene plasticity recently, and that the observable characteristics of genes are not fixed but can respond to both physical and social environment. So, everything from our genes, to the slow heat death of our sun, is a story of change, of fluidity. Change can feel violent or it can be barely felt at all. Yet it is happening all the time. I am interested in its possibilities and what difference can look like. Part of my job as an artist is to stare hard at how we live in the world, and to also imagine how we might live better in the universe.

Suba Das

Suba Das is a British theatre director and artistic director and chief executive of HighTide Theatre in London. This interview was conducted over email from mid-November to mid-December 2020.

CS *How has lockdown been for you?*

SD The first UK lockdown in March 2020 began about a month before I was due to announce my first series of programs as Artistic Director at HighTide, having taken up the post in October 2019. As we'd headed towards March, I had been asking myself, my team, our Board, artists, audiences and funders what our core mission was; what unique space we occupied in the British theatre landscape. While we're renowned for launching the careers of incredible writers such as Jack Thorne, Ella Hickson and Vinay Patel, there are many other companies and venues doing the same across the UK. For HighTide, with our annual festival of new work taking place in the East of England; what felt, and still feels, the real 'USP' for us, and our opportunity for greatest growth, was our impact in our home region and how this could reach beyond appearing for a week or so each year and offering a programme of work for a relatively 'traditional', affluent, theatre-going audience.

Having already undertaken this reflection, as Covid-19 hit the UK we found ourselves ready to roll with a series of writer training programs and access initiatives for young people in the East of England, that we were able to rapidly tweak, adjust and shift online, launching our 'Lighthouse Programme' by the end of the first lockdown week. We established training for first-time playwrights; digital storytelling resources into primary schools; create a digital youth theatre for the county's most vulnerable young people in partnership with the local youth health service, supported our playwrights already under commission to create a film monologue series for our audiences; and we connected with, advised and counselled as many artists as we could – some 400 over that first lockdown period. Unencumbered by the overhead costs of a building; and operating as a lean team of four core staff in any case; with no need to furlough and no work imminently scheduled to go into rehearsal; it really felt like our duty to provide some signal of hope – to underline that self-isolation did not need to mean silence.

The frenzy of that was quite gorgeous in many ways – it was certainly distracting. In the midst of such anxiety, we were very proud to be offering concrete, positive, inclusive opportunities and certainly for me personally – very much not a key worker, and not facing the extent of the horrors on the front line of the pandemic response – it felt like making some useful contribution. And that's certainly soul food in such times.

Quite apart from that, on a much more personal level, with the incredible, good fortune of having a regular income, a leadership role and my own place to live throughout this time, I have found that I was able to put down some of the armour I've worn on a daily basis for as long as I can recall. As a gay, brown man from a working-class background, this world isn't necessarily always the most welcoming place. Liberated from so many micro-aggressions; the space to think deeply, to breathe and to consider what world I wish to make for myself, was quite astonishing and life-changing.

CS *What advice do you have for people entering the field right now?*

SD I'll focus on writers, because that's who we serve first and foremost. I'd say, first and foremost – continue to tell the stories you want to tell and that matter most to you. We're hopeful of course that vaccination and improved testing programs will in time obviate the need for social distancing; but while this is in play, I understand that writers are fearful of writing for large casts that might have to 'bubble'; writing intimacy; writing any form of physical contact – why on Earth write something right now that feels like it would be difficult to produce? I would counter that fear saying it is the job of directors, designers and the full creative family that makes work live to find the solutions that make a writer's work sing; to make limitations feel like choices. So please, always, write what you must and trust that those of us fortunate enough to weather the storm in jobs and organizations will do the work to honour your authentic voice.

CS *During a time of global collective trauma, what are theatre's healing properties, if any?*

SD We need to honestly ask ourselves for whom theatre truly is that space of healing? Of course, Covid-19 has collided squarely with the Black Lives Matter movement; and I'm heartened that there has been what feels like the mist sustained reflection on racial injustice in the UK in my lifetime. As Angela Davies noted, this timing is not coincidental. While the world found itself trapped at home; experiencing the privations of limited contact; limited joy; a sense of constant behavioural scrutiny; we all more keenly discovered our empathy for those for whom these indignities have been a part of their lived experience long before Covid-19, let alone Covid-19.

I would argue that, in the UK at any rate, theatre has much more profoundly connected with its responsibility to heal in these circumstances. I think we see this within the sector in the new solidarity that has sprung up, with formidable initiatives such as Freelancers Make Theatre Work and Scene/Change agitating for enduring sector change. It's a stark acknowledgement of the fact that the practices, schedules and processes we have become used to are far from 'healing' but rather evidence of a sector that has thrived on exploitative, low-paid practices that too often privilege the independently wealthy or well-connected; and much too often rely on the extreme, unsustainable emotional labour of artists to paper over the cracks in an exceptionally creaky production system that hasn't notably evolved or innovated in decades. And that's where the work now lies.

CS *Can you talk about your work currently as a director and artistic director at HighTide?*

SD I write in the UK as we're in the midst of our second lockdown in December 2020; and candidly it's getting harder on many fronts. The adrenalizing shock of that first lockdown, the leaping into responsiveness and new ways of working, much of that has lost its charm by now. By this stage, as the situation has contorted and rolled forwards in unexpected ways, with an erratic government response, we continue to try to build foundations on sand, with more versions of budgets and schedules than I had ever thought possible.

But if it's like that for us, then we can't even begin to imagine how it is for our freelance community. Consequently, over our next phase of work, these next six months until we see how infection rates pan out and what a vaccine might do; our focus is resilience and demystification. We have launched our School of HighTide which will specifically support a cohort of writers of colour with not only the 'creative' end of writing but tackling all of the invisible barriers I described earlier, barriers which will not simply vanish with a vaccine, but which run the risk of becoming even more entrenches as Brexit grips our purse strings and national psyche. Going forwards, our agenda is holding ourselves and our sector to ongoing account.

CS *What are your hopes and dreams for theatre's future?*

SD One of the most important things to hold on to in all of this is that – in fact – those organizations who have most sought to commercialize themselves, who have worked hardest to toe the line of diversifying income streams, minimizing their reliance on subsidy – in fact those organizations are the ones who have found themselves amongst the most endangered as their box office, café and bar sales, galas and the like have dried up. This ever-encroaching capitalism, the insistence that we define ourselves according to our bottom line and prove to our governments how much 'value' and 'return' we're generating – these cannot be the accepted conditions for a thriving cultural sector. Of course, there must be accountability; and of course, we can't fund to resource inefficiency; but art and profit are not natural bedfellows and it's worth us all holding on to that thought as we think about how we rebuild our budgets and funding structures.

Above and beyond this, I try as much as possible not to separate my dreams for the sector from my dreams from society as this speaks into the unhelpful presumption that theatre is in some way immune from the contagion around us all – by which I mean racism, sexism, ableism and the many more and various structural inequalities besides. And really no part of our world is. As we see that the countries who are at the vanguard of the great neoliberal experiment, coincidentally or causally, look to now have the highest death tolls from Covid-19, I wonder if we find ourselves at a major cultural crossroads around our ideas of employment, social safety net, access to medical aid. Looking at the way furlough schemes have worked across the world, I wonder if there is now a much more real possibility of moving towards a universal basic income and what this might make possible. I wonder too how we as artists can further embark on our real work – that of helping us all imagine better worlds – in support of such necessary social change.

Lauren Gunderson

L auren Gunderson is an American playwright, screenwriter,
librettist and short story author, born in Atlanta and based
in San Francisco. She was recognized as America's most produced
living playwright in 2017. This interview was conducted over
email in November 2020.

CS *How has lockdown been for you?*

LG The lockdown has been alarming, unsettling, exciting, boring,
creative and vacant. At time it felt good to not have to be anywhere,
which let me focus on my writing, my kids, the food I'm cooking
for my family, the books on my night table and the backyard. It
also elicited a strange fear of other people, of crowds, of indoor
spaces – of the exact stuff that fuels theatre. That continues to
send me into a despairing mindset. My husband is a virologist, so
I am always close to an expert in outbreaks and pandemics. I am
privileged to have him to fact check and think through safety
protocols for our family. But it does not take an expert to tell you
how bad it is to have a President refuse to wear a mask and hold
unsafe rallies during a pandemic. That also sent me into a despairing
space. Yet I am an optimist by nature. I write because I want to test
the future, a future that is better for more of us. After two weeks of
shut down, I wrote. I wrote about lots of things.

But all of this was before George Floyd was murdered for all to
see. My entire mindset shifted after that and the ensuing uprising
of brave activists from the Black Lives Matter movement. It shifted
my sense of what was possible, what theatre must do, what I must
do to continue the lifelong work of choosing every day to be on the
right side of history and on the right side of those who don't have
the privileges I was freely and undeservedly born into.

CS *What advice would you give to people entering the field
right now?*

LG My advice is as follows:

1. Don't settle. You deserve to be paid, to be produced, to be heard, to work in a safe and affirming and supportive environment. You deserve power and agency and real respect. You deserve to say, 'You also deserve to take a break and not fight every battle and not to be burdened with other people's issues.'

2. Collaborate. Most of the projects I started during this time were collaborations. With one other writer, with three other writers, with six creators. All different projects, all of them were built in conversation, in connection, in collectivity. This has been a true gift of this time for me. There is power and vision in the collective.

3. There is theatre that can be made and developed right now. If you want to make art, make it. The gates of traditional American Theatre have been thrown open by this pandemic, so walk in and own it. Put your new musical online, do a Zoom reading, make an audio drama. Put it out there, surprise us, shock us, disrupt the way things have been done before and do it your way. Theatre is iterative, so let's all iterate on what theatre 'is' and should be, on who gets to see it, on how much it costs, on who our audience is, on the many experiences in which they might enjoy the play.

CS *In a time of global collective trauma, what are theatre's healing properties, if any?*

LG If theatre is not working for the good of the public, it is not working. It is a non-profit and that should make us think beyond the business models and into a civic-minded model of theatre making. If we believe theatre matters and engages hearts and minds to the end of making us better people, then our goal should not be how many tickets we sell but how many we give away. It should not be about who *pays us but* who *joins us*, not who donates money but who gifts us with their time and presence. I know theatre institutions need to pay bills too, but not at the cost of audiences or artists.

Everything *We See You White American Theatre* has put forth is good for our industry, not just for BIPOC artists but for white ones too! Once we all know making theatre is safe, welcoming, power-sharing, beneficial for all creative parties who are paid equally and collectively generative then we can all make work we can stand behind. We will start to live up to theatre's potential and defy the scarcity mentality we have come to expect.

CS   *What are your hopes and dreams for theatre's future?*

LG   The big hope is one John F. Kennedy articulated in his 1963 speech at Amherst College:[1]

> I look forward to an America which will reward achievement in the arts as we reward achievement in business or statecraft. ... which will steadily raise the standards of artistic accomplishment and which will steadily enlarge cultural opportunities for all of our citizens.

I hope for an America where art of every kind is seen as essential work, as critical civilization-building work, as a respected oracle and trusted moral compass this nation requires to know a better future for all.
I hope this means artists are paid comfortable living wages and given benefits to live well and fully, are welcomed into all the places decisions are made, are given agency for their own artmaking and are looked to as creative ethical advisors.
I hope, too, that art is widespread, easy, accessible, democratized. If we believe that theatre is so important then we should be making sure it gets to every American, not just the ones who can pay $100 a ticket.

> When power leads men towards arrogance, poetry reminds him of his limitations. When power narrows the areas of man's concern, poetry reminds him of the richness and diversity of his existence. When power corrupts, poetry cleanses. For art establishes the basic human truth which must serve as the touchstone of our judgment. – JFK, 1963[2]

CS   *What do you think has been the impact of digital theatre during this time?*

---

[1]https://www.jfklibrary.org/archives/other-resources/john-f-kennedy-speeches/amherst-college-19631026. Accessed 1 November 2020.
[2]Ibid.

LG   When the lockdown started I found it hard to concentrate and think in a with a scope that I require for storytelling. But I got that verve and vision back and I credit a lot of that with the online classes I was offering three on Facebook. I started doing one class a week but that quickly expanded to include interviews with either makers or all kinds of topics. The chance to process the craft of writing and the source of inspiration was quite galvanizing in part because it built a community that was curious and present even virtually. I was also lucky to have lots of projects in various stages of development at that time, so I could jump from world to world and keep different parts of my creative brain working.

The darker thoughts came in waves as I begin to fully grasp what the shutdown of public life meant for the art form I so loved and admired. Why was I even writing for the theatre if there is no theatre? Why would I bother crafting something meaningful when it is inability to be realized would just break my heart?

The impact of Virtual Theatre – whether on Zoom or twitch or streamed – was not fully satisfying to me and mostly made me miss live theatre. But that perception was challenged several times throughout the shut down by various performances that – even delivered to me on a screen or through my headphones – were riveting, intimate, profound. I have not been fully won over by Zoom theatre, but I have been won over deeply by stream-able, filmed theatre. I find its democracy, affordability and accessibility unparalleled in our field. I want that part of this immersive experiment making art in crisis to continue, so the breadth of our art form can expand.

CS   *What is theatre's role in times of crisis?*

LG   My instincts with theatre's power is always its intimacy and its extremely tight focus on a handful of individual lives. I think that kind of human theatrical microscopy allows for us to really stand next to another life-in-progress, step into each other's shoes, really question the decisions we would make if that character's situation was ours, really lean into a lived experience that isn't ours. If my supposition is correct then the way to use the superpower of theatre to connect and comprehend is to share the storytelling power and make sure our stories are as diverse as America is. This work is in specific alignment with the brilliant maxims behind We See You White American Theatre. The possibilities that come through when we expand those who get to tell the stories is what will keep theatre powerful, relevant and life-changing.

CS   *How do you instigate joy in work processes when working with traumatic narratives?*

LG   Thinking about joy as a principle is important especially when it comes to stories of women and BIPOC characters. So often the stories that feel the most powerful hinge on the terrible abuses perpetrated against those who are not white, straight and male. I think the way to combat this is to simply combat it! Fill the stage with all women instead of just a few! Fill the stage with all Indigenous characters not just a few! Feel the stage with all trans or non-binary characters not just a token character to represent an entire diverse community! Our multiplicity and manifold versions of humanity are our power because they are our sources of joy.

Philip Howard

Philip Howard is a theatre director and artistic director of Pearlfisher in Edinburgh, Scotland. He was the dramaturg on Hope Leach's film *Ghost Light*, which premiered online during the pandemic and was conceived as a love letter to theatre. This interview with conducted over Zoom on 1 September 2020.

CS   *How has lockdown been for you?*

PH   I've been lucky, unlike others, because I've been teaching mostly at the University of Glasgow, but I know a lot of playwrights, for instance, have struggled in lockdown. Their emotional ecosystem has been completely unbalanced by all the horrors of the pandemic. I do a lot of work too which circles the boundaries of dramaturgy and playwriting, editing and adapting, and somehow the work has continued, including work on a commission from the theatre company Stellar Quines here in Scotland on a new version of *Richard III* with a female Richard at the centre. Not a woman playing a man, but a female Richard. But I do suffer from survivor guilt about having work during this time, when so many do not.

CS   *How did* Ghost Light *come to be?*

PH   The whole thing was put together quite quickly because Edinburgh International Festival decided they wanted to commission the five national companies (ballet, opera, orchestras and theatre) to make a piece of online work, which would have premiered on the same night that the Edinburgh International Festival would have normally opened. Jackie Wiley, the artistic director and chief executive of the National Theatre of Scotland, commissioned filmmaker Hope Dickson Leach and brought me in as the 'theatre' person to work on the film to pieces together a variety of texts by Scottish playwrights – some historical, some contemporary, some brand new – in a collage of performances for the short movie. The film has had a positive reaction. Hope is a brilliant filmmaker and was the core lead artist on the project. The reviews have said it is maybe a hybrid of film and theatre, but it absolutely is not a hybrid. It is a film which happens to be set in the world of theatre and celebrating the art form in a loving manner.

I assembled the texts for the shooting script with Jackie Wiley's support as overseeing producer. There is a thematic narrative through the arrangement of the texts that reveal a construction of national identity. It starts with a non-binary Peter Pan and it moves quickly to a Scottish king, and then the ground is taken from under his feet by a very loud-mouthed Glaswegian woman and so forth. There is a gender narrative at work in the collage that subtly suggests a new world order that is centred on female-identified, and non-binary bodies leading the way and shaping the narratives of power.

CS   *What are your hopes and dreams for theatre's future?*

PH   When people are all allowed to return to the physical space of theatre, I think they will value it more. If we survive long enough to be able to come back, I also think that in the Western world at least theatre may return to the ancient Greek model and become an arena for debate. I wouldn't go so far as the actual Greek model of it being one's public duty to go to the theatre, but I do think that there is a need for a public space, which is live and non-digital, where ideas can be explored and debated by writers in front of an audience and that it's not just going to be about entertainment.

In Scotland, there's support for the arts from the government, but in England, the Tory government is still based on a distant idea that theatre is something you go to in the West End after a workday in stocks and shares. It is seen as entertainment and not as something that people earn a living from or want to go to for more than just entertainment. Nonetheless, I dream rather quixotically that there will be the return of the big play – big roaring plays that tackle huge ideas – and that there will be a hunger for them instead of two-handers all the time, which it was becoming.

We are obviously much better off here than in England. There's extra funding coming specifically from the Scottish government to many of the building-based companies. I think both big and small theatres will survive. What will be the deciding factor is what proportion of their turnover relies on box-office revenue. Bigger theatres tend to have more government subsidy. Smaller theatres tend to be nimbler. The mid-sized theatres are the ones that will be hurting the most and may not make it through this, sadly.

CS *What advice do you have for people entering the field right now?*

PH There is a pressing need to come out of lockdown with something to show for it. Not just in terms of one's income. But in terms of one's own peace of mind, sanity, and pride. I think it important to find any strategy to keep your morale up and indeed come out of the whole ghastliness with your artistic muscles in fit shape somehow. My advice is to keep up your practice however you can. It is not just about keeping the physical instrument fit but also the intellectual instrument.

CS *What are theatre's healing properties, if any?*

PH In theory theatre should be well placed to contribute to regeneration. The problem is that we are living, especially in England, through a terrible government that simply does not care for or understand its people, and as a result, also does not truly value its theatre. I also think artists need to learn to articulate why art matters in a way that is convincing to precisely those in government that do not care. Artists do not need to convince others in the arts, but people that are not in the arts, and they need to come up with tough and imaginative and persuasive language to do so. We think everybody already knows that theatre is good for you and can be good for your emotional well-being. But that is not true. So, we need to make the case. And reach across the aisle, so to speak.

CS *How do you see the interaction between live and digital theatre?*

PH We must balance the contradiction. We have got to be proud of the best of the online work. But at the same time admit, and even and I use this word advisedly, celebrate its limitations. We need harness some enthusiasm about the power of doing work in a live context. The National Theatre of Scotland has had much success with *Ghost Light* and their *Scenes for Survival* series of short films, but they have been clear that they do not wish to become a film company as a result of this but invest time and energy into planning a return to live theatre. No doubt the art form will learn from the success of the best digital work, but we cannot take our eye off the ball, and not prepare to ever present live work again.

Jennifer Jackson

Jennifer Jackson is a British Bolivian movement director, actor and theatre-maker. This interview was conducted via email on 6 November 2020.

CS *How has lockdown been for you?*

JJ I was in rehearsal with Roy Alexander Weise for *Antigone: Burial at Thebes* (Lyric Hammersmith), when the PM advised people not to go to the theatre. We were devastated and frightened. The week leading up the cancellations were full of anxiety and fear of this unknown threat, unsure if we were compromising our families and colleagues. There was so much collective grief and so much sadness. I felt acutely aware of it early on, as I had lost my dad three months prior to the pandemic and I was still in the early stages of grieving. It was a very wrought time.

In addition to this, I remember being in varying states of fight/flight/freeze, as I balanced a fear for my family's welfare, and the consequences of the lockdown. As the weeks went on, I realized the level of precariousness that we had all been operating at, and the huge problematic hierarchies that play out in our industry. As freelancers we had no security and no visibility. It was frightening.

I also remember the first slew of online work that seemed to come from every angle, and the overwhelming pressure to deliver digital content. There was a feeling of missing out or losing your relevance in this new digital landscape. I did not watch very much theatre. I found only three moments that really spoke to me during this time. The first was the National Theatre Live at Home streaming on YouTube of Inua Ellams's 2017 play *Barber Shop Chronicles*, which captured the audience in their archive recording, and in doing so, caught the energy of what it was like to experience that piece in the flesh. Second was Quarantine's *White Trash*, which reunited the original cast members and creative team in the group Zoom watch. Quarantine had really thought about the experience they were giving to the audience and mixed the footage with rehearsal shots, so I felt like I was inside the process. The last one was the reading of Katori Hall's *The Mountaintop*, streamed by the Royal Exchange. I had worked with Roy on this production at The Young Vic (and tour) and it had been brought back to raise money and awareness for Black Lives Matter in the wake of George Floyd's murder. Katori Hall's words shooting an arrow into the future and our humanity. I struggled to make sense of the murders of Breonna Taylor, Ahmaud Arbery and George Floyd. I struggled to make sense of the murder of Vanessa Guillen. I put this rage and sadness into working with other artists and manifestos were written, meetings were had and I joined the Freelance Task Force. The work continues; the rage is still burning.

CS   *What advice do you have for people entering the field now?*

JJ   I didn't have very much access to a range of theatre in my hometown. I was the first 'Jackson' to go to university, and as such, I was encouraged to study a subject which would give me financial security.

My advice is to be open minded about where you can make work, and how you make it. This time is about thinking outside the parameters of what has been. Focus your attention on training, reading, watching and learning. Your expression is unique to you, and only you can nurture it. Time spent investing in enriching your creative well of experience is a life's investment. Remember too, that although we are told theatre is a meritocracy, it is not. A successful actor told me when I was starting out that trying to change yourself for the powers that be will take its toll. You cannot be everything to all people. The most important thing is to stay true to yourself. Reach out and ask like all those average white men have done in the past, the worst that can happen is that they will say no.

CS   *What are your hopes and dreams for theatre's future?*

JJ   Dealing with Covid-19 safety measures has meant that we have been acutely aware of people's boundaries and consent in the rehearsal room like never before. I have been lucky enough to be in rehearsal rooms as a performer, and as a movement director during the pandemic. The anxiety and sense of responsibility is a complex cocktail of emotions, and in the past, there has been an assumption that actors and their bodies are always available. This has been thrown into sharp focus. My hope is that what we have learned from this time is carried forward and becomes best practice. Intimacy direction has been pioneering this sort of work for years; it has taken a pandemic for the industry to listen.

I want to see artists have more agency over the work they make and how they are commissioned. There is such little transparency about who gets to do what, and at what level. It can often feel like a secret club. I would love to see this turned on its head. I want new stories.

I want to see the industry, and our society learn from the Black Lives Matter movement. I do not mean reacting to the 'noisiest' problem the buildings are dealing with, which just results in a simple change in optics. I want full out, systemic change. I want us all to embody it and make those changes so that we can build some equity.

Selfishly, I want to see more Latinx stories on stage. I am British Bolivian, and I have never seen anyone who looks like my mother represented on a UK stage. South America is just not on the radar in the UK, and yet, whenever it is, the people are not treated with respect. Artists with no connection or understanding of these countries are cast, and pieces are directed without understanding the complex cultural legacy.

One last dream, inclusion will be the starting point of all practice.

CS *Can you talk about your work currently?*

JJ In terms of my artivism, I see all my work as a challenge to the presented history and dynamics that society offers us. My primary focus is on creating work that interrogates the female body in performance, my relationship with the UK, and the duality of living between races and cultures.

Growing up in the UK as a mixed-race Latinx womxn and watching my mother deal with racism gave me an early education into how people are categorized and labelled by the dominant white culture in the UK. The world of South America and Bolivia provided a rich tapestry of colonial and Indigenous history, folkloric dance and ancient landscapes, which stand in stark contrast to the market towns and brutalist concrete structures of Coventry and the surrounding area where I grew up. I feel more than ever the drive and urgency of making work that speaks to a contemporary British experience, and the legacy of colonial histories.

CS *This is a time of massive illness and death. What kind of invitations can art create now?*

JJ It is clear we are dealing with more than one pandemic; one is the Novel Coronavirus, and another is white supremacy. Our bod(y)ies have become a battleground. If we have become disconnected from our mortality, then this year has brought it into hard focus. Preserving our lives meant we could not share space and be together, and yet it revealed an insatiable and necessary part of what it is to be human. We are now acutely aware of the space between us. This is seen as a negative, but it is also a reminder that there is an uncrossable divide of unknowing between us. How much can we ever really know someone or be known. The space between us offers us a void, both of emptiness and of possibility. We are aware of our desire to cross the void, to reach out, to communicate something about what it means to be alive. Art often occupies this void, and can create possibility between experiences, between people, between minds.

Dan Rebellato

Dan Rebellato is an English dramatist and academic born in South London. He is Professor of Contemporary Theatre at Royal Holloway, University of London, and has written extensively for radio and the stage. This interview was conducted over email in November 2020.

CS *How has lockdown been for you?*

DR In our dreams, we walk through impossible, contradictory, nightmarish worlds that are sometimes just like our familiar waking lives but twisted and doubled and overlaid and distorted and mostly we accept them as normal. I do anyway. There are just occasional moments in my dreams, when I notice how strange it is that someone that I know to be dead is talking to me, or that the place I'm in is both my dad's front room and an old classroom. Sometimes, at those moments, I might even realize that this is a dream and often, if I think that, I wake up.

I feel like that about our Covid-19 world. The world is both recognizably the same and utterly different – shopping centres overlaid with scenes from zombie movies, twenty-first-century high streets mashed up with images from 1970s Soviet Moscow – and I've mostly accepted it as normal. But just moments, maybe when I'm thinking of something else and not expecting it, I'll step across a sticker on the floor showing me where to stand, see a hand-sanitizer dispenser at a coffee stall or catch sight of people shopping as normal but everyone wearing masks, I think we're in a nightmare and I experience a horror that there's no waking up that this is what being awake is like now.

CS *During first half of lockdown you created the interview series* Playwrights in Lockdown *on your YouTube channel. Over twenty-five interviews with some of the best UK playwrights in the field. How did the series impact you?*

DR There's a Latin aphorism I love and live by, which concerns drinking wine. It goes something like this: 'There are only five reasons to drink wine: 1. The excellence of the wine; 2. The arrival of a friend; 3. One's present or future thirst; 4. To promote cleverness; 5. Or any other reason.'

I think of this when I think about how to write a play: there are only five ways. 1. Through careful research; 2. By imagining hard; 3. Through meticulous structural planning; 4. In a rush of creative improvisation; 5. Or any other method.

The more I've spoken to other playwrights over the years, I've been cheered by how different people's methods are, because, as the late Adrian Howells used to say, 'it's all allowed'. So many connections and links seemed to spring up through the series. Mostly – because I did quite a bit of reading to fill in gaps in my knowledge – I was staggered by the continuing vigour and creativity of British playwriting. One thing that fascinates and intrigues me is the vitality of Scottish feminist writing; plays like Linda McLean's *Sex & God*, or Stef Smith's *Enough*, or Zinnie Harris's *Meet Me at Dawn*, all written in the 2010s, have a playful, poetic, painful but sometimes exhilarated quality, not tied down to simple ideological commitments but lifted out of a particular sense of space, into a world of experiences imagined or remembered, words carving out visionary futures for sex, love, identity, hope and desire. I adore Scotland and look longingly at it from Brexit-y England and would love to know what has been happening in Scottish theatre and society to produce these three masterpieces. Writing the introductions and reading or rereading the back catalogue, as it were, of these writers, I've been amazed by the tendency of British playwrights restlessly to reinvent themselves and the form of the play; it's true of every playwright I interviewed, from Roy Williams to Alan Ayckbourn, from Mark Ravenhill to Winsome Pinnock. No one repeats themselves; the journey perpetually seems open and unfinished.

CS *The upheaval that the global pandemic has caused has been massive (financial, systemic, etc.) – and the rebuilding process will likely be slow. Are there hopeful signs?*

DR The government announced a £1.57 billion fund to keep cultural institutions going and, although it took months for that process to work through, a lot of institutions have been given a chance to breathe, at least until April 2021. But what happens after that. The last few days have seen promising news about vaccines, but how quickly they can be rolled out, how long they last, how and whether, in terms of future cultural participation, one could make distinctions between the vaccinated and the unvaccinated seems hard to talk about yet. And, as you say, Brexit looms with the chaos that will bring. I don't want to predict: this crisis may hasten the extinction of the monumental civic playhouse in favour of smaller, pop-up, hyper-responsive, quicksilver theatre ventures; but we may find that, through this crisis, we have longed to gather in crowds at the heart of our cities and tell each other stories again.

I hope that we learn from this, that we learn how much theatre means in our culture and how hard it was to do without it. I worry the culture may remember how it managed to cope without it for a while and that it may take a long time to get back into the theatre habit. I also hope that we don't reinvent the wheel: while this could be a moment to take stock, to take a breath, to look around and see what we do and what we might do differently, there were some important things happening in the pre-Covid-19 theatre, particularly in the representation of Black and Global Majority theatre-makers in our theatre. I would be concerned if starting again set back these advances.

CS   *What's inspiring you these days?*

DR   Resistance. The last four years, since 2016, have been the most politically depressing of my life, no contest. I spent my teenage years under Thatcher, and it was nothing like this. The stupidities of Brexit and the bullying cruelties of Trump have raised my blood pressure like nothing I can remember. (I wonder if there will be a long-term health impact on the progressive left tracked to these years.) But I find myself moved to tears by resistance.

I do a playwriting class about structure where I ask students to plan the perfect football match – one that will create the purest, most giddy and wild joy at the final whistle. They have to figure out when the goals go in, where the off-the-ball incidents go and so on. Typically, we find that the match starts badly, gets worse and only in the second half do a couple of decisions go our way, allowing hope to blossom with a careering upward trajectory in the last ten minutes with a last-minute, freak winning goal, usually accompanied by some genial humiliation for the other team. This was my experience of the US Presidential Election. I stayed up that night, saw the Florida result, had the sick feeling that this might be 2016 all over again and then feverishly watched CNN over the next few days as gradually, I found myself daring to hope, possibly for the first time in four years. And then Pennsylvania came in, magnificently accompanied by the comic humiliation of the Four Seasons Total Landscaping fiasco. It was the winning goal, and it was priceless. The dramaturgy of your election will buoy me through many projects for many years.

CS *Because of Brexit, I fear we'll likely not see touring work from Europe and abroad for a very long time. Unless it is streaming digitally. How can we forge new exchanges?*

DR First, it seems plausible that the current restrictions under which we live will be significantly eased a year from now. Second, is it too much to hope that the power and prestige of the populist right, with their preference for walls and barriers, is on the wane? The thwarting of Trump is not the end of all that, but it is a signal that the most powerful leader in the world is no longer on their side and this is a good moment for the forces of internationalism to regroup and reassert themselves. Third, I think these nationalist forces have provoked a resistant counter-formation that has more actively sought out connections. Certainly, in the UK, I think the pro-EU side of the Brexit argument has greatly sharpened its knowledge and valuation of our international ties. (Who knew we'd all get so interested in trade agreements and customs unions?) I advise complacency. The theatre has never waited in line at passport control; it's never been honestly stamped with a place of origin; audiences travel, and theatre moves and plays circulate and techniques and stories are swapped promiscuously backstage and on it always goes.

For the UK the salt grain on the cornea is Brexit, of course, which will make touring more arduous, expensive, frustrating, unpredictable and, perhaps, ultimately unsustainable. But theatre finds its ways through. Maybe those ways will be online for a while or maybe we'll write letters to each other or maybe we'll find illicit moments to meet in secret and whisper ideas, but it won't stand still. Like Galileo (didn't say but it would be so good if he did say it that we just keep on preferring to believe that he) said, *eppur si muove*.

Rajni Shah

Rajni Shah is a British performance maker, writer, producer and curator who works across disciplines, countries and thought structures. Their work ranges from large-scale performance installations made through an in-depth collaborative process to small solo interventions in public spaces. This interview was conducted over email between October and November 2020.

CS *How has lockdown been for you?*

RS Rich. Quiet. Challenging. Hopeful. Unbearable. Demanding. Reckonful.

I kept contact with those I love. I meditated. I cried. I howled. I mourned. I walked every day on a mountain. I surrounded myself with teachers who were already practicing the end of the world. I made food for people who couldn't cook or didn't have access to a kitchen. I left notes for my neighbours. I slowly started trying to unravel my own internal hierarchies. I let go of the very rich plans I had for this year. I let go of many things.

CS *What advice do you have for people entering the field right now?*

RS In 2013, after completing my most ambitious project as a performance maker, I walked away from my ideas of being a successful artist within the UK Live Art and experimental theatre scenes. This is how I survived.

My advice? Find your own field, your own story, your own right to exist. Walk away if you need to. Look and listen carefully for your allies. They might be right beside you, though it may take years for you to notice them. Trust process. Trust yourself.

CS *In what ways is it possible to instigate joy in artwork and its processes in order to prise it away from the heaviness of traumatic* *narratives, especially when those are centred on stories about Black, Indigenous, and People of Colour, and LGBTQIA people?*

RS   I have been obsessed with the concept of joy for some years now, and how it sits differently within different bodies, or that your own version of joy work will vary depending on what kind of body you bring, and what stories you carry. I have been thinking about joy as resistance in relation to the exhaustion of living inside a racialized body. I've been thinking about 'trans joy' as a phrase that feels dangerous (and important) to claim because it sits so far outside the realm of mainstream reality/media. Related to joy work is recognizing where the work begins. For me, the work of claiming joy is in the details, in the bloodstream, in the casual remarks, in the ways we curl our tongues. The work of reclaiming joy in the face of violence and erasure is relevant and makes a difference. It might feel small, it might feel irrelevant, but the small and the big live inside each other. What is happening inside me is also happening outside me. Of course, as I write this, I am aware of the ways in which the narrative of joy has been co-opted by capitalism, as a celebration of individualism and consumerism. But I think you already know; this is not the joy work I am talking about.

CS   *Poetry is the language of resistance. It can be the language of the street and the language of divinity. Language of muscle and sinew, and language of air and light. What use is poetry these days for you?*

RS   I am writing letters. Some are postal packages, dream writings and drawings posted with stamps. Others are voice notes spoken into existence, daily, or weekly, or whenever we are awake. And with one friend, a weekly exchange of letters we have been doing since 2015, in which we write by hand (and scan) or type or speak our week to each other. I have come to think of these practices as the work that is at the centre of my life.

   I have been sleeping a lot. I used to romanticize the one who cannot sleep, who wakes late and writes into the night. Then a friend reminded me that dreaming is an excellent kind of work to do at night. And I realized, yes. It's okay. I have been sleeping, processing things through my body, tuning into other worlds. I meet friends in my dreams, I feel out my own existence. I find safety there, and unforeseen knowledges. This is also the work.

All of which is to say that poetry is a kind of truth for me, and a constellation of secret languages that slip right past if I am moving too quickly in the moment of encounter. These days, I try to allow myself to be close to poetry all the time, tuning into its frequencies. In words, reading, sleeping, drawing, dancing, gesture and writings.

CS *What are your hopes and dreams for the future of theatre, especially given that the arts sector has been suffering from, and has incurred suffering upon many people due to systemic racism, economic injustice and massive inequities in working practices and in matters of access? What kind of dreamwork is possible?*

RS When you asked me to be a part of this project, I asked you who was involved, how you were working, what was required of me and whether you could pay me. I mention this because I cannot write about any of the issues you have raised without first acknowledging the conditions within which this piece of work is happening. It is a dream book. I believe strongly in the work of dreaming. I've taken dreamwork and slowly placed it at the centre of my life since I abandoned my ambitions of being a career artist. But dreamwork goes both ways. I dream because the conditions are untenable, but I do not dream in order to ignore. I do not want my dreaming to contribute to sustaining inequities. I dream from within failed systems that have shaped me and will never leave me. I dream as if to expand those systems, to break them open from the inside. But I have to acknowledge the outside in order for that to be possible. I begin here:

I am not being paid for this writing.

Presumably none of the authors are being paid.

The people at Methuen are, presumably, being paid.

Presumably this affects us all differently.

This is not a project that exists outside of monetary or hierarchical systems.

So this book is a dream book caught within a system.

This is where we begin our dialogue.

I am not being paid, but I chose to say 'yes'. Why?

Because I wanted to be heard.

I wanted to be heard, and I felt my perspective was important here. And I could.

I am able to respond to your invitation with 'yes' because

I am just coming out of two years' salaried work and I am being paid for another project right now
I have savings, and family who are able to support me if need be
I have had educational and passing privileges
because
I am racialized, but with fairly light skin
My mum's skin is almost white
My dad was adopted into a wealthier part of the family, where he was the only male
This is where I begin.
Attached to all the beginnings before me.
I responded to your invitation to contribute because
I am worried about the representation that happens within the UK Live Art and experimental theatre sector and have been sickened by the sameness of the names that appear on that roster.

I am worried about the whiteness of queer stories within this sector, and the ways in which there are so many queer people who are completely unable to access that world.

I am worried about the DIY aesthetic that is so lauded in this sector, but is so often an excuse to underfund, undercare and exclude certain bodies and minds from the discourse.

I am worried about whose stories really get told, and why.

I am worried about the extent of the ignorance (by which I mean ignoring). I am worried about White Niceness (which is not only performed by 'white people'). I am worried about what never gets spoken. I am worried about the ways in which almost every time I bring these things up, I end up doing all the work while others shut down, walk away or centre their own fragility.

Having walked away from the UK arts scene, I can speak to some of these things. And so here I am, writing this for people who fail to recognize themselves in what you refer to as 'the field'. I am writing this for those who do not understand what makes 'the field', whether they are within it or how it operates. I am writing this for people who are not celebrated or successful. I am writing this for those who veer between invisibility and being consumed, with no space between. I am writing this as a queer non-binary person of colour who never dared to claim any of those terms when I was working in 'the field'.

My hopes and dreams are of reorientation. A future that is rooted in deep past. Indigenous sovereignty. Listening. My hopes are for fluidity, inarticulacy, for not knowing and for being led by the wisdoms outside of human construct. I dream of theatres as places for gathering and listening, the tiniest theatres are held between us, in our calm and open hearts. I dream of working together across difference. I dream of us all being able to imagine generations past and future. I dream of us all being able to rest and work and play to our own rhythms without questioning what has most value. I dream of artist in us all. I dream of lying on the ground, acknowledging land and knowing that we are held. I dream of deep respect, for self and other, that shows up in every detail of every encounter.

Jose Solís

Jose Solís is a Honduran critic based in New York City, whose work has appeared in the *New York Times* and *American Theatre*, among others. He is founder of the BIPOC Theatre Critics Lab. This interview was conducted via email on 30 October 2020.

CS *How has lockdown been for you?*

JS The first thing I did on 12 March, when theatres in New York City shut down, was to go to my calendar and delete every single show I was scheduled to see for the next month or so. With my calendar now an empty canvas, I allowed myself the chance to paint a new picture.

One early evening in my apartment in Brooklyn I noticed my entire living room was filled with an otherworldly pink light. Considering I never am home between the hours of 5 pm and midnight (I saw shows every single night) it took me a while to realize what I was seeing was the sunset! The curtains on each side of my window made me think of a stage, I was witnessing the most spectacular show I had seen in ages. I had no choice but to surrender to the universe and thank it for the graces it was giving me.

CS *What advice do you have for people entering the field right now?*

JS Rules are meant to be broken. Those rules that you abide by? Most likely a dead white man made them up to preserve his power and maintain the status quo. Dismantle the system. Challenge everything. Ask yourself why more often than how. Stop believing in the quixotic myth that you need to 'find your voice'. You were born with a voice. It is the voice that comes across in your writing, social media posts and conversations with friends. You have that voice already. Cherish it. Someone out there needs to listen to it.

CS *What are your hopes and dreams for theatre's future, if any?*

JS American theatre is rotten at its core. It is the artistic field that congratulates itself the most for its progress and achievements, but, it is a field of silence, where the powerful often quiet those whose voices they fear. The theatre industry has for too long tried to upkeep this illusion of perfection and love. Theatre will be able to heal when it gives in to the will and desires of the less powerful, and becomes a place of community, rather than the preservation of the status quo.

I want equity. I want to see faces that look like mine when I attend critics' events. I want to sit at the theatre next to someone who speaks a language I do not know. On stage I want artists from different cultural backgrounds to transport me to new worlds. Diversity and inclusion have become buzzwords deployed by predominantly white institutions that do not care about either, so it is essential BIPOC people go outside the system. We must build community and cherish each other.

I also hope to see a future where the theatre capitals of the world are decentralized. I adore New York City, but it is far from being the sophisticated theatre mecca it is made to be. I find theatre here extremely provincial in so many ways. Broadway continues celebrating franchises and film adaptations, while claiming to be more progressive than Hollywood. The lives of shows are determined by merely financial interests. Would it be foolish to dream of theatre backed by federal funds?

CS *Can you talk about your work currently as a critic and activist?*

JS Although I was disappointed to see theatres close and heartbroken by the thousands of people who lost their livelihood, it was always clear to me that theatre was not paused. I was inspired by the creativity and resilience of artists who immediately took to different mediums and platforms to deliver their work. I do not mean Zoom readings. Instead, I was captivated by those who were thinking outside the box. Within a few days of the closure of NYC theatres, I was seeing a live performance online by the British artist Brian Lobel called *you have to forgive me you have to forgive me you have to forgive me* just for me in the comfort of my couch! I was constantly renewed by seeing playwrights deliver works in the shape of Instagram posts. Erin Mee's This Is Not a Theatre Company even did a three-day-long play on a video gaming platform! Yet, mostly white critics were writing articles saying nothing was happening!

This lack of coverage by critics reminded me one of the things I love the most about our field is that we are chroniclers and historians. This led me to take the Token Theatre Friends, which is a web series and podcast I created, outside of the umbrella of a non-profit at Theatre Communications Group and launch it as its own outlet. I found it imperative to celebrate the works of those who, like me, did not believe in that pause.

I also was inspired to launch the BIPOC Critics Lab, an educational program I created, developed and executed without any funding or help from organizations. Although believe me, I tried endlessly to rally people behind me. The pilot program took place from August to October of 2020. The recruitment took place on Twitter; from over 100 entries I selected eight BIPOC aspiring critics from across the United States. For three months we went over the importance of decolonizing the canon, deprogramming outdated ways of criticism and celebrating alternative mediums to celebrate the critic as an artist. The key element for me was to have each cohort member finish the salon with their first paid published piece; I achieved that by creating alliances with theatre companies who asked the cohort members to write season previews, interviews, material for their newsletters and more. At the heart of my programme is the notion that critics need to rejoin the ecosystem, rather than being outsiders. I figured if theatre companies helped nurture new critical voices, they would be more inclined to stop relying on the mighty word of elderly white critics from major outlets.

Halfway through the pilot programme I was invited by the Kennedy Center to hold the second version of the lab in their institution. With the financial and administrative backing of such a prestigious cultural institution, I was able to invite guest instructors, and curate salons open to the public. With enough funding, I plan to do at least two sessions each year, and continue having theatre companies involved in shaping a richer cultural field.

It is strange to say it, but this has been the most meaningful year for me as a professional.

The pandemic has forced us all to sink or swim, I swam by creating community, by sharing my knowledge, by cherishing those who are rarely cherished.

CS   *How can and/or will the theatre industry reckon with the fact that many of its freelancers live in the starving class, while some top-tier administrators are making six figures?*

JS I call 2020 the Mirror Year. It has forced us to take a long, deep look at who we are. Ugly truths have come up, and we are forced to deal with unspoken facts that used to be protected at all costs. The lack of financial support for artists has been an issue, but that is rooted in the larger structure of the country. The abandonment of theatre by the powerful is simply a reflection of a culture that celebrates greed, rather than spirit.

This year I was inspired by the work of Congresswoman Alexandria Ocasio-Cortez, who reminded me of what my grandma raised me on: the notion that there is nothing the powerful fear more than to see the oppressed work together and unify. This year I have found support from people who do not have much money to give, but still give something. Token Theatre Friends runs entirely on crowdfunding. I dream of one day being able to bring more BIPOC colleagues into the fold and to be able to pay them for their work. In the meantime, I have been marvelled at the power of kindness, the thrill of empathy and the joy of community.

CS *What are ways to parse through these times and do the work of deep listening but also take actionable steps to address the wide-ranging volatile state the United States is in?*

JS One of my least favourite things about American culture (I migrated from Honduras as an adult so I can identify the differences with nuance; they never shock me because I grew up on American film and TV) is the idea that having a conversation is enough. I appreciate conversation as a starting point, but conversation in America is like a diving board that becomes longer and longer, with people rarely taking the plunge.

The problems in America stem from the incapacity people must see themselves for who they are. The media has aided this by perpetuating the idea that there are two sides to everything. BIPOC know our existence does not have two sides. We do not need to justify our right to live. Politeness needs to be set aside. People need to be uncomfortable. It is only from there where meaningful change can rise.

I believe in radical change. Conversation and listening to each other has not been enough when we are not walking the talk. The white establishment needs to step aside. It is clear by now they cannot create meaningful change, because consciously or not, they have been raised to protect whiteness at all costs. It is time for white editors, artistic directors and powerful people to step aside and allow for the creation of a new world.

NOTE ON
THE AUTHOR

Caridad Svich is a playwright and theatre-maker. She is associate editor for *Contemporary Theatre Review* and founder of NoPassport theatre alliance and press. She received the 2012 OBIE for Lifetime Achievement, the 2011 American Theatre Critics Association Primus Prize for *The House of the Spirits*, based on Isabel Allende's novel, and the 2018 Ellen Stewart Award for Career Achievement in Professional Theatre from the Association for Theatre in Higher Education. She has edited and/or authored several books on theatre including *Fifty Playwrights on Their Craft* (2018), *Audience Revolution and Innovation in Five Acts* (2015 and 2016), *Out of Silence: Censorship in Theatre & Performance* (2014) and *Trans-Global Readings: Crossing Theatrical Boundaries* (2004). She also authored a book on *Mitchell and Trask's Hedwig and the Angry Inch* (2019). She is co-screenwriter of the independent feature film *Fugitive Dreams*, which has been seen at the Fantasia Film Festival in Montreal, the Austin Film Festival, Tallinn Black Nights Film Festival, Manchester Film Festival and Maryland Film Festival.